Old English Literature
in its
Manuscript Context

MEDIEVAL EUROPEAN STUDIES V

Old English Literature
in its
Manuscript Context

Edited by
Joyce Tally Lionarons

West Virginia University Press
Morgantown 2004

West Virginia University Press, Morgantown 26506
© 2004 by West Virginia University Press

First edition published 2004 by West Virginia University Press
Printed in the United States of America

10 09 08 07 06 05 04   9 8 7 6 5 4 3 2 1

ISBN 0-937058-83-1 (alk. paper)

Library of Congress Cataloguing-in-Publication Data

Old English Literature in its Manuscript Context/ edited by
Joyce Tally Lionarons.
          p. cm. – (Medieval European Studies ; 5)
        1. Libraries–Great Britain–History–400-1400. 2. Libraries-
        -Great Britain–History–1400-1600. 3. Scriptoria–Great
        Britain. 4. Paleography, English. 5. Manuscripts, Latin
        (Medieval and modern) 6. Books–Great Britain–History-
        -400-1400. 7. Manuscripts, Medieval–Great Britain. 8.
        Civilization, Anglo-Saxon, in literature. 9. Christian
        literature, English (Old)–History and criticism. 10. English
        literature–Old English, ca. 450-1100–History and criticism.
        I. Title. II. Lionarons, Joyce Tally. III. Series

IN PROCESS

Library of Congress Control Number: 2004110389

Cover design by Alcorn Publication Design
Cover motif: Detail of 1678 Engraving of 1661 portrait of
     King Alfred at Oxford University overlaid with detail of
     Cambridge, Corpus Christi College, MS 173.
Typeset by P. W. Conner
Printed in USA

TABLE OF CONTENTS

FOREWORD

THE ESSAYS IN THIS VOLUME result from a 1997 NEH Summer Seminar on "Old English Literature in its Manuscript Context," which we directed at the Parker Library, Corpus Christi College, Cambridge. The Richard Rawlinson Center for Anglo-Saxon Studies and Manuscript Research at the Medieval Institute, Western Michigan University, provided administrative support and structure for the project. As Joyce Lionarons indicates in her introduction, the seminar took its major theme, and indeed part of its title, from Fred C. Robinson's seminal 1980 article wherein he considers the issue of textual identity and the (unreliable) intervention of editors in the process of textual transmission. The broader background of the seminar comprised the special issues, problems, and methodologies that have arisen in the last two decades of Anglo-Saxon manuscript studies. "Manuscripts in context" encompassed a wide-ranging set of related themes: textual identity, the idea of the author, the boundary of prose and poetry, the idea of translation, canon formation, standards and expectations for editing, and the reception and transmission of Old English texts. To these were added the remarkable developments of technology and the challenges posed by the initiatives to digitize manuscripts. During the seminar these initiating and enabling ideas took several different directions, including postmodern challenges to any idea of editing, which this collection reflects. It is clear that "manuscripts in context" is a formulation that has many applications to what is arguably the "first subject" in the study of Anglo-Saxon England.

The Parker Library and its remarkable treasures provided the working laboratory for testing the directions of current scholarship. Affording a focused research atmosphere within the larger resources of Cambridge University, the Parker collection is the longest established of the three major collections of Old English manuscripts. Entrusted to the College in 1575 by its former Master, Archbishop Matthew Parker, the collection has always commanded the admiration of Anglo-Saxonists. The manuscripts include the earliest surviving copy of the Anglo-Saxon Chronicle and definitive copies of the Old English Bede, the Old English Pastoral Care, and the homilies of Ælfric and Wulfstan. The manuscripts were closely studied and copiously annotated by

Parker and those associated with him, and several of the manuscripts served for the production of the earliest Old English printed texts. The collection therefore afforded a unique opportunity to study the sixteenth-century origins of Anglo-Saxon studies and the transition of texts from manuscript to printed context.

It goes without saying that the co-directors and the participants owe a deep debt of gratitude to the Master of Corpus Christi College at the time, Sir Tony Wrigley, and to the Librarian, Dr. Fred Ratcliffe, for giving us special access to the Parker Library for six weeks. Ms. Gill Cannell made day-to-day work a pleasure, as did her associates Ms. Pat Aske and Mrs. Catherine Hall. The Cambridge University community, particularly the University Library and University Computing Services, were most hospitable to the needs of the seminar participants. The co-directors are equally grateful to Professor Lionarons for selecting and editing essays for this volume to represent the work of the group. We also appreciate the six weeks of stimulating interchange and conversation, which continue even now.

Paul E. Szarmach
Timothy Graham
The Medieval Institute
Western Michigan University

Introduction: Manuscript Context
and Materialist Philology

Joyce Tally Lionarons

IN THE SUMMER OF 1997, a diverse group of fifteen American college
and university professors gathered to study "Old English Literature
in Its Manuscript Context" at the Parker Library at Corpus Christi
College, Cambridge, under the aegis of a National Endowment for
the Humanities-sponsored seminar directed by Paul E. Szarmach and
Timothy Graham. Although most of us regarded the study of Old
English literature and/or history as our primary fields of endeavor, we
also included Middle English scholars, a mathematician, a professor of
Japanese language and literature, and an historian of early modern England. For the next six weeks, all of us worked at a fever pitch — reading
primary and secondary sources, examining manuscripts, reflecting, discussing, and, finally, writing. The eight essays in this volume comprise
some of the fruits of our efforts.

Serious students of the Middle Ages have never, of course, entirely neglected the study of its manuscripts. But the relative inacces-
sibility of the manuscripts themselves, coupled with the proliferation
of critical editions of medieval texts based on clearly articulated and
widely accepted principles of textual scholarship, has allowed most
scholars to rely on those editions unless there were compelling reasons
not to do so. In recent years, however, medievalists of all disciplines
have come to realize that critical editions, for all their virtues, can at
best provide a useful tool that mediates between the reader and the
work, and at worst can seriously misrepresent or even falsify what is
found in the material context of a manuscript. For Anglo-Saxonists,
the starting point may perhaps be found in Fred C. Robinson's 1980
article, "Old English Literature in its Most Immediate Context," with
its startling example of how the meaning of a work of literature can be
lost or distorted by severing it from its "immediate [i.e. manuscript]
context" and studying it in isolation in a print edition. The article was
a call for a return to the study of the manuscripts themselves, based on
Robinson's seemingly self-evident thesis:

1

> ... when we read an Old English literary text we should take
> care to find out what precedes it in its manuscript state and
> what follows it. We should know whether it is an indepen-
> dent text or part of another, larger text. We should have
> some sense of the [text]'s *mise-en-page* and some concep-
> tion of the manuscript as a whole. For medieval books often
> constituted composite artifacts in which each component
> depended on its environment for part of its meaning.[1]

The simplicity of his suggestions belies the complexity of the tasks, however, as numerous scholars have found. For to read a medieval work in its manuscript context raises fundamental questions about the ways in which we read and understand literature, questions not only about a work's textual meaning, but about the nature of textuality, questions not only about authors and scribes, but about what Michel Foucault has called the "author function" as it applies to a manuscript culture. It raises questions as well about generic boundaries (particularly those between poetry and prose), about the interplay between Latin and the various vernaculars of the Middle Ages, about translation theory and canon formation, about the uses of texts at various stages in their history, and about the transmission of those texts from one hand to another. At the very least, reading the manuscripts raises questions about the editorial principles behind the print editions of medieval texts.

Attempts to answer these questions have given rise to what Siegfried Wenzel and Stephen J. Nichols have called "materialist philology," that is, the study of a "single manuscript as an historical artifact."[2] Materialist philology is an enterprise that is not intended to replace traditional philology, but rather to supplement and enhance the study of the texts within a manuscript by a close consideration of

[1] In *Old English Literature in Context: Ten Essays*, ed. John D. Niles (Woodbridge, Suffolk: D. S. Brewer, 1980), p. 11.

[2] Wenzel and Nichols, eds., *The Whole Book: Cultural Perspectives on the Medieval Miscellany* (Ann Arbor: University of Michigan Press, 1996), p. 1.

... the relationship of the individual version to its historical context in a given manuscript. In order to understand the principles upon which the manuscript has been organized, materialist philology postulates the possibility that a given manuscript . . . may well present its text(s) according to its own agenda . . . . The manuscript agency — manuscript kind or identity — can thus offer social or anthropological insights into the way its texts were or could have been read by the patron or public to which it was diffused.[3]

However, as Ralph Hanna III points out, any attempt to reconstruct the way a text was or could have been read by its medieval audience(s) inevitably involves the modern scholar in a double act of mediation: first because the language we use to explain the text is necessarily modern, not medieval, reflecting "our own estrangement from the objects of our interest," and second because a medieval codex does not participate in textuality as it is conceived of in the modern world. Manuscript books do not provide "publicly available renditions of texts;" rather, "they represent defiantly individual impulses — appropriations of works for the use of particular persons in particular situations."[4]

Cambridge, Corpus Christi College MS 41 provides a good example of one such "defiantly individual impulse." The manuscript contains as its main text a version of the Old English translation of Bede's *Historia Ecclesiastica*; however, copied into its margins is an eclectic group of miscellaneous works: liturgical texts, a martyrology, *Solomon and Saturn*, six homilies, and various Latin and Old English charms. In "Nostalgia and the Rhetoric of Lack: The Missing Exemplar for Corpus Christi College, Cambridge, MS 41," Sharon Rowley focuses on the manuscript's primary text, the Old English translation of Bede. Because the manuscript contains the most complete extant version of the work, but a version most scholars find unreliable because of its inconsistencies with other manuscripts and its numerous scribal errors, Rowley argues that CCCC 41 provides "a rich site for theorizing

---

[3] Wenzel and Nichols, p. 2.

[4] "Miscellaneity and Vernacularity: Conditions of Literary Production in Late Medieval England," in Wenzel and Nichols, p. 37.

what, precisely, scholars since Robinson have been trying to get at by returning to material contexts." Critical studies of the manuscripts containing the Old English translation of Bede in general and studies of CCCC 41 in particular, she asserts, reveal a "pervasive sense of lack," a lack that scholars perceive as residing in the texts themselves rather than in "our uncertainty about their translation, origination, dialect, and provenance." The result is that critical studies are permeated with "a rhetoric of the second-rate and the other," filled with unarticulated nostalgia and "images of . . . desire" for a non-existent exemplar. Rowley's analysis of the desire for the absent original revises and develops Allen Frantzen's theorizing of the "desire for origins" in Old English studies in general,[5] extending his argument to the materialist-philological study of an individual manuscript. Rather than using CCCC 41 to continue the pursuit of an absent Old English Bede archetype on the one hand, or falling into "endless semiotic drift" as a result of the acknowledgment that the manuscript texts do not signify the origins we want them to on the other, Rowley suggests that scholars explore "the complexities of the material text to sound out what CCCC 41 can tell us about textual culture, authority, and orthodoxy in eleventh-century England," and she offers this essay as a starting point for such an exploration.

In a complementary essay, Nancy M. Thompson addresses many of the same questions while focusing on the manuscript's purpose and organizational principles as a whole. Her particular emphasis is on the marginal homilies, most of which deal with heterodox and apocryphal material that one scholar has termed "wild and extravagant"[6] and another "ecclesiastical fiction."[7] Thompson suggests that the "apparent incongruity" of CCCC 41's textual juxtapositions is a problem "of our own making," based in "an anachronistic standard of orthodoxy that

---

[5] Allen J. Frantzen, *Desire for Origins* (New Brunswick, NJ: Rutgers University Press, 1990).

[6] Mary Clayton, *The Cult of the Virgin Mary in Anglo-Saxon England*, Cambridge Studies in Anglo-Saxon England 1 (Cambridge: Cambridge University Press, 1990), p. 234.

[7] Raymond Grant, *Three Homilies from CCCC 41: The Assumption, St. Michael, and the Passion* (Ottawa: Tecumseh Press, 1982), p. 15.

misleads us about the nature of Anglo-Saxon Christianity." Through an examination of the manuscript's anonymous marginal homily on the Assumption of the Virgin, Thompson reconsiders the question of religious orthodoxy in Anglo-Saxon England, asking us "to shed unhelpful presuppositions about what Anglo-Saxon Christians should have believed and look instead at what they did believe."

As both essays make clear, manuscript culture did not, indeed could not, produce identical versions of medieval works in the way a text is mechanically reproduced in the age of print. Medieval texts are "performative" in the sense that each rendition by an individual scribe represents a unique (re)performance of the work that may reflect the preferences and creative abilities of the scribe in addition to or instead of those of the author.[8] Traditional editing practices seek to erase such scribal "corruptions" and "interpolations" in order to establish a recon-structed, originary, authorial text. In so doing, these practices not only disguise the very information about the manuscript works that mate-rialist philology seeks to recover, but they also create a modern text in place of the medieval work. As Joyce Tally Lionarons points out in her essay, "Textual Appropriation and Scribal (Re)Performance in a Com-posite Homily," one unintended result of traditional editorial practice is that modern readers may find themselves reading "a fundamentally different work from that encountered by medieval readers." Scholars returning to the manuscripts to study the immediate context of their texts have been inspired by the discrepancy between manuscript and print to question long-established editorial principles, resulting in a flurry of conferences and publications. Fred Robinson's seminal essay was reprinted with eleven later articles in 1994 in *The Editing of Old English*; the same year saw the publication of D. G. Scragg and Paul E. Szarmach's collection, *The Editing of Old English: Papers from the 1990*

---

[8] See A. N. Doane, "Oral Texts, Intertexts, and Intratexts: Editing Old English," *Influence and Intertextuality in Literary History,* ed. Jay Clayton and Eric Rothstein (Madison: University of Wisconsin Press, 1991), pp. 75-113; and Fred C. Robinson, "Print Culture and the Birth of the Text: A Review Essay," *Sewanee Review* 89 (1981), pp. 423-30. See also Joyce Tally Lionarons, "Textual Appropriation and Scribal (Re)Performance in a Coposite Homily: The Case for a New Edition of Wulfstan's *De Temporibus Anticristi*," pp. 67-93 in this volume.

Manchester Conference, followed by Shuji Sato's *Back to the Manuscripts* in 1997, along with numerous unanthologized articles.[9] In her essay in this volume, Lionarons discusses the related issues of textuality, authorship, and manuscript authority in preface to a newly re-edited text of Wulfstan's homily *De Temporibus Anticristi* that restores a lengthy passage excised from the text in Dorothy Bethurum's long-standard edition on the grounds of authorial inauthenticity.[10] The restoration of the interpolation not only gives the modern reader the entire work as found in two of the three manuscripts in which the homily appears, but also "provides Wulfstan's homily with a temporal depth and typological sophistication that is not found either in his sources for [the homily] or in the two Old English analogues to [the interpolation]." Lionarons's edition of *De Temporibus Anticristi* is "an attempt to walk a fine line between a simple manuscript transcription and a version of the manuscript work edited for easy accessibility to the modern reader."

But as the material philologists argue, studying the manuscript context of a work can also tell us more than simply the intrinsic form or meaning of a text: it can often provide clues as to how Anglo-Saxon (and later) readers used the texts they found in the manuscripts. In "Multilingual Glosses, Bilingual Text," Melinda Menzer looks closely at the Latin, French, and Old English glosses found in three manuscripts of Ælfric's *Grammar* in order to ascertain not only the uses to which medieval readers put the text, but also what the glosses can tell us about the interplay among the three languages in Anglo-Saxon England and later. She notes that some scribes and glossators seem equally at home in two or even three languages, while others do not, indicating

---

[9] Robinson, *The Editing of Old English* (Oxford: Clarendon, 1994); Scragg and Szarmach, eds., *The Editing of Old English: Papers from the 1990 Manchester Conference* (Cambridge: Cambridge University Press, 1994); Sato, ed., *Back to the Manuscripts* (Tokyo: Center for Medieval English Studies, 1997). Articles include Mildred Budny's "Old English Poetry in Its Material Context," in *Companion to Old English Poetry,* ed. Henk Aertsen and Rolf H. Bremer, Jr. (Amsterdam: VU University Press, 1994), pp. 19-44; and A. N. Doane, "Oral Texts, Intertexts, and Intratexts: Editing Old English," in *Influence and Intertextuality in Literary History,* ed. Jay Clayton and Eric Rothstein (Madison: University of Wisconsin Press, 1991), pp. 75-113.

[10] Dorothy Bethurum, ed., *The Homilies of Wulfstan* (Oxford: Oxford University Press, 1957).

that the boundaries between languages were "porous and fluid." Menzer argues that the glosses show that the *Grammar* functioned variably for different users: it was used to teach Latin, but could also function to teach English grammar. One of the Anglo-Norman glossators may have been using the text as a prototype for a French grammar designed for non-native speakers, but another seems to have been using the text to teach himself English verbs, a procedure that "reverses our usual assumptions about the interaction between French and English in post-Conquest England." Similarly, Paul Acker's examination of the three tables of contents in Cambridge, Corpus Christi College MS 178 reveals the uses to which the manuscript was put in three different centuries: the tenth, when it was written; the thirteenth, when the Tremulous Worcester Hand glossed it; and the sixteenth, when Matthew Parker put his indelible stamp on the manuscript by adding to and reordering its contents during rebinding.

Even a cursory examination of the manuscripts containing Old English texts reveals one incontrovertible fact: the overwhelming majority of the extant works are in prose, in spite of which most of the study of Old English literature in the past century has focused on the poetry. Thus another question raised by the re-examination of the manuscripts is that of canon formation within the discipline. Anglo-Saxonists have in the past decades striven to rectify the balance: one may cite the emphasis placed on the prose texts in recent introductory anthologies such as *The Cambridge Companion to Old English Literature* and Katherine O'Brien O'Keeffe's *Reading Old English Texts*,[11] as well as several volumes devoted entirely to prose works.[12] However, a reconsideration of the prose raises yet another problem within the canon: many Old English prose works contain poetic passages, some

[11] O'Brien O'Keeffe, ed., *Reading Old English Texts* (Cambridge: Cambridge University Press, 1997); Malcolm Godden and Michael Lapidge, eds., *The Cambridge Companion to Old English Literature* (Cambridge: Cambridge University Press, 1991).

[12] See, for example, Bernard F. Huppé and Paul E. Szarmach, eds., *The Old English Homily and Its Backgrounds* (Albany: State University of New York Press, 1978); Paul E. Szarmach, ed., *Studies in Earlier Old English Prose: Sixteen Original Contributions* (Albany: State University of New York Press, 1986); *Holy Men and Holy Women: Old English Prose Saints' Lives and Their Contexts* (Albany: State University of New York Press, 1996); Karen J. and

of which are regarded by modern scholars as poetry, some as merely rhythmic prose, and others as "irregular" or "debased" verse, with little clear distinction among the three categories. Passages falling into the second two categories have been for the most part excluded from the canon of Old English poetry as defined by the standard edition in the field, *The Anglo-Saxon Poetic Records* (ASPR). In "The Boundaries Between Verse and Prose in Old English Literature," Thomas A. Bredehoft examines a series of manuscript works that juxtapose prose and poetry to determine how and when scribes demarcated the boundaries between the two and what sorts of passages merited such demarcations. He concludes that many of the distinctions modern critics have made between the genres have no basis in Anglo-Saxon thought, and that at least some of the poetic passages omitted in modern anthologies of Old English poetry (especially but not exclusively the ASPR) should be included with canonical works in order to provide us with a full idea of the forms and cultural value of Old English poetry. He notes, however, that the poems should be edited "from a perspective that does not see them as flawed examples of 'classical' verse, but rather as examples of a different kind of Old English verse," and in such a way that they are not separated from their poetic contexts.

Not all study of Old English manuscripts is primarily literary, however, and the final two articles in this collection are historical rather than strictly literary in focus. Robert M. Butler's essay, "Glastonbury and the Early History of the Exeter Book," is a reconsideration of the evidence for the provenance of the Exeter book that suggests a Glastonbury origin. He brings considerable paleographical and historical knowledge to his task, examining not only the manuscript of the Exeter Book itself, but also following up some unlikely clues in a second manuscript: the marginal notation of two proper names, Æthelwine and Ælwe, in the upper corners of London, Lambeth Palace Library, MS 149. Last but not least, Nancy Basler Bjorklund's article focuses

Kenneth B. Quinn, *A Manual of Old English Prose* (New York: Garland, 1990); Clare A. Lees, *Tradition and Belief: Religious Writing in Late Anglo-Saxon England* (Minneapolis: University of Minnesota Press, 1999); and Gregory Waite, *Old English Prose Translations of King Alfred's Reign,* (Woodbridge, Suffolk: D. S. Brewer, 2000).

not on the manuscripts of the Parker Library per se, but on Matthew Parker himself, the man responsible for collecting and preserving many of the manuscripts discussed in this collection. Although scholars have often decried the uses to which Parker put his manuscripts — uses that included marking, cutting and pasting pages, and re-arranging and rebinding quires in the order he felt best (for examples see Paul Acker's essay in this volume) — Bjorklund defends Parker's actions by focusing on the historical context in which they occurred. Parker was neither primarily an editor nor an antiquarian, she asserts, but rather a scholar and reformer interested in "us[ing] his manuscript collection and publications chiefly to advance his reform interests," including the "rejection of transubstantiation, acceptance of clerical marriage, and elimination of non-scriptural teachings," in addition to the promotion of vernacular scriptures. Parker "followed the practices he knew, those of the medieval scribes and editors before him who at their discretion repeatedly added to, deleted from, and reassembled parts of manuscripts." Because he wanted to use the manuscript texts as "vehicles for ecclesiastical reform," he needed to make them clear for his sixteenth-century audience and therefore "boldly rectified textual problems . . . correct[ing] errors made by medieval scribes in grammar, wording, and composition" and "fill[ing] in missing or damaged parts as he saw fit." Like Parker's manuscripts, Bjorklund concludes, Parker the man is best understood in his own context — that of his own century.

I believe I may speak for all the contributors to this volume, as well as for those seminar participants who are not represented here, in saying that we owe a tremendous debt of gratitude to the National Endowment for the Humanities for sponsoring the Cambridge Seminar, and most especially to Paul Szarmach and Timothy Graham for their generosity in giving us their time and expert advice both in the seminar itself and in the preparation of these essays. In addition, I would like to thank the seminar participants for entrusting me with the editing of this volume, as well as the anonymous readers from West Virginia University Press for their invaluable comments. Any errors or infelicities that remain are, of course, those of the authors and editor.

9

Nostalgia and the Rhetoric of Lack:
The Missing Exemplar for Corpus Christi College, Cambridge, Manuscript 41

Sharon M. Rowley

[I]t is not possible to translate verse, however well composed, literally from one language to another, without some loss of beauty and dignity. — Bede, *Historia ecclesiastica*[1]

IRONICALLY, THE ANGLO-SAXON TRANSLATOR of Bede's *Historia ecclesiastica gentis anglorum* decided to omit Bede's recognition of the difficulties of translation, quoted above from the Latin version of the text. While the *HE* is not verse, one move a reader of the Old English Bede could make would be to accept its differences from the Latin text as the marks and limits of translation. The problem remains, however, that the Old English Bede as we know it does not exist in its material contexts. Rather, we have five manuscripts that differ to varying degrees, among which we can establish no clear stemma. The Parker Library's copy, now Cambridge, Corpus Christi College MS 41,[2] while famous for its extensive marginalia, has been treated historically as a second-rate manuscript that presents, according to Thomas Miller in *The Old English Version of Bede's Ecclesiastical History of the English People*, a mediocre text in the wrong dialect.[3]

---

[1] Bede, *Historia ecclesiastica gentis anglorum*, ed. and trans. Bertram Colgrave and R. A. B. Mynors (Oxford: Clarendon, 1992), 4.24, p. 417. Hereafter cited as *HE*. Translations from Old English are my own.

[2] Ker, no. 32; Gneuss, no. 39; Budny 32. Hereafter cited as CCCC 41. Neil Ker, *A Catalogue of Manuscripts Containing Anglo-Saxon* (Oxford: Clarendon 1957); Helmut Gneuss, *Handlist of Anglo-Saxon Manuscripts* (Tempe, AZ: Arizona Center for Medieval and Renaissance Studies, 2001); Mildred Budny, *Insular, Anglo-Saxon, and Early Anglo-Norman Manuscript Art at Corpus Christi College, Cambridge: An Illustrated Catalogue* (Kalamazoo, MI: Medieval Institute Press, 1997).

[3] Thomas Miller, ed. *The Old English Version of Bede's Ecclesiastical History of the English People*, EETS, o.s. 95, 96, 110, 111 (New York, 1890).

Despite the fact that Fred Robinson uses the metrical epilogue to CCCC 41 to demonstrate the need to read texts in their manuscript contexts in his influential essay, "Old English Literature in Its Most Immediate Context," no such return has really been made to the material contexts of the Old English Bede.[4] *Cædmon's Hymn*, which has sparked extensive discussion of its history and contexts among scholars — including Kevin Kiernan, Katherine O'Brien O'Keeffe, and Allen Frantzen — is a notable exception.[5] The Old English Bede as a whole compounds the material and theoretical problems attested by the Cædmon scholarship. While an examination of the complete text is beyond the scope of this article, I would like the essay to serve as an exploration of Old English Bede scholarship and of some of the key problems specifically facing readers of the Old English Bede in CCCC 41. These problems include unresolvable stemma complications, a lack of correspondence between the texts and the lists of chapter-headings, the missing Old English exemplar, questions of authority surrounding *Cædmon's Hymn*, and the pervasive sense of lack that characterizes the study of CCCC 41. Because these are also some of the same troubles that complicated Miller's reconstruction of an Anglian archetype of the text, they also make the manuscript a rich site for theorizing what, precisely, scholars since Robinson have been trying to find by returning to material contexts.

Rather than reading CCCC 41 in pursuit of evidence for an Old English Bede archetype, this essay explores the complexities of the material text to sound out what CCCC 41 can tell us about textual culture, authority, and orthodoxy in eleventh-century England. After providing an overview of the history and scholarship of CCCC 41, including Miller's treatment of the text, I will discuss the problems of the table of chapter-headings and *Cædmon's Hymn* in order to demon-

---

[4] Fred C. Robinson, "Old English Literature in Its Most Immediate Context," *The Editing of Old English*, ed. Fred C. Robinson (Oxford: Blackwell, 1994), pp. 3-24.

[5] Kevin Kiernan, "Reading Cædmon's *Hymn* With Someone Else's Glosses," *Representations* 32 (1990), pp. 157-74; Katherine O'Brien O'Keeffe, *Visible Song* (Cambridge: Cambridge University Press, 1990), pp. 23-46; Allen J. Frantzen, *Desire for Origins* (New Brunswick, NJ: Rutgers University Press, 1990), pp. 130-167.

strate the ways in which CCCC 41 complicates Miller's assessment of the text and stemma. The place of *Cædmon's Hymn* in the Old English Bede also raises questions concerning authority, textual transmission, and marginalia. The authority of the *Hymn* contrasts not only with the perceived lack of authority of the Old English Bede in relation to the Latin, but also with CCCC 41 in particular, because of the anonymous homilies copied into the margins of the manuscript. Finally, for the most part scholars have viewed the anonymous homilies in the margins of CCCC 41 as heterodox and Irish, and, therefore, as reflecting an inaccurate picture of Anglo-Saxon spirituality. However, reconsidering the anonymous homilies of CCCC 41 in the context of the visions of St. Fursa and Dryhthelm, both in the Old English Bede, I argue that the anonymous homilies, along with CCCC 41 itself, reflect a specifically Anglo-Saxon synthesis of interests and textual practices.

Cambridge, Corpus Christi College 41 and the B Text

CCCC 41 is one of five manuscripts containing an Old English translation of Bede's *Historia ecclesiastica* (*HE*). I follow the convention of citing the Old English Bede text in CCCC 41 as the B text. The other Old English Bede manuscripts are: Oxford, Bodleian Library, MS Tanner 10 (T); London, British Library, Cotton MS Otho B.xi (C); Oxford, Corpus Christi College, MS 279, part ii (O); and Cambridge University Library, MS Kk.3.18 (Ca). London, British Library, Cotton MS Domitian ix (Zu) also contains three brief extracts.[6] Laurence Nowell made a transcript of C beginning at Book I before it was burned in the Cottonian fire of 1731. Nowell's transcript is now London, British Library Additional MS 43703 (CN). Both Abraham Wheelock and John Smith, who edited the Old English version of the *HE* in 1643 and 1722, respectively, supply some variant readings from C.

CCCC 41 dates from the first half of the eleventh century and was made in an unidentified, but probably southern, English scriptorium. Two scribes working simultaneously copied into the manuscript

---

[6] T (Ker 351, Gneuss 668) is from the first half of the tenth century; C (Ker 180, Gneuss 357) dates to the mid-tenth century; O (Ker 354, Gneuss 673) dates to the early eleventh century; and Ca (Ker 23, Gneuss 22) dates to the second half of the eleventh century. Zu dates to c. 900. These dates are paleographical.

13

an Old English translation of Bede's *HE* as the manuscript's main text. Sometime in the middle of the eleventh century, a different scribe added extensive liturgical and homiletic materials in Old English and Latin into the margins and endleaves; a third scribe added the record of Bishop Leofric's gift of the manuscript to Exeter Cathedral.[7] The manuscript was acquired by Matthew Parker during the sixteenth century and shows signs of use by Parker, by his secretary John Joscelyn, and by Abraham Wheelock, Cambridge University Librarian from 1629.

Notably, CCCC 41 remains key to the editing of the Old English Bede because it contains the most complete text extant. It includes both the preliminary list of chapter headings (the only other extant list is in Ca, although we have variants from C via Wheelock) and Book 3, Chapters 19-20 (which are missing from all other texts but T).[8] Despite B's relative completeness, the text is not always consistent with the other Old English Bede texts. As Grant observes, "the scribes of the Bede text are careless fellows whose negligence extends beyond the usual haplography and homoeoteleution."[9] While the B text has been collated and considered in most of the editions of the Old English Bede, it has been edited as a main text only once, in Jacob Schipper's parallel edition of the B and O texts, which, according to Raymond Grant, is unreliable.[10] Miller's treatment of the Old English Bede texts, however, has obscured some of the virtues of B at the same time as it has glossed over some of the differences in T.

In his EETS edition, Miller emphasizes the Anglian nature of the Old English Bede and dismisses the late-West-Saxon shift and

---

[7] Bishop Leofric gave the manuscript to the library of the cathedral at Exeter sometime between 1069 and 1072. See Raymond Grant, *The B Text of the Old English Bede: A Linguistic Commentary* (Amsterdam: Rodopi, 1989), p. 8.

[8] B and T lack a passage from the end of 3.17. For a detailed account of the Old English Bede in comparison with the Latin, see Dorothy Whitelock, "The Old English Bede," Sir Israel Gollancz Memorial Lecture, 1962, rpt. in *British Academy Papers on Anglo-Saxon England*, ed. E. G. Stanley (Oxford: Oxford University Press, 1990), pp. 227-61.

[9] Grant, *B Text*, p. 10.

[10] Grant, *B Text*, p. 15. Jacob Schipper, ed., *König Alfreds Übersetzung von Beds Kirchengeschichte*, Bibliothek der Angelsächsischen Prosa IV (Leipzig: Wigand, 1897 and 1899).

scribal activity apparent in the other texts. He discards B as "comparatively useless" because "the Bede was an Anglian and not a West Saxon work" and because "the scribe or editor of B's text has dealt very freely with his author, changing forms and recasting sentences."[11] Miller bases his conclusions about the origins of the work on the Anglian colorings present in all five manuscripts, although, as Grant points out, "all five texts have, to varying degrees, been altered to accord more closely with the late-West-Saxon Schriftsprache."[12] Miller goes on to attempt to "exhibit a text representing, as far as possible, the Anglian archetype" by adopting what he refers to as a "'contamination' of texts founded on T.C.O.Ca, in order of preference."[13]

Miller's focus on reconstructing the Anglian archetype, however, leads him to misrepresent the quality of his main text, T. In *The B Text of the Old English Bede*, Grant points out that Miller's extensive apparatus remains incomplete because it does not include a version of the Latin, and that his "reliance on T for his main text inevitably obscures one point, namely that instances of agreement between B, O, Ca, C and the Latin show that T has errors to which Miller has not drawn attention and which demonstrate that T is just the best of the surviving Old English Bede texts and not necessarily as good a version as Miller might be held to imply."[14] Grant's observation that T may be just the "best surviving" text rather than a "good" one signals the complexity of reading and editing the Old English Bede.[15]

Unlike many Old English poetic texts, which, as Paul E. Szarmach points out, mostly allow editors to avoid the optimist-recensionist trap by being "sole and unique survivors,"[16] the Old English

---

[11] Miller, pp. v-vi.

[12] Grant, *B Text,* p. 4.

[13] Miller, p. vi. Punctuation of the list of mss is Miller's.

[14] Grant, *B Text,* p. 17.

[15] In *B Text,* Grant offers a linguistic study of B in comparison to T based on Miller's data. I am currently collating the Old English manuscripts with the Latin to reconsider textual variations, focusing on the issues of language and culture in all of the manuscripts.

[16] Paul E. Szarmach, Introduction to *The Editing of Old English* (Cambridge: D. S. Brewer, 1994), p. 2. Also, see Szarmach for a fuller discussion of traditional

Bede offers a particularly tangled reminder that Old English scholars cannot avoid the question, even as readers of edited texts. As Szarmach points out, "the old, apparently clear distinction between 'what a text says' and 'what a text means' is, as post-modern theorists help us understand, not quite so disjunctive, for determining what a text says is not a simple, objective, or scientific enterprise, but rather is already mediated by a tendency towards some instantiation of meaning."[17] For Miller, the Old English Bede says what it really has to say in an Anglian dialect covered over by late-West-Saxon corruptions; his task, which he catalogues with invaluable detail in four volumes, is excavating the "real" text from what the manuscripts say. At the same time as the Old English Bede manuscripts offer recensionists like Miller several irreconcilable puzzles, they offer texts so tantalizingly and inconsistently different from each other and from the text of Bede's Latin *Historia ecclesiastica* that they demand a recognition of difference. Any optimistic presentation of one of the texts would require an apparatus at least as weighty as that of Miller, and could run the risk of reading like a New Critical denial of historical context and intertextuality for a text with no clear claims to authority. As Szarmach suggests, an electronic version of the texts could solve this problem by allowing editors to present all the options, so that "the user/reader will have his/her day and democracy, not expertise, will rule."[18] Theoretically, however, democracy

and contemporary editorial theory. For an historical overview of Latin and Old English Bede editions, see Frantzen, *Desire for Origins*, Chapter Five: "Polemic, Philology, and Anglo-Saxon Studies in the Renaissance." While Frantzen's account is mostly useful, CCCC 41 has become more accessible since he published *Desire for Origins*, and readers should note that Frantzen is mistaken on some points relevant to the manuscript. The hand of the envoi is not larger than that of the main text (Frantzen, p. 133), though it is larger than some of the other marginalia. Similarly, his claim that the homily on the end pages is there because "a later copyist ran out of room" (p. 134) suggests that the marginal scribe had filled up all of the margins, which he had not. Also, Frantzen gives the date of the writing of the Moore MS (734) as the date of the Latin Bede (p. 136), although Bede writes that he completed the *HE* in 731.

[17] Paul E. Szarmach, "The Recovery of Texts," *Reading Old English Texts*, ed. Katherine O'Brien O'Keeffe (Cambridge: Cambridge University Press, 1997), p. 125.

[18] Szarmach, "Recovery," p. 143.

requires actively critical participants. The readers of an electronic version of the Old English Bede, CCCC 41, or both, will still seek to read the texts, and it will remain the responsibility of the editors to make active, critical participation in those texts possible. Although Miller was able to generate four volumes of text and apparatus that appear to present textual variants objectively, they nonetheless present his particular critical apprehension of the texts. And although Miller is quite open about his belief in the Anglian nature of the Old English Bede, he still manages to gloss over his bias towards T. Problems that will continue to confront readers (even readers of an electronic text), and that must be confronted by editors of CCCC 41 and the Old English Bede texts, are the differences and resistances that surface in the images of lack, strangeness, and desire that run through the textual and material scholarship of those texts.

For example, although Grant has written three books about CCCC 41, one on the late-West-Saxon dialect of the B text, and two on the marginalia, the rhetoric of the second-rate and of the other nonetheless pervades his treatment of the texts and manuscript.[19] He describes CCCC 41 as a "second-rate, working copy" and regrets that the scribes are "careless," "recalcitrant," and "negligent" fellows.[20] Although Grant admits that there is no clear line discernible between the "arbitrary errors" of "recalcitrant scribes" and the deliberate alterations of conscientious scribes trying to "adapt the exemplar to a particular audience in a given time period and cultural context," he concludes that "one cannot but wish that its scribes had read and taken to heart Ælfric's plea that scribes should copy according to their exemplar."[21] He reiterates that the poor quality of the vellum, the carelessness of the copying, and the unusual use of the book marked by the presence of the marginalia all "suggest that the manuscript is either the project

---

[19] In addition to *The B Text*, see Grant, *Cambridge, Corpus Christi College 41: The Loricas and the Missal* (Amsterdam: Rodopi, 1979), and *Three Homilies from CCCC 41: The Assumption, St. Michael, and the Passion* (Ottawa: Tecumseh Press, 1982).

[20] Grant, *B Text*, p. 10.

[21] Grant, *B Text*, p. 11; p. 445.

of a poor, minor foundation or the second-rate product of a major scriptorium intended as a working copy of the OE Bede."[22]

While Grant's scholarship is invaluable, his speculation about the state and shape of the exemplar characterizes the study of the Old English Bede. With Dorothy Whitelock's recognition of the need for reconsideration of the evidence in the Old English Bede being a key exception, most of the scholarship reiterates a sense of lack in the texts.[23] Miller's theory of the missing archetype has been accepted and developed: J. J. Campbell points out that "the MSS . . . differ greatly among themselves in orthography and vocabulary, and none of them is a direct copy of the archetype."[24] Sherman Kuhn adds a second intermediary text, arguing that the mixture of dialects present in the manuscripts may derive from the translator's use of a copy of the Latin with interlinear glosses in a Mercian dialect.[25] Returning to the B text and CCCC 41 specifically, Sarah Larratt Keefer suggests that "the nature of the marginalia suggests that the additions, as . . . perhaps the book itself, [were made] in a provincial scriptorium of no great size." She also notes that "the use of the margins of the text indicates a shortage of available vellum, thus suggesting that the original text of the Old English Bede may have been made for a smaller center with a minimal library, or possibly for an individual."[26] While Keefer concludes that the liturgical marginalia "are important to our understanding of Anglo-Saxon liturgical practice,"[27] the scholarly consensus about the B text seems to be that it remains "comparatively useless."

---

[22] Grant, *B Text,* p. 445.

[23] See Whitelock, "The Old English Bede," and "The List of Chapter Headings in the Old English Bede," *Old English Studies in Honour of John C. Pope,* ed. Robert B. Burlin and Edward B. Irving, Jr. (Toronto: University of Toronto Press, 1974), pp. 263-84.

[24] J. J. Campbell, "The Old English Bede: Book 3, Chapters 16 to 20," *Modern Language Notes* 67 (1952): p. 381-86 .

[25] Sherman M. Kuhn, "The Authorship of the Old English Bede Revisited," *Neuphilologische Mitteilungen,* 73 (1972), pp. 172-80.

[26] Sarah Larratt Keefer, "Margin as Archive: The Liturgical Marginalia of a Manuscript of the Old English Bede," *Traditio* 51 (1996), p. 147.

[27] Keefer, p. 166.

I have summarized the treatment of CCCC 41 and the B text in this way so as to emphasize that even with a return to the material text of CCCC 41, the myth of presence and the presence of absence remain. Somehow, despite our having several old, good, clean copies of the Latin Bede on top of substantial evidence that the Old English Bede is based on the Latin branch exemplified by London, British Library, Cotton MS Tiberius C.ii, these fail to supply a sufficient "original text."[28] Instead, scholarship since Miller has focused on reinforcing his theory of the missing exemplar, the non-existent, original translation.[29] I do not mean to suggest that the comments above about the material quality of CCCC 41 are inaccurate or that the theory of an intermediary Old English manuscript is unfounded, but I would like to suggest that such emphases influence the way we read the Old English Bede. I see my analysis of the scholarly emphasis on the archetype as developing and revising Frantzen's application of critical theory and desires for origins in Old English studies. Frantzen articulates issues crucial to the study of Bede as an "eventful" and originary text, but, at the same time as he works toward recovering the history of textual scholarship, he collapses the Old English Bede into his discussion of the Latin Bede.[30] The texts and the critical reception of the Old English Bede differ quite markedly from those of the Latin; I am interested here in exploring scholarly denial of authority to the Old English Bede along with the insistent space carved out between the Old English and Latin versions.

The Dilemma of the Chapter Headings

Part of the difficulty of reconstructing an archetype for the Old English Bede derives from the existence of several apparently unresolvable differences among the manuscripts. A review of the scholarly

[28] Whitelock, "Chapter-Headings," p. 266.

[29] Despite Grant's initial claim that his specific study of B and T will not "simply re-tread the ground covered by such skilled commentators as Deutschbein and Klaeber, who concentrated upon the archetype" (p. 14), the first of the "useful conclusions" he draws is that "the present study has demonstrated the Anglian nature and relatively early date of the archetype" (*B Text*, p. 447). Also see Whitelock, "The Old English Bede," p. 227, especially notes 5 and 6.

[30] Frantzen, p. 131.

treatment of the chapter-headings of the Old English Bede demonstrates not only how complicated the textual relationships among the extant manuscripts are, but also how resistant to study the differences and omissions among and within the manuscripts are.

Of the Old English Bede texts, two versions, B and Ca, include lists of chapter headings. Wheelock collated the list in C before it was burned, and there is no way of knowing whether T or O ever had lists. One result of Miller's silence about the differences between the Latin Bede and his Anglian reconstruction is that the list of chapter-headings fails almost completely to correspond to the text of his edition. Although Miller does note that T, his main text, is corrupt at the beginning and that he supplies the table of contents and first few chapters from Ca and B, only his cryptic introductory list of omissions provides information about the discrepancies between chapter headings and actual chapters. The problem remains not only that the Old English version differs from the Latin by breaking some sections differently, collapsing some chapters together, and omitting others, but also that the Old English versions differ from each other. [31] The Old English list of chapter-headings reflects only some of these differences, so that the chapter numbers and headings in Miller's edition become less guides to his text than indices marking that his attempt to recreate an archetype has escaped his control.

Wheelock's 1643 table of contents, in contrast, attempts to reflect the state of the Old English text in a way that Miller's edition does not. With his parallel text of the Latin and the Old English, Wheelock notes omissions and numbers accordingly, so that his readers can identify where chapters in the Old English are omitted or where more than one chapter-heading corresponds to the Latin and vice versa. The reader can navigate Bede's text, with Wheelock's apparatus clearly marking the complicated relationship between the Latin and Old English texts.[32]

Whitelock analyzes the problems presented by the chapter headings in her essay, "The List of Chapter-Headings in the *Old English*

[31] Whitelock, "Chapter-Headings," pp. 275-77.

[32] Abraham Wheelock, ed., *Historia ecclesiastica gentis anglorum* (Cambridge, 1643).

Bede." She points out that up until Book 1, Chapter 23, the translator of the chapter-headings translates directly from the Latin, including headings for chapters omitted in the Old English text. After this point, the translator seems to have made an attempt, albeit an inconsistent one, to reflect the state of the Old English Bede in the lists. Contrasting the apparent carelessness and inconsistency of the chapter-headings with the comparative care and consistency of the main text, Whitelock concludes that the lists and the main text were probably translated by different people. However, the similar vocabulary leads her to suggest that the list of chapter-headings came from the same place of origin as the main translation, and that the translator of the list may have been a pupil or colleague of the main translator.[33]

Whitelock and Grant agree that a comparison of the chapter-headings with the surviving texts confirms that "the whole stemma is much more complicated than the traditional hypothesis holds."[34] The following diagram shows the traditional view of manuscript relationships that Whitelock developed for her 1962 lecture on the Old English Bede:[35]

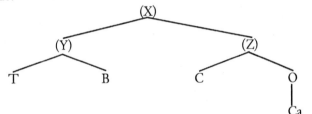

The first major problem discussed by both Whitelock and Grant comes in Book 3, Chapters 17-20, chapters dealing primarily with Bishop Aidan and the vision of St. Fursa. They point out that Miller bases his division of the existing manuscripts into two groups according to

[33] Whitelock, "Chapter-Headings," p. 270. For Whitelock's account of the skill and consistency of the Old English translator, see "The Old English Bede." See also Raymond C. St-Jacques, "'Hwilum Word Be Worde, Hwilum Andgit of Andgiete'? Bede's *Ecclesiastical History* and Its Old English Translator," *Florilegium* 5 (1983), pp. 85-104.

[34] Grant, *B Text*, p. 399. The "traditional view" is basically that of Miller.

[35] Whitelock, "Old English Bede," p. 251, n. 22. See also Miller, I, xxiv.

the different versions of this section. Whitelock explains that in the Y group (T and B), these chapters are complete except for part of Chapter 17, while the Z group omits Chapters 19 and 20, but has "the rest of this section, including the part of Book 3, 17 omitted by Y, in a completely different translation."[36] As Whitelock points out, however, the chapter-headings for 17-20 "are omitted, not only from the list in Ca, a manuscript of the Z branch, where it was a later translator who filled in part of the missing portion, but also from the list in B, whose version . . . never lacked this section." On the basis of this evidence, teamed with her assessment that Miller's list of agreement of error in T and B is not impressive, Whitelock then suggests that "one may doubt whether there ever was an archetype Y."[37]

The problem that B's list agrees with Ca of the Z branch is compounded by further textual evidence. Chronologically, B could not have copied the list from Ca. Also, there are places in which B retains better readings of the Latin than Ca — better readings that, according to Wheelock, were sometimes also present in C. These problems continue to multiply. Whitelock points out that at the ends of Books 1 and 4, the chapter breaks "vary between [the branches of] the manuscripts" as well as where headings are occasionally supplied. While she is willing to suggest that the list "fits a text set out like that in . . . O and Ca better than T or B," she also concludes that "one can only speculate" about the numbers of originals, the timing of the omissions of text, and the additions of chapter headings. The problem that B shares some errors with the Z group — but avoids others — mainly leads Whitelock to determine that the whole question "requires reconsideration" and allows us to ascertain only that the relationship between these manuscripts is as complicated as it seems to be.[38]

Authority and Cædmon's Hymn

The chapter-headings mark the complexity of the relationships among the extant Old English Bede manuscripts. Considering the difficulty of ascertaining the number of originals, the timing of the omis-

---

[36] Whitelock, "Chapter-Headings," p. 264.
[37] Whitelock, "Chapter-Headings," p. 264.
[38] Whitelock, "Chapter Headings," pp. 264-78.

sions, and the addition of the chapter-headings, in conjunction with scholarly frustration with the quality of the texts, it becomes clear that at least part of the desire to find an exemplar for these manuscripts arises from trying to negotiate the split between our sense of the originality of CCCC 41 as a manuscript — that is, as being something like a work of art — and the contradictory status of the manuscript's also being a copy or a translation — or, worse, a translation of a copy of a translation. As Umberto Eco points out in "Fakes and Forgeries," "the modern notion of a work of art as irreproducible and unique assigns a special status both to its formal and material complexity, which together constitute the concept of *authorial authenticity.*"[39] At the same time that we invoke the status of the Old English manuscript as an original material text, however, CCCC 41 forces us to acknowledge its status as mediated and to recognize the activity of scribes, translators, and editors. The manuscript, then, cannot really be "authentic," as Eco puts it later in the same essay, because "authentic [also] means historically original. To prove that an object is original means considering it *as a sign of its own origins.*"[40]

No matter how diligently one tries to smooth out the differences among the Old English Bede manuscripts themselves and then to rearrange the results in the order of the Latin, the result is neither a closer approximation of the Latin original nor a purer version of the Old English. Rather, the harder we press on the text, the more it refuses to signify the origins we desire it to signify. In *On Longing*, Susan Stewart characterizes this pull towards and deferral of authenticity as a form of nostalgia. Stewart sees nostalgia as arising from the symptoms of two assumptions:

> [f]irst ... that immediate, lived experience is more 'real' bearing with itself an authenticity which cannot be transferred to mediated experience; yet second, the assumption that the mediated experience known through language and the temporality of narrative can offer pattern and insight by virtue of its capacity for transcendence.

[39] Umberto Eco, "Fakes and Forgeries," *The Limits of Interpretation* (Bloomington, IN: Indiana University Press, 1994), p. 179.

[40] Eco, p. 193.

23

> . . . By the narrative process of nostalgic reconstruction the
> present is denied and the past takes on an authenticity of
> being, an authenticity which, ironically, it can only achieve
> through narrative.[41]

For Stewart, the search for context privileges situation in such a way
as to direct a romanticism "toward a lost point of origin, a point where
being-in-context supposedly allowed for a complete and totalized understanding . . . [a] point before the splitting of the signifier and signi-
fied, the point of union between utterance and context."[42] Traditional
scholarship's desire for and reconstruction of a non-existent Old English Bede exemplar participates in a desire to close this gap and regain
the lost authenticity of the original. Continued frustration with the
texts that we have, and our own careful documentation that the B text
is not the original that we want, inscribes what Stewart calls "an internal relation between past and present which is made possible by their
absolute disruption."[43]

Our ambivalence towards the status of CCCC 41 as only almost
the thing itself — as a second-rate manuscript with its lacks meticu-
lously catalogued — marks the death of the thing itself to create an object that we can consume: the exemplar. We attempt to reconstitute a
real Old English Bede from what CCCC 41 and the other manuscripts
are not. Our failure, of course, is a function of our nostalgia for the
complete and totalized understanding theoretically present in the historically original. To discuss the history of the criticism of CCCC 41
in terms of revealing a version of the crisis of the sign, however, is not
simply to switch our reading options from a search for the lost autograph copy of the exemplar to endless semiotic drift. As Eco observes,
"these two options are both instances of epistemological fanaticism."[44]
Stewart's formulation of nostalgia, which allows for the "pattern and
insight" offered by narrative despite its mediated existence, also allows

---

[41] Susan Stewart, *On Longing* (Durham, NC: Duke University Press, 1996),
p. 22-23.

[42] Stewart, p. 19.

[43] Stewart, p. 143.

[44] Umberto Eco, "Unlimited Semiosis and Drift," *Limits of Interpretation*
(Bloomington, IN: Indiana University Press, 1994), p. 24.

for the generative capacity of narrative in practice. The fact that Bede marks his Latin paraphrase of *Cædmon's Hymn* with an acknowledgment of the inadequacy of his translation and the loss of the beauty and dignity of the original verses does not reduce his account to a secondary status; rather, *Cædmon's Hymn* has become a famous point of origin in Old English studies.

At the same time that engaging critical discussion of Cædmon reflects the impact of scholarly activity on reading and reception, looking at Cædmon in the context of CCCC 41 also demonstrates the generative potential of material context and quotation. As both Kiernan and Frantzen point out, in a very real sense, Cædmon today bears as much, if not more authority than Bede. As Kiernan puts it in "Reading Cædmon's 'Hymn' with Someone Else's Glosses,"

> [n]owadays scholars are generally convinced that we have inherited by this process authentic witnesses of Cædmon's debut as a poet; in fact, they print the "Hymn," in both scholarly editions and general anthologies, as *the* central text, with Bede's *Historia Ecclesiastica* relegated to the margins. The textual history of Cædmon's "Hymn" provides an unmiraculous case history of how re-productions of literary texts both purposely and unintentionally re-present our past.[45]

Kiernan goes on to argue, on the basis of his examination of the hand of the gloss as well as the size and placement of other, surrounding marginal glosses in the Moore MS, that prioritizing *Cædmon's Hymn* represents an ahistorical reconstruction of the texts, and that "the possibility that the Old English versions we have inherited in this way began as glosses, or reverse translations of Bede's Latin paraphrase, warrants more attention than it has yet received."[46] For Kiernan, *Cædmon's Hymn* is, in the Latin Bede manuscripts, a marginal text.

The narratively marked but visually seamless insertion of a text from the margins of the Latin Bede into the main body of the Old

---

[45] Kiernan, p. 157.

[46] Kiernan, p. 162. Kiernan also argues that the hand of the Old English version of the *Hymn* in Moore is actually different from that of the main text (p. 172n.).

English Bede signals two interpretive problems. First, as Whitelock observes, the translator of the Old English Bede no longer needed to include Bede's acknowledgment of the poverty of translation. Second, the authority of the Old English version of *Cædmon's Hymn* resonates in contrast with the lack of authority of, and scholarly frustration with, its immediate Old English prose context. In *Visible Song*, Katherine O'Brien O'Keeffe discusses *Cædmon's Hymn* as unpunctuated and unmarked in contrast with Bede's Latin poetry because of the familiar orality of Old English poetry; readers of Old English knew how to read it.[47] In a sense, we still do, but *Cædmon's Hymn* evokes a different kind of familiarity today. Most Old English scholars today are so familiar with the text that in almost any version of *nu sculon herigean* one comes across, the phrase resonates with authority and originality.[48] Ironically, the separate, anthologized, authority of *Cædmon's Hymn* in Old English scholarship and our familiarity with the text as a quotation demonstrate the independent sense of originality we want in the missing exemplar: "the quotation appears as a severed head, a voice whose authority is grounded in itself, and therein lies its power and its limit."[49]

CCCC 41, however, undermines even this brief flash of authority because its version of *Cædmon's Hymn* contains the problematic *we* as the subject of *sculon*, so that the *Hymn* begins *nu we herigan sculon*.[50] Notably, among the Old English Bede texts, Ca, O, and B show *Nu we* — providing yet another instance in which the texts resist the traditional stemma.[51] Kiernan argues that the inclusion/exclusion of the

---

[47] O'Keeffe, "Orality and the Developing Text of Cædmon's *Hymn*," *Visible Song*, pp. 23-46. And as Thomas Bredehoft points out in his essay in this volume, CCCC 41's version of the *Hymn* begins with a rather prominent capital.

[48] Miller, p. 344.

[49] Stewart, p. 19.

[50] CCCC 41, p. 322.

[51] O'Keeffe addresses the variants in CCCC 41's *Hymn* in *Visible Song*, pp. 39-41. See also Dan O'Donnell, "Manuscript Variation in Multiple-Recension Old English Poetic Texts: The Technical Problem and Poetical Art," Unpublished Ph.D. diss., Yale University, 1996.

pronoun troubles both theories of the oral-formulaic nature of the *Hymn* and proponents of the text as the foundation of Old English poetry. As Mitchell points out, although the *we* is present in most of the seventeen versions of the *Hymn*, it is missing from "the two 'oldest Northumbrian texts' and 'the best West Saxon text.'"[52] Kiernan suggests that Mitchell articulates — and immediately dismisses — the idea that "if the Latin version with *debemus* had come first, *scylan* alone could be explained as a careless gloss for it."[53] Whereas Mitchell writes that he "finds [him]self in a predicament reminiscent of that which led Dr. Johnson to write 'Some words there are which I cannot explain because I do not understand them',"[54] Kiernan argues that the lack of the pronoun "strongly suggests that the gloss moved from Latin to English."[55]

Although *Cædmon's Hymn* may initially seem like an oasis of authority and origination in B, upon closer examination, it becomes yet another moment in which the book resists signifying the origins scholars want it to signify. While I find Kiernan's arguments compelling, I include them here not to engage in a full-blown discussion of orality and the origins of Old English poetry, but to suggest the possibility that our examination of Cædmon and Bede needs to find an alternative to the dichotomies of original/translation, oral/written, marginal/central. The version of *Cædmon's Hymn* in CCCC 41 is one of the places where the "recalcitrant scribes" may have altered their text, not necessarily so as to "adapt the exemplar to a particular audience in a given time period and cultural context," but on the level of

---

[52] Bruce Mitchell, "Cædmon's *Hymn*, Line 1: What is the Subject of *Sculan* or Its Variants?" *On Old English* (London: Blackwell, 1988), p. 89. Mitchell argues whether the subject of *scylan* may have been "*weorc uuldurfadur*" (p. 91). On this question see also O. Arngart, *The Leningrad Bede*, EEMF 2 (Copenhagen: Rosenkilde and Bagger, 1952), pp. 30-31; Richard Wülker, "Über den Hymnus Caedmons," *Beiträge zur Geschichte der deutschen Sprache und Literatur* 3 (1876), pp. 348-57; and Julius Zupitza, "Über den Hymnus Cädmons," *Zeitschrift für deutsches Alterum und deutsche Literatur* 22 (1878), pp. 210-23.

[53] Kiernan, p. 172.

[54] Mitchell, p. 95.

[55] Kiernan, p. 164.

basic comprehension. At the same time, however, the scribes have also marked the text for modern readers as intertextual and layered with the activity of other readers. But regardless of their intentions, the scribes of CCCC 41 have generated a text legible both on the level of comprehension and as a sign of difference.

The Marginal Homilies, Texts and Mediation

Like *Cædmon's Hymn*, the marginal texts of CCCC 41 signal intertextuality and difference at the same time as they reflect a view of Anglo-Saxon spirituality, as does the book as a whole. In fact, while I agree with Whitelock's assertion that the translator of the Old English Bede was mainly concerned with "the ecclesiastical history of the *English* nation," I would go so far as to highlight *ecclesiastical* as well as *English*.[56] As Whitelock herself points out, the carefully abridged Old English version of the *HE* includes all but one of Bede's miracle stories, while it lacks most of the "historical" matter (copies of historical documents and letters, Bede's careful concern for chronology) that has allowed scholars to claim that Bede manifests a proto-modern, scientific sense of history.[57] Indeed, Whitelock argues that "Bede's attitude to evidence has sometimes been described as modern; it lay outside the conception of the translator" and that the Old English Bede supports Alfred's complaints of the decline of scholarship.[58] Although in the eyes of later scholars the Old English translator loses Bede's sense of evidence, the miracle stories in his translation most likely still carried the stamp of Bede's authority into the eleventh century. Because the authority of Bede's miracles and visions contrasts so markedly with the reputed heterodoxy of the marginal texts, however, the juxtaposition of the miraculous Otherworldly visions in the Old English Bede and those in the margins of CCCC 41 warrants discussion.

The marginal texts of CCCC 41 begin on the problematic table of chapter-headings, marking, as they fill the lower margins of the page, the fact that the list of chapter-headings really does not sup-

[56] Whitelock, "Old English Bede," p. 232.

[57] See Bertram Colgrave, "Bede's Miracle Stories," *Bede: His Life, His Times, His Writings*, ed. A. Thompson (New York, 1966), pp. 201-29, and Wilhelm Levison, "Bede as Historian," also in Thompson, pp. 111-51.

[58] Whitelock, "Old English Bede," p. 244-45.

ply the reader of CCCC 41 with anything like a guide to the book's contents. The marginal texts seem to have no direct connection to the text of the Old English Bede, though O'Keeffe's observation that the way *Solomon and Saturn* "physically frame[s] and contain[s]" the account of Sigehere's apostasy is a "splendid graphic accident" hints at some imponderable resonance.[59] There is no way to know if the scribe of the marginal texts in CCCC 41 intended them to be "marginal," that is, secondary or supplementary to the Bede, if he was using the book as a commonplace book of texts meaningful to him, or if he — unlike Kiernan's Moore scribe — was using extra space to archive texts with "primary" cultural significance. While the occasional rubrication of the marginal texts may indicate their significance, a Latin charm text interpolated into the Last Judgment homily may also indicate that the scribe was not always careful or systematic in his copying.[60]

Although the margins of CCCC 41 also contain extensive liturgical texts, several charms, part of *Solomon and Saturn*, and selections from a Martyrology, I will focus on the scholarship surrounding the six homiletic texts in the context of the Old English Bede's accounts of Dryhthelm and Fursa.[61] The marginal texts include a version of the Last Judgment, homilies on the Assumption and Doomsday (based on the *Gospel of St. Thomas* and the *Vision of the Seven Heavens*), a Homily for Easter (based on the *Gospel of Nicodemus*), and homilies on St.

---

[59] O'Keeffe, *Visible Song,* pp. 69-70.

[60] CCCC 41, pp. 373, 272.

[61] On Fursa and Dryhthelm, see Aron Gurevich, *Medieval Popular Culture,* trans. János. M. Bak and Paul A. Holingsworth, Cambridge Studies in Oral and Literate Culture (Cambridge: Cambridge University Press, 1988), pp. 116-17; also Jacques Le Goff, *The Birth of Purgatory,* trans. Arthur Goldhammer (Chicago: University of Chicago Press, 1981); Peter Dinzelbacher, *Vision und Visionsliteratur im Mittelalter* (Stuttgart: Hiersemann, 1981); Claude Carozzi, *Le Voyage de l'âme dans l'au-delà d'après la littérature latine* (Rome: Ecole français de Rome, 1994); Richard K. Emmerson, "The Apocalypse in Medieval Culture," *The Apocalypse in the Middle Ages,* ed. Richard K. Emmerson and Bernard McGinn (Ithaca: Cornell University Press, 1992). For a critical edition of the Latin version of Fursa's vision, see Maria P. Ciccarese, *Visioni dell'Aldilà in Occidente* (Florence, 1987).

Michael and the Passion.[62] As I have mentioned, these texts have been labeled as part of the "colorful" anonymous tradition, often described as different, marginal, heterodox at best, in some characterizations "wild," and, for those who would rather imply alien through national stereo-typing than confront the contents of the texts, Irish. [63] The apparent heterodoxy of the marginal texts, combined with scholarly focus on their Irish affiliations, serves further to undermine the authority of CCCC 41 and, as a result, that of the B text of the Old English Bede. Reconsidering the marginal texts in the context of the Otherworldly journeys of Fursa and Dryhthelm recounted by Bede, however, makes the marginal texts seem less wild.

Notably, Whitelock's observation about the number of miracles in the Old English Bede needs revision: three out of five of the Old English Bede manuscripts contain all of Bede's miracles but two, as only T and B contain Bede's account of St. Fursa's miraculous visions in the troublesome Book 3, Chapter 19, which remains unaccounted for in the list of chapter-headings. (There is, in fact, no chapter break or initial at this point in CCCC 41; rather, there is a point just before the "mid" that corresponds with the opening of the chapter in Latin.) The explanation of why Book 3, Chapters 16-20 are partly missing and

---

[62] For the homilies on the Assumption, St. Michael, and The Passion, see Grant, *Three Homilies.* See also Max Förster, ed., "A New Version of the Apocalypse of Thomas in Old English," *Anglia* 73 (1955), pp. 6-36; William Hulme, ed., "The Old English Gospel of Nicodemus," *Modern Philology* 1 (1904), pp. 579-614; and Rudolph Willard, ed., "Two Apocrypha in Old English Homilies," *Beiträge zur englischen Philologie* 30 (Leipzig: B. Tauchnitz, 1935).

[63] Mary Clayton describes these homilies as "a wild and extravagant collection with a marked interest in apocryphal material." Mary Clayton, *The Cult of the Virgin Mary in Anglo-Saxon England,* Cambridge Studies in Anglo-Saxon England 1 (Cambridge: Cambridge University Press, 1990), p. 234. See also Milton McC. Gatch, *Preaching and Theology in Anglo-Saxon England: Ælfric and Wulfstan* (Toronto: University of Toronto Press, 1977, 1992). Grant follows Willard in describing the homilies as "ecclesiastical fiction" in *Three Homilies,* p. 15. One voice of dissent is John C. Pope. In a review of Gatch's book, Pope cautions that "the contrast drawn between the anonymous homilies and Ælfric's on the score of orthodoxy seems to [him] exaggerated." John C. Pope, review of *Preaching and Theology in Anglo-Saxon England: Ælfric and Wulfstan,* by Milton McC. Gatch, *Speculum* 54, no. 1 (1979), p. 136.

partly present in another translation in C, Ca, and O may be as simple as that someone realized that a quire was missing, looked at the Latin, and filled in what he thought was left out.[64] Although there is no real way of ascertaining what happened between texts with this section, one result of the differences is that they highlight the presence of Fursa's visions in B and T, and, like the *we* in the Cædmon episode, mark the complexity of transmission.

In the context of the marginalia in CCCC 41, however, the sense of intertextuality, difference, and spirituality marked by the presence of Fursa's vision becomes especially resonant. Fursa's vision, after all, is one of the visions recommended by Ælfric in the homily he preaches against the authority of the *Vision of St. Paul*.[65] I mention Ælfric here to question the scholarly habit of automatically labeling Old English anonymous homilies and apocrypha as "heterodox" based on an anachronistic view of inappropriate content. In fact, while Malcolm Godden initially reads Ælfric's concerns about orthodoxy in vernacular homilies as being based on content,[66] he later argues that Ælfric's "criterion is authority rather than historicity."[67] Similarly, in *The Cult of the Virgin Mary in Anglo-Saxon England*, Mary Clayton argues that Ælfric's "acceptance or rejection of legendary matter was based on whether or not he had any cause to doubt its authenticity rather than on independent

---

[64] Whitelock suggests the solution of a missing quire, "Chapter-Headings," p. 277. As the chapter-headings include the rubric *Đæt se ylca bisceop to þæt gewehgene fyr þære cynelican burh gebiddende [and] on weg gewende* (Wheelock, p. 13), in which *se ylca bisceop* refers to Aidan, who is named in Chapter 15, it makes sense that the person filling in went back and supplied all the missing information about Aidan, including the final bit of Chapter 16 that remains missing from T and B.

[65] Ælfric, "Item in Letania maiore. Feria tertia," *Ælfric's Catholic Homilies: The Second Series*, ed. Malcolm Godden (Oxford: Oxford University Press, 1979). Hereafter cited as *CHII*.

[66] In "Ælfric and the Vernacular Prose Tradition," Godden writes: "What Ælfric objected to in these earlier homilies was not primarily their theological ideas or their views on religious practices, but rather their use of sensational narratives which were clearly fictitious and in some cases of dubious morality" (p. 102).

[67] Godden, "Ælfric's Saint's Lives and the Problem of Miracles," *Leeds Studies in English* 16 (1985), p. 88.

31

suspicion of its theological content."[68] This view has, in fact, been gaining currency, though the full implications of this shift in thought in relation to the anonymous homilies still need to be explored. In relation to the texts in CCCC 41, however, this shift at least qualifies some of the claims about the colorful, heterodox nature of its compilation.

Bede's account of the vision of Dryhthelm provides further evidence as to the Anglo-Saxon acceptance of, and interest in, Otherworldly visions such as the ones included in the margins of CCCC 41. The vision of Dryhthelm is, in fact, the *"Alio Visio"* offered as acceptable by Ælfric after his condemnation of the *Vision of St. Paul*.[69] In CCCC 41, Dryhthelm's vision begins towards the end of the marginal St. Michael text and is marked with one of the most elaborate initials in the manuscript.[70] The vision gives an account of a man who dies for a night, receives a tour of the Otherworld, and returns to live out his life in penance. William McCready notes that Dryhthelm's vision, along with the two other Otherworldly visions in Book 5, has analogues in Gregory's *Dialogues*.[71] Notably, like *Cædmon's Hymn*, Bede's account of Dryhthelm in Latin and Old English has its own history of scholarship and has developed a separate, anthologized authority.[72] Dryhthelm's vision became the object of extensive scholarly interest in the late nineteenth and twentieth centuries among scholars exploring vision literature or the apocryphal Irish tradition. Rudolf Willard, St. John Seymour, Jacques Le Goff, and Aron Gurevich have all discussed Dryhthelm's vision more or less independently of its context in Bede — like the severed head that floats in the small space between the text of the vision and the marginal St. Michael text in CCCC 41 — as an

[68] Clayton, p. 239. See also Nancy Thompson's essay in this volume, "Anglo-Saxon Orthodoxy," on Ælfric's treatment of the *Transitus Mariae*.

[69] Ælfric, *"Alio Visio,"* CHII, pp. 199-203.

[70] CCCC 41, p. 417.

[71] McCready speculates that Bede appropriates the visions in Book V from Gregory, but his own evidence suggests the more likely possibility that the two writers report analogues influenced by earlier sources. William McCready, *Miracles and the Venerable Bede, Studies and Texts* 118 (Toronto: Pontifical Institute of Medieval Studies, 1994), pp. 176-94.

[72] Eileen Gardiner, ed. *Visions of Heaven and Hell Before Dante* (New York: Italica, 1989).

important, early analogue to the medieval visionary tradition.[73] Seymour, especially, is interested in what he sees as Dryhthelm's testimony to the four-fold division of the afterworld present in the Irish tradition. He treats Dryhthelm's vision, which Bede dates around 696, as a transparent episode and as the earliest extant example of this division.[74] Though Seymour excises the vision from any question of its relation to Bede's *Historia ecclesiastica*, his treatment of it remains imbued with the authority of Bede. The conjunction of Bede's authority and precedent in relation to the "Irish" content in Dryhthelm's vision problematizes our notion that the questionable content of the anonymous homilies always moved in one direction: from Ireland to England.

The repeated association of Dryhthelm's vision, the marginal texts of CCCC 41, and other anonymous Old English homilies with an Irish tradition mark a desire for origin as a means of accounting for materials scholars have deemed troublesome, provincial, or at least not properly Anglo-Saxon. In a general essay on the anonymous homilies, for example, Milton McC. Gatch wonders "whether . . . there are occasional notes of nervousness on the part of the anonymous authors themselves about the apocryphal matter which they use in their work," and he goes on to point out that "when apocrypha are mentioned, the most mysterious matter of Anglo-Irish literary relationships is raised again."[75] In light of the texts in CCCC 41, I would argue that the mystery and the notes of nervousness belong to scholars like Gatch rather than to the anonymous authors.

---

[73] See St. John D. Seymour, "Studies in the Vision of Tundal," *Proceedings of the Royal Irish Academy* 37 C (1926): pp. 154-63; "Notes on Apocrypha in Ireland," *PRIA*, 37C (1926), p. 108; and "The Eschatology of the Early Irish Church," *Zeitschrift für Celtische Philologie* (1923), pp. 196, 205-10; C. S. Boswell, *An Irish Precursor to Dante* (London: D. Nutt, 1908); Willard, *Two Apocrypha;* Gurevich, *Medieval Popular Culture;* and Le Goff, *Birth of Purgatory.*

[74] Seymour, "Tundal," pp. 100, 103-04.

[75] Milton McC. Gatch, "A Decade of Studies of Old English," *Anglo-Saxon England* 8 (1976), p. 240. For an overview of Irish apocrypha, see David Dumville, "Biblical Apocrypha and the Early Irish," *Proceedings of the Royal Irish Academy* 73 (1973), pp. 299-338. See also Charles D. Wright, *The Irish Tradition in Old English Literature*, Cambridge Studies in Anglo-Saxon England 6 (Cambridge: Cambridge University Press, 1993).

Notably, most of the texts of the medieval apocryphal tradition that these scholars discuss as Irish, including versions of the *Apocalypse of St. Thomas*, along with the Signs of Doomsday, the Seven Heavens, Nicodemus, the visions of Adamnan and Tundal, and the Assumption, have analogues in CCCC 41 — that is, if one includes the text of the Old English Bede itself. Willard is especially interested in the relationship between the Irish and the Old English; and Grant, in his edition of *Three Homilies of CCCC 41*, eagerly attempts to track down Irish homilies of St. Michael in an attempt to draw a connection between the Irish texts and the marginalia. While such correspondences seem as good a lead as any to the impetus behind the accumulation of the marginal texts, the fact that there exist analogues in Latin, Greek, Syriac, and Coptic, as well as Old English analogues in the Blickling and Vercelli Homilies and in the Old English and Latin versions of the *HE*, should caution against any attempt to draw a direct relation.[76] In fact, despite his endeavors, Grant acknowledges that he cannot find any direct Irish analogues. Willard, who publishes part of the *Vision of the Seven Heavens* section of the Homily on Doomsday, ultimately concludes that the version of the *Seven Heavens* in CCCC 41 "can neither have been derived from the other versions, nor have the others been derived from [it]."[77] Willard points out that Seymour, too, concludes that the textual evidence warrants no sure relationship between the Old English and Irish versions. James E. Cross and Joyce Bazire's caution in relation to Willard's desire to regard as Irish the apocrypha of "The Three Utterances of the Soul" serves well to summarize the general consensus here. They write, "what is clear is that the Latin homily was widely disseminated, extremely well known within the insular area, and popular among insular writers."[78]

As we have substantial Old English material that corresponds to the marginal texts, and as we have, in the Old English account

---

[76] See Donald Scragg, "The Corpus of Vernacular Homilies and Prose Saints' Lives Before Ælfric," *Anglo-Saxon England* 8 (1976), p. 223-78. See also Pope's review of Gatch, cited in note 63 above.

[77] Willard, p. 30.

[78] Joyce Bazire and James E. Cross, *Eleven Rogationtide Homilies* (Toronto: University of Toronto Press, 1982), p. 116.

of Dryhthelm, one of the earliest and most authoritative versions of this kind of vision, I would suggest that in CCCC 41 there is a small claim for textual evidence that challenges our conception of orthodoxy and authority in relation to Anglo-Saxon spirituality. Reading all of CCCC 41 reveals a greater range of interest and a more vivid image of the afterworld than we generally attribute to Anglo-Saxon England. The profound and sometimes troubled influence of Ireland on Anglo-Saxon Christianity is well-documented; however, this survey of the textual scholarship seems to reiterate that the Irish analogues to the anonymous homilies in CCCC 41 are precisely that: analogues. In the patterns and contexts generated by the juxtaposition of the B text of the Old English Bede and the marginal homilies of CCCC 41, the manuscript reflects an Anglo-Saxon spirituality that, like the language, derives from a blend of cultures and a "synthesis of heterodoxies."[79]

Although scholars have treated the texts in CCCC 41 as mediocre and mediated because of their marginality or their manuscript context (or both), the texts are mediated as all texts are. While the scholarship on CCCC 41 to date remains invaluable to any consideration of the texts in their material contexts, this overview of some of the material complexities of CCCC 41 suggests that some of the assessments of and assumptions about the manuscript — specifically its Irishness and the inferiority of the B text — do not hold up well in the face of the manuscript evidence. While further study of the material text may supply answers to questions about the precise nature and status of the marginal texts and the questions surrounding the authority and transmission of the Old English Bede, such issues may not be resolved unless further evidence is discovered. Yet the question remains whether further manuscript evidence would provide any such resolution. In the meantime, the patterns and insights generated by CCCC 41 as we have it must be explored further for what they are, rather than for what they are not.

---

[79] "There is more here than [an] 'intersection,' a meeting. There is a synthesis of heterogeneities." Marshall Sahlins, "The Return of the Event, Again," *Clio in Oceania*, ed. Aletta Biersack (Washington, DC: Smithsonian Institution Press, 1991), p. 68.

Anglo-Saxon Orthodoxy

NANCY M. THOMPSON

C AMBRIDGE, CORPUS CHRISTI COLLEGE MS 41 offers a number of
scholarly puzzles. Academic interest first centered on the main
text, an early eleventh-century copy of the Old English Bede.[1] Was the
translation of the *Historia ecclesiastica* Alfred's work, part of his program
of rendering into English "books most necessary for all men to know"?[2]
Then there is the enigma of the material crammed into the margins by
a slightly later hand: liturgical texts, a martyrology, the poetic *Solomon
and Saturn*, six homilies, and various Latin and Old English charms.
The marginalia have no obvious connection to the main text, nor even
much of a relationship to one another. The *Solomon and Saturn* breaks
off abruptly; the martyrology is a fragment. What motivated the compiler to assemble these varied materials? Were the marginalia intended
for some sort of practical use — reference or reading aloud — or was
this manuscript simply medieval scratch paper, a place to jot down
notes for later transcription into another volume?[3]

There is also the larger question of how this manuscript fits into
the history of later Anglo-Saxon spirituality. To many critics, the combination of texts seems peculiar, reflecting a religious view at odds with
the mainstream English church. While the prayers and martyrology
are unexceptionable — one can envision a priestly compiler, recording things useful for his profession in the pages of the Bede[4] — some

---

[1] The manuscript is described in N. R. Ker, *Catalogue of Manuscripts Containing
Anglo-Saxon* (Oxford: Clarendon Press, 1957; repr. with supplement, 1990),
no. 32; Helmut Gneuss, *A Handlist of Anglo-Saxon Manuscripts* (Tempe, AZ:
Arizona Center for Medieval and Renaissance Studies, 2001), no. 39.

[2] Dorothy Whitelock, "The Old English Bede " (Sir Israel Gollancz Memorial
Lecture), *Proceedings of the British Academy* 58 (1962), pp. 57-90; Sherman
Kuhn, "The Authorship of the Old English Bede," *Neuphilologische
Mitteilungen* 73 (1972), pp. 172-80.

[3] Sarah Larratt Keefer, "Margin as Archive: The Liturgical Marginalia of a
Manuscript of the Old English Bede," *Traditio* 51 (1996), p. 148.

[4] See Christopher Hohler, review of *Cambridge, Corpus Christi College 41: The
Loricas and the Missal* by Raymond J. S. Grant, in *Medium Ævum* 49 (1980),

of the other items included appear incongruous, calling into question the orthodoxy and piety of the scribe. The charms, which come trailing clouds of a pagan past, seem especially suspect,[5] but the homilies present problems as well. Although one comes from the Gospel of Matthew, others translate apocryphal material: the *Apocalypse of Thomas*, the *Gospel of Nicodemus*, and the *Transitus Mariae* or Assumption of the Virgin.

The inclusion of such seemingly discordant material has caused scholars to characterize the CCCC 41 marginalia as survivals from an unreformed past, perhaps Irish-influenced, but in any case not representative of the religiosity of the late Anglo-Saxon church. For example, in his edition of the liturgical matter of CCCC 41, Raymond Grant refers to the marginalia as "rather strange bedfellows for the Old English Bede;" elsewhere he associates the homilies with "apocryphal and apocalyptic" subjects "of the type liked so much by the Celtic church."[6] Writing in a similar vein, Richard Johnson stresses Irish influences in this "seemingly odd assortment . . . of texts" and Mary Clayton describes the homiletic portions of the manuscript as "a wild and extravagant collection with a marked interest in apocryphal

---

pp. 275-78. Hohler speculates that the scribe was a secular priest living near Glastonbury and summoned by the bishop of Wells to update his liturgical books, which he did, using the margins of the Bede because he had not brought writing materials with him.

[5] So regarded by Godfrid Storms and a generation of early scholars who sifted through them looking for evidence of a pagan Germanic heritage. See Storms, *Anglo-Saxon Magic* (The Hague: Nijhoff, 1948), pp. 6-11. Hohler, however, argues that the charms are not folklore at all, but "characteristically 'bad' Anglo-Saxon texts of widely used liturgical prayers." On the place of charms in Anglo-Saxon religion, see also Karen L. Jolly's excellent study, *Popular Religion in Late Saxon England* (Chapel Hill: University of North Carolina Press, 1996). Jolly numbers the charms among what she terms "middle practices" that are not inconsistent with a Christian world view, and she argues convincingly that they cannot be taken as evidence of persistent heathen survivals.

[6] Raymond J. S. Grant, *Cambridge, Corpus Christi College 41: The Loricas and the Missal* (Amsterdam: Rodopi, 1978), p. 2; and *Three Homilies from Cambridge, Corpus Christi College 41: The Assumption, St. Michael and the Passion* (Ottawa: Tecumseh Press, 1982), pp. 5-6.

material."[7] Their characterizations of the manuscript echo the assessments of an earlier generation. Godfrid Storms studied the charms for evidence of pagan survivals.[8] Robert Menner suggested an Irish transmission for the *Solomon and Saturn*.[9] Rudolph Willard spoke of the homilies as "belong[ing] to an earlier period, to what one might call the unreformed, or pre-Ælfric, period . . . . Practically all of them abound in apocryphal material of an uncanonical nature, what, indeed, might be called ecclesiastical fiction."[10]

[7] Richard F. Johnson, "Archangel in the Margins: St. Michael in the Homilies of Cambridge, Corpus Christi College 41," *Traditio* 53 (1998), pp. 63-91 at p. 66; Mary Clayton, *The Cult of the Virgin Mary in Anglo-Saxon England*, Cambridge Studies in Anglo-Saxon England 1 (Cambridge: Cambridge University Press, 1990), p. 234. While this is not the place to take up the issue of Irishness at length, the contrast drawn between English restraint and Celtic "apocryphal content and stylistic extravagance" (Johnson, p. 85) seems much too automatic. Johnson's article reveals the difficulties of this approach. He demonstrates a clear Irish connection in one part of one of the homilies he discusses (the Seven Heavens motif that is appended to the *Apocalypse of Thomas*, pp. 76-79) and a possible connection in another (the St. Michael), although that case is not proven. Johnson himself, pp. 87-88, suggests other, non-Irish, potential sources; and Hildegard L. C. Tristam, *Early Insular Preaching: Verbal Artistry and Method of Composition* (Vienna: Osterreichischen Akademie der Wissenschaften, 1995), p. 5n, argues that there is no Irish connection there at all. In Johnson's two additional cases (the Assumption and the Easter homilies), the argument is clearly strained. Unable, by his own admission, to show direct Irish influence, Johnson falls back on a Irish "spirit" (p. 75), or a (presumably uniquely?) Irish "concern with the ultimate fate of individual souls" at Judgment (p. 85). In short, the arguments for the Irishness of CCCC 41's homilies are not compelling. Cf. Charles D. Wright, *The Irish Tradition in Old English Literature* (Cambridge: Cambridge University Press, 1993), pp. 3-6 and 47-48, who argues for a distinctive Irish style, but who cautions (p. 48) against the assumption that "every weird motif or baroque feature of style . . . is an Irish symptom."

[8] Storms, pp. 6-7.

[9] Robert J. Menner, in his edition of *The Poetical Dialogues of Solomon and Saturn* (New York: MLA; London: Oxford University Press, 1941), p. 25, states: "The Celtic church, because of its isolation and independent tradition, may have preserved apocalyptic legends savoring of demonology which disappeared elsewhere when condemned by ecclesiastical authority."

[10] Willard, "Two Apocrypha in Old English Homilies," *Beiträge zur Englischen Philologie* 30 (1935), p. 2.

In this paper I wish to suggest that this collection is incongruous only from a modern perspective, and that what seems to us a bizarre assortment of heterodox materials would have been regarded by its compiler as an anthology of useful religious texts. Historians have placed considerable weight on Ælfric's criticism of contemporary beliefs, assuming a standard of orthodoxy that is anachronistic for Anglo-Saxon Christianity. My focus here will be on CCCC 41 and its apocrypha, especially the *Assumption of the Virgin*, for this text represents one of a number of cases in which scholars have tended to read the past backwards, approaching the anonymous homilies with a set of presuppositions about what Anglo-Saxon Christians should have believed, rather than looking at what they did believe.

Ælfric's criticisms of the Assumption apocrypha are well known. In the *Catholic Homilies*, First Series, he says he fears lest his listeners encounter a false but widespread story and accept it as the truth, when in fact no book gives us a clear certainty (*nan swultere gewissung*) of the Virgin's last days.[11] In the Second Series, he objects to heretical books in Latin and English that lead foolish people astray.[12] His comments (and modern, especially Protestant, Christian doctrine) have colored the reaction of editors to Assumption accounts, who then frame their discussion in terms of Ælfric's condemnation. Hence Grant prefaces his edition of the CCCC 41 *Assumption* with a lengthy quotation from Ælfric's works, then comments:

> It is important to read what the orthodox and scholarly Ælfric has to say about the standard belief in the Assumption in Old English times and to bear in mind his warning about heretical narratives when reading the ecclesiastical fiction of the CCCC 41 homily.[13]

[11] Peter Clemoes, ed., *Ælfric's Catholic Homilies: The First Series* EETS, s.s. 17 (Oxford: Oxford University Press, 1997), p. 431.

[12] Malcolm Godden, ed., *Ælfric's Catholic Homilies: The Second Series* EETS, s.s. 5 (Oxford: Oxford University Press, 1979), p. 259: "Sind swa ðeah gyt ða dwollican bec ægðer ge on leden, ge on englisc, and hi rædað ungerade menn . . . . Læte gehwa aweg ða dwollican leasunga ðe ðe unwæran to forwyrde lædað."

[13] Grant, *Three Homilies*, p. 15.

Grant acknowledges the widespread belief in the Assumption, citing
Blickling Homily 13:

> That apocryphal accounts were widely known in Anglo-
> Saxon times may be inferred from the opening of Blickling
> 13, 'Men þa leofestan, gyhyraþ nu hwæt segþ *on þissum bocum*
> [emphasis Grant's] be þære halgan fæmne.'[14]

But having conceded this point, Grant quotes yet another paragraph
of Ælfrician objections, so that Ælfric's condemnation becomes the
context in which to consider the CCCC 41 Assumption homily. All in
all, it makes it sound as though this text — this *marginal* text — has
somehow eluded a censor. Such handling presumes a test for a standard Christianity, with Ælfric as the measure, and renders this piece
immediately suspect: why do we find it here, crowded onto the pages
of the saintly Bede?

"Heretical narratives" and "ecclesiastical fiction" are rather odd
terms to use in connection with the translation of a Latin text that
Dom André Wilmart called "la version quasi officielle dans l'Église
latin."[15] But behind Grant's choice of terms lies a commonly held paradigm of Old English ecclesiastical history, as a story of decline and
restoration. According to the paradigm, under pressure of the ninth-
century Viking invasions, England fell away from the high Christian
standards established by Bede and his school, leaving Christianity
"withered and lifeless."[16] In the dark age that followed, superstition

---

[14] "Dearly beloved, now listen to what it says in these books about the blessed
Virgin." Grant may have misinterpreted the significance of this remark,
however. The reference is not to multiple copies of the *Transitus* in
circulation; rather, the original translator referred to books in the plural
because he literally had two books before him as he translated: the two
different versions of the *Transitus* that he combined to create the composite
homily that appears in both the Blickling book and in CCCC 198. On the
compilation of this homily see Rudolph Willard, "The Two Accounts of the
Assumption in Blickling Homily XIII," *Review of English Studies* 14 (1938),
pp. 1-19; and Mary Clayton, "Blickling Homily XIII Reconsidered," *Leeds
Studies in English* 17 (1986), pp. 25-40.

[15] Dom André Wilmart, "L'ancien récit de l'assomption," *Analecta Regensia,*
Studi e Testi 59 (1933), 323. Granted, Dom Wilmart probably accepted the
doctrine of the Assumption, although it was not yet dogma when he wrote.

[16] R. H. Hodgkin, *A History of the Anglo-Saxons* (London: Oxford University
Press, 1952) 2:531.

and ignorance pervaded the church, as the "heterodox" Vercelli and Blickling homilies attest.[17] Then came the reform initiated by Dunstan in the mid-tenth century. Originally monastic in focus, by the end of the tenth century it had taken on broader implications, resulting in a more disciplined secular clergy and a greater concern for the spiritual well-being of the faithful. With Wulfstan and Ælfric, orthodoxy was restored; therefore, literary remains that do not measure up to the revived standards are either relics of an earlier period or aberrant examples of tenacious superstition. The paradigm allows for a tidy and simple division of texts into two easily distinguished "traditions": the apocrypha-filled anonymous works that predate the Reform and a later post-Ælfric and Wulfstan group that can be dated by its orthodoxy. Clare Lees describes the conventional split and its implications:

> The tendency to subdivide the prose corpus into anonymous and named collections results in a hierarchy of critical value, which in this case is confirmed by dating and the methods of source study. Relatively speaking, the prose is easier to date than the poetry, since the implementation of the Benedictine Reform offers a practical guideline to homiletic production. The earlier Blickling and Vercelli collections represent the anonymous tradition of homiletic prose, most often held to be prereform. Evidence of source study for these works indicates an emphasis on apocrypha, often featuring Insular or Irish concerns and topoi and a generally unremarkable Latinity. The later authored collections of Ælfric and Wulfstan represent the newer tradition of homiletic prose, influ-

---

[17] Alternatively, some scholars have attributed Blickling and Vercelli to the first stage of the reform, since both manuscripts date from the later tenth century. Donald Scragg, for instance, notes that the several of the Vercelli homilies bear traces of the vocabulary preferred by the reformers around Æthelwold; see D. G. Scragg, ed., *The Vercelli Homilies and Related Texts*, EETS, o.s. 300 (Oxford: Oxford University Press, 1992), p. xxxix. Yet elsewhere Scragg speaks of these manuscripts as witnesses of a pre-Ælfrician tradition, suggesting that their antecedents, if not the manuscripts themselves, lie in the unreformed past; see Scragg, "The Homilies of the Blickling Manuscript," *Learning and Literature in Anglo-Saxon England*, ed. Michael Lapidge and Helmut Gneuss (Cambridge: Cambridge University Press, 1985), pp. 299-316 at pp. 308, 315.

enced by the revival of Latinity and ecclesiastical orthodoxy
generated by the Benedictine reform. These works consistently demonstrate a much higher level of Latin scholarship,
a concern with accuracy, and a more consistent use of form,
whether exegetical or catechetical.[18]

That abundant surviving homilies, most coming from manuscripts of
the eleventh century and later, do not measure up to the supposed "revival" of orthodoxy should warn us of the problems of this paradigm,
although it has the weight of tradition behind it.[19] Ælfric has been held

---

[18] Clare A. Lees, *Tradition and Belief: Religious Writing in Late Anglo-Saxon England*, Medieval Cultures, vol. 19 (Minneapolis: University of Minnesota Press, 1999), p. 25. This paradigm also informs Willard's division of English homilies into "the unreformed" and the post-Ælfric periods (above, n.10); see also the works cited at nn. 84 and 85 below. Cf. Tristram, *Early Insular Preaching*, p. 5n: she leaves the dating open, but still maintains the division into two traditions, a "heterodox tradition" that made use of apocryphal materials and an "orthodox Benedictine tradition" that supposedly avoided them. Although his name is often coupled with Wulfstan's, Ælfric in particular becomes the standard bearer for of a new way of thinking, and it is commonplace to contrast his standards of orthodoxy with his predecessors'. Peter Clemoes, "Ælfric," *Continuations and Beginnings*, ed. E. G. Stanley (London: Nelson, 1966), pp. 176-209, states at p. 184: "Tradition as it came to Ælfric did not ensure success [in his plan to provide orthodox preaching]. Later writers had not shown a single-minded respect for orthodoxy. Vernacular prose did not in fact present Ælfric with ready made standards. Both intellectually and artistically he had to find his own." Clemoes goes on to contrast Ælfric's works with the anonymous collections: "The Blickling and Vercelli Books give us some idea of what Ælfric was complaining about. They contain texts in which material derived from apocrypha . . . is mingled indistinguishably with material based on scripture, texts in which the distinction between orthodox dogma and popular theology is lost sight of behind a dazzling display of rhetoric. Ælfric set his face against all this." Cf. James Hurt, *Ælfric* (New York: Twayne Publishers, 1972), who notes Ælfric's attempt to "counter the widespread decline in learning in his day" (p. 33) and who contrasts Ælfric's work with Blickling's "endless popular superstitious embellishments, often crudely materialistic in character . . . a whole series of clearly superstitious fabrications" (p. 243). In Hurt's estimation, Ælfric's "work so well reflects that quality of his age that we may speak of . . . the Age of Ælfric."

[19] Lees notes that the traditional division needs modification, for "anonymous homilies circulate[d] side by side with those of the reform period" (p. 27). Even so, by contrasting the anonymous and reform homilies, the implication

up as a champion of orthodoxy, defined in contemporary terms, since the days of Archbishop Parker.[20] While modern scholars have moved well beyond the archbishop's partisanship, their assessment of late Anglo-Saxon religiosity remains influenced by two lingering attitudes toward Ælfric and his views. The first is the perception of orthodoxy as a constant, unchanged through time. Scholars can therefore describe Ælfric as "orthodox," especially in contrast to the anonymous homilists. The very use of the term, undefined and unelaborated, implies an agreed-upon understanding of what orthodoxy entails. The second is the associated tendency to turn Ælfric into the arbiter of belief for his contemporaries, so that his expressed views signal the restoration of orthodoxy in the late Anglo-Saxon church. Only a few scholars have questioned the extent of Ælfric's influence,[21] and despite their caution, critical discussion continues to be framed in terms of contrast between heterodox and orthodox, anonymous and known author, early or pre-reform works and late ones.

One can easily understand the casual and unreflective use of the term *orthodox*. Orthodoxy has been traditionally regarded as adherence

is that only Wulfstan and Ælfric's homilies are from the reform period. Cf. "[k]nowledge of the Benedictine Reform and, to a lesser extent, the Viking incursions is thus essential to the formulation of dating criteria" (p. 80). Lees may have in mind specifically the Blickling and Vercelli homilies, which are of course relatively early (though perhaps not pre-reform), but there are other anonymous homilies with similar features that circulated with Ælfric's or Wulfstan's work that are unique items, appearing only in manuscripts of the eleventh or twelfth century. These may be copies of much earlier works; some may also be contemporary to or even postdate the reform.

[20] In the sixteenth century, Archbishop Parker began his study of Old English in order to support his Protestant polemic. In a comparable example, Samuel Harvey Gem, writing during World War I, found Ælfric an early advocate of "Christian Education, Temperance, and Home Defense" in *An Anglo-Saxon Abbot, Ælfric of Eynsham* (Edinburgh: T. & T. Clark, 1912), p. xiii.

[21] Joyce Hill, "Reform and Resistance: Preaching Styles in Late Anglo-Saxon England," *De l'homélie au sermon: histoire de la prédication médiévale: actes du Colloque international de Louvain-la-Neuve (9-11 juillet 1992)*, ed. Jacqueline Hamesse and Xavier Hermand (Louvain-la-Neuve, Belgium: Université catholique de Louvain, 1993), pp. 15-46 at pp. 33-34; Mary Clayton, *Cult*, calls Ælfric a lone voice, a maverick (pp. 260-65). Lees also rightly states that Ælfric was "maintaining an orthodoxy . . . that verges on the heterodox" (p. 91).

to a set of beliefs both static and eternal. At times beset by heresy or error, orthodoxy nonetheless seems to remain unaltered. In the words of R. A. Markus, it is "a rock buffeted by the waves, the light of the sun hidden by the clouds."[22] From a religious standpoint, this is not an unreasonable point of view. After all, when religious disputes arise, both sides contend for the belief that they hold true; and when a victor eventually emerges from the fray, he will understand the conflict, not as the defeat of another equally plausible opinion, but the triumph of right — i.e., that which, from his perspective, was always and absolutely true. There is a problem, however, when historians adopt this point of view. By taking on the interpretation of the past as determined by the winners, they impart an air of inevitability to the outcome and miss the fact that the establishment of orthodoxy is a process carried out over time. Traditions grow up, disputes arise and are settled, new ideas or foreign influences are encountered and absorbed. Teachings considered heterodox or even heretical in one period may be accepted belief in another.[23] Certainly that was the case with many aspects of Mariology: doctrines debated in the Middle Ages were not pronounced Catholic dogma until the modern era.[24]

And as doctrine changes with time, so it changes with place. The medieval church was not the monolith sometimes assumed by popular opinion — certainly not in the early eleventh century, and probably not even later.[25] Here again there is a tendency to read history

---

[22] R. A. Markus, "The Legacy of Pelagius: Orthodoxy, Heresy and Conciliation," *The Making of Orthodoxy: Essays in Honour of Henry Chadwick,* ed. Rowan Williams (Cambridge: Cambridge University Press, 1989), p. 214.

[23] Cf. Markus on the controversy over Pelagianism: "They [the Pelagians] were breaking rules not yet made. The orthodoxy they were thought to have offended was only defined in the course of the conflict with the African church between 411 and 418" (p. 215).

[24] Pius XII asserted the Assumption of Mary, body and soul, into heaven in 1950; the Immaculate Conception became dogma a century earlier, in 1854. On the medieval debates over Mariology, see, e.g., Jaroslav Pelikan, *Mary through the Centuries: Her Place in the History of Culture* (New Haven and London: Yale University Press, 1996), pp. 191-95.

[25] See, e.g., Robert Brentano, *Two Churches: England and Italy in the Thirteenth Century* (Princeton: Princeton University Press, 1968), pp. 346-52.

backward, looking at questions of doctrine as though there were some centralizing power capable of establishing and enforcing belief. Ælfric's world predated the Gregorian Reform. In his day the great lawyer-popes and church-wide councils were still several generations in the future; a push to systemize doctrine and punish deviance would not occur until well into the twelfth century, the outgrowth of profound changes in European society.[26] In the late Anglo-Saxon period, real authority remained largely local — within a diocese, or occasionally a little further if a particularly ardent abbot or bishop was supported by an effective and powerful king.[27]

I do not mean to imply that the English clergy felt no concern for orthodox belief. One aspect of faith on which all medieval Christians could agree was the idea of one unchanging truth, "perpetually instituted by God in the reasonable order of things."[28] But belief in a single truth did not lead automatically to the development of a discriminating sense of what should or should not be believed, or the elaboration of a fixed set of standards for distinguishing pure from heretical doctrines. None seemed necessary. Most Christians assumed that there was a unified and harmonious body of doctrine set out in scripture, attested by the Fathers, and shared by the whole church

[26] See R. I. Moore, *The Formation of a Persecuting Society* (Oxford: Blackwell, 1987; paperback, 1990), pp. 68-70.

[27] On episcopal independence before the Gregorian Reform, see Frank Barlow, *The English Church, 100-1066: A History of the Later Anglo-Saxon Church*, 2nd ed. (London: Longman, 1979), pp. 236-39, 242-44, and 289; R. W. Southern, *Western Society and the Church in the Middle Ages* (Harmondsworth, Middlesex: Penguin, 1970); p. 170; Margaret Deanesly, *The PreConquest Church in England*, 2nd ed. (London: Adam and C. Black, 1963), pp. 319-20; F. Donald Logan, *A History of the Church in the Middle Ages* (London: Routledge, 2002), pp. 90-91. For an instance in which episcopal efforts were extended beyond diocesan boundaries, there is the case of Æthelwold himself, whose monastic reform centered in his own diocese, but was extended with the support of King Edgar, to several foundations in the east of England. See Barbara Yorke, "Introduction," *Bishop Æthelwold: His Career and Influence*, ed. Barbara Yorke (Woodbridge, Suffolk: Boydell, 1988; rpt. paperback, 1997), pp. 1-12 at pp. 3-4 and 9-10 (Æthelwold's influence is contrasted with Archbishop Dunstan's).

[28] Augustine, *De doctrina christiana* 2.32.50, D. W. Robertson, trans., *On Christian Doctrine* (Indianapolis: Bobbs-Merrill, 1958), p. 68.

without disagreement. This perception of unity, based in what Jaroslav Pelikan has called the Augustinian synthesis,[29] impeded the recognition of contradictions or inconsistencies in the tradition. Christians knew that the Holy Spirit, who had inspired the Scriptures and the Fathers, continued to guide the church. How then could there be contradictions between the authorities?[30] This comfortable conviction prevailed until the Renaissance of the twelfth century, when thinkers such as Peter Abelard pointed to discrepancies in the tradition and the revival of dialectic generated theological debates.[31] But before that intellectual shift, the assumption of consensus governed the determination of orthodox opinion.[32] True doctrines were those held by the church as

---

[29] Jaroslav Pelikan, *The Christian Tradition: A History of the Development of Doctrine*, vol. 3, *The Growth of Medieval Theology (600-1300)* (Chicago and London: University of Chicago Press, 1978), pp. 41-44. For the dissolution of this view in the later eleventh and twelfth centuries, see pp. 215-29.

[30] One can see this principle at work in Ælfric's own writings, where in discussing the Real Presence, he cites both Paschasius Radbertus and Ratramnus as authorities, even though the two Carolingian theologians held opposing views. As Lynne Grundy correctly points out in *Notes and Queries* 235 (1990), pp. 265-69, "Ælfric moves back and forth over the boundary line apparently without noticing it" (p. 266) and "Ælfric must have believed that no contradiction was implied by his use of [both Radbertus and Ratramnus] . . . by quoting the Paschasian example he was seeking to support his argument" (p. 268).

[31] Colin Morris, *The Discovery of the Individual, 1050-1200*, Medieval Academy Reprints for Teaching 19 (Toronto: University of Toronto Press, 1972), p. 60.

[32] According to the promise of scripture (Matt. 18.20), the Holy Spirit acted "where two or three are gathered in [Christ's] name." So important was the concept of unity that the *Liber pontificalis* reports that every ninth-century pope (Leo III to Stephen V) was elected *una voce* — unanimously, with the Holy Spirit present and active — even though contentions arising soon after such elections showed that no such unanimity existed and that the papacy was in fact the plaything of aristocratic factions. See L. Duchesne, ed., *Le Liber Pontificalis: Texte, Introduction, et Commentaire* (Paris: Éditions E. de Boccard, 1955; rpt. 1981) 2: 1, 49, 52, 69, 71, 73, 86-87, 107, 140, 152, 173-74, 191 (after which the papal *vitae* become brief notices of regnal dates). Similarly, as Karl Morrison notes, Pseudo-Isidore claimed "antiquity, universality and consensus" as the guarantors of authenticity for his collection of canons, including some he knew were regarded as apocryphal. And while he knew that there were inconsistencies in the provisions of the

a whole — to use the formula of Vincent of Lérins, they were beliefs held "ubique, semper, et ab omnibus."[33]

As a standard for measuring orthodoxy, this formula has obvious flaws, for few Christian doctrines have been believed *semper* and *ab omnibus*.[34] Even the Nicene creed was hammered out over time and in controversy. In practice, however, there were few problems. Theological disputes were rare,[35] but if a challenge arose, the bishop bore the primary responsibility for protecting the faith in his see.[36] He might convoke a council to address questions of doctrine — for instance, in the occasional cases when wandering preachers stirred up contro-

canons, this did not trouble him, "for diverse interpretations had led to variant statements, some longer, some shorter, but all with the same sense." See Karl F. Morrison, *Tradition and Authority in the Western Church, 300-1140* (Princeton: Princeton University Press, 1969), p. 237; cf. Morrison on the importance of consensus over papal authority in the years before the Gregorian Reform (p. 264).

[33] See Jaroslav Pelikan, *The Christian Tradition*, vol. 1, *The Emergence of the Catholic Tradition* (Princeton: Princeton University Press, 1971), p. 333; Morrison, pp. 4-5.

[34] Cf. Morrison, pp. 5-6: "Vincent of Lérins showed the flaw in his all-too-clear definition when he said that universality could deceive if the whole Church fell into heresy. His ultimate canon was universal consensus; his argument was in fact tautological." Even the appeal to tradition, which Vincent proposed as a guide to orthodoxy, was not "an appeal to a timeless abstract standard, but to various modes of thought formed by particular circumstances of time and place." Even later, after the push to systematize canon law in the twelfth century, the definition of heresy did not become much more precise. Gratian defines it as a teaching "chosen by human perception, contrary to holy scripture, publically avowed and obstinately defended" (qtd. by Moore, p. 68).

[35] After the dispute between Radbertus and Ratramnus over the Real Presence in the ninth century, there was no significant theological controversy until the Gregorian reform.

[36] Moore, pp. 69-70. Morrison stresses episcopal autonomy from early in the history of the church, resulting in tension between ecclesiastical theory and the real state of affairs: "The fact was that every bishop was in effect autocephalous. He could repudiate even the decrees of episcopal synods and councils if he judged them heretical or unjust. The theory was the ancient idea of the faith's essential unity" (p. 70). By the tenth century, however, theory had developed to support the reality: to Pseudo-Isidore and others, all bishops shared the power to bind and loose; see Morrison, pp. 239-40, 252.

versy.[37] As the members of a council understood their role, they were the conduit for the actions of the Holy Spirit; therefore, they were articulating what the church had always believed. But they could only make that determination based on their own experience and practice of Christianity, identifying the customs or beliefs prevailing locally as the "consensus of the whole church."[38] This does not mean that orthodoxy became entirely arbitrary or that there were radical shifts in doctrine or practice from place to place. Consensus was assembled from sources deemed authoritative: the traditions handed down from earlier generations or recorded in books. Some authorities might be shared with other churches or other sees — e.g., the Bible, or the works of Augustine or Gregory — while others might be fairly local, as the records from local councils or treatises of limited circulation. Certainly Christians held many basic ideas in common, but a decentralized church[39] also permitted the growth of regional variations in saints venerated, feasts celebrated, ecclesiastical organization, and numerous other matters.[40]

If we define orthodoxy as consensus in this sense (i.e., based on tradition as understood and supported by ecclesiastical authority) and admit that it can change with time and place, our next step should be

[37] Bishops or episcopal councils dealt with most of the half-dozen cases of heresy documented in the late tenth and early eleventh centuries. See Moore, pp. 13-19.

[38] Hence one has the odd case of Ramihradus of Cambrai, burned by servants of the bishop for his claim that sacraments administered by a simoniac were invalid (an essentially Donatist view), yet celebrated as a martyr by the reform party around Gregory VII. See Moore, pp. 18-19; Walter Wakefield and Austin P. Evans, *Heresies of the High Middle Ages* (New York: Columbia University Press, 1991), pp. 95-96.

[39] Or, as Morrison puts it (pp. 37ff.) a church with "multiple centers of cohesion" — an expression which conveys both the prevailing conception of unity and the reality of localized autonomy.

[40] Diversity of practice was accepted as the norm in the ninth and tenth centuries. Regino of Prüm (d. 915), for example, remarked that "just as divers nations differ among themselves in descent, habits, language and laws, so also does the whole universal Church dispersed throughout the earth differ in ecclesiastical customs, though it is unified by a common faith" (qtd. in Morrison, p. 232); see also Morrison, pp. 258-59, for the similar views of Fulbert of Chartres (d. c. 1028) and pp. 269-70 for a more general assessment of attitudes to diversity before the Gregorian reform.

to ask what consensus prevailed in Ælfric's day. There had, of course, been objections raised to the legend of the Assumption. Bede, for example, did not like the story on chronological grounds: in the version he knew, the Assumption occurred two years after Christ's passion, which did not allow enough time for the chain of events recorded in Acts. Bede also rejected the claim that John had to be miraculously transported to Mary's bedside.[41] He should have already been near at hand, since the Lord had commended her to his care.[42] But despite Bede's skepticism over the *Transitus* narrative, he seems to have accepted the doctrine of the Assumption — at least, his word choice admits the possibility that Mary was not awaiting the general resurrection with the rest of humanity.[43]

Reservations about the *Transitus* apocrypha became still harder to maintain in the decades after Bede's death, when the Feast of the Assumption became a regular part of the liturgical calendar in the Eng-

---

[41] Indeed, in some versions of the *Transitus*, Mary had to *remind* John of his obligation. For example, in Tischendorf's A-version, Mary says: "O carissimi fili, cur tanto tempore me dimisisti et praecepta tui magistri non attendisti, ut me custodias, sicut praecipit tibi dum in cruce penderet?" ("Oh dearest son, why have you sent me off for so long a time and ignored the orders of your master that you take care of me, as he bid you while he was hanging on the cross?") See Constantinus Tischendorf, *Apocalypses Apocryphae* (Leipzig: Hermann Mendelssohn, 1866), p. 116. Bede's version (he quotes from it) was not quite so forcefully expressed, but one can still understand his unwillingness to credit this portrayal of an apostle. See Clayton, *Cult*, p. 17.

[42] See Clayton, *Cult*, pp. 16-19, for full discussion of Bede's objections. To such a notion, Bede responds, "Absit, autem ut credamus."

[43] Clayton notes that Bede, in *De sanctis locis*, abridged Adamnan, his source, which reads: "Sed de eodem sepulchro quomodo vel quo tempore aut a quibus personis sanctam corpusculum eius sit sublatum vel in quo loco resurrectionem expectat, nullus, ut refert, pro certo scire potest." ("But when and by whom her holy body was carried off from that tomb or in what place she awaits resurrection, no one, they say, knows for sure.") Bede eliminated the *in quo loco resurrectionem expectat* line and referred instead to the empty tomb "in quo sancta Maria aliquando pausasse dicitur, sed a quo vel quando sit ablata, nescitur" ("in which St. Mary is said to have rested awhile, but by whom or when she was carried away is unknown"). See Clayton, *Cult*, pp. 14, 16-17.

lish church.[44] It was necessary, after all, to know something about the occasion one celebrated. Where could one turn for information about the event being commemorated, if not to the apocryphal accounts? It is not surprising, therefore, that we have numerous versions of the *Transitus* in manuscripts that suggest use in a variety of contexts.

The earliest, from the Blickling book, is a composite homily that combines two different versions of the Latin *Transitus* (B and C) in a badly garbled translation (at one point, the apostles grab Mary around the waist; later her corpse is told to walk around town).[45] A variant of this homily occurs in Cambridge, Corpus Christi College MS 198, a manuscript of the early eleventh century.[46] The two texts are clearly closely related, but if Willard is correct, neither is a copy of the other.[47] We must therefore assume another Old English exemplar behind them, which despite its dreadful deficiencies in sense, was considered useful enough to be copied more than once. Since in both manuscripts the homilies follow (more or less) the order of the ecclesiastical calendar, they seem intended for liturgical use.[48] Since they are

---

[44] On the gradual acceptance of the feast in the eighth century, see Clayton, *Cult*, p. 38.

[45] Richard Morris, ed., *The Blickling Homilies*, EETS, o.s. 58, 63, 73 (London: N. Trübner, 1880; rpt. Oxford: Oxford University Press, 1967), pp. 141, 147. Ker (no. 382) dates the manuscript to the end of the tenth or beginning of the eleventh century.

[46] Ker, no. 48; Gneuss, no. 64. On the compilation of this manuscript and its relation to the Blickling book, see Scragg, "Homilies of the Blickling Manuscript," pp. 309-15.

[47] Rudolph Willard, "On Blickling Homily XIII: *The Assumption of the Virgin*: the Source and the Missing Passages," *Review of English Studies* 12 (1936), pp. 5-6; Scragg, "Homilies of the Blickling Manuscript," pp. 313-15.

[48] Ker, no. 48; Scragg, "Homilies of the Blickling Manuscript," pp. 311-12. CCCC 198 was compiled in three parts, the earliest running from Christmas to June. Other sets of homilies were added later to make a collection which roughly covers the church year, but with additional homilies interposed. Scragg suggests that the compilers intended to supply a Temporale sequence from Christmas to Pentecost and a Sanctorale for the rest of the year. Blickling is less comprehensive than CCCC 198 in the occasions that it covers, but it too is arranged *per circulum anni* with some pieces out of order.

in the vernacular, they may have been meant for preaching *ad populum*, although other audiences are certainly a possibility.[49]

The version in CCCC 41 is based on the same source as the latter part of the Blickling Assumption, but it offers a much more accurate translation.[50] It is different in other respects as well. It is squeezed into the margins of the manuscript in a rather cramped hand, and it lacks the hortatory address that frequently marks homilies intended for public delivery. Whatever the scribe intended to do with it, we are fairly safe in assuming that it was not meant to be read aloud. In its present state, this version looks like someone's private notes, perhaps jotted down as a temporary expedient until more parchment could be obtained, or perhaps recorded by a reader who had only one book in which to preserve this text, along with the other marginal material, for personal devotional reading. But while the intended use of the CCCC 41 *Transitus* remains obscure, we do have some indication of the milieu in which it circulated. According to a note added at the end, the manuscript was the gift of Bishop Leofric (1046-1072) to Exeter. Since the hand that wrote the marginalia predates the notice of gift, it seems

[49]The question of audience is vexing. See Milton McC. Gatch, "The Unknowable Audience of the Blickling Homilies," *Anglo-Saxon England* 18 (1989), pp. 99-115; Mary Clayton, "Homiliaries and Preaching in Anglo-Saxon England," *Peritia* 4 (1985), pp. 207-42; Nancy M. Thompson, "The Milk of Doctrine: Translation and Homiletic Method in Early England" (Ph. D. diss., Stanford University, 1994), pp. 70-78. I am no longer as convinced as once I was that most of our surviving manuscripts make good candidates for public preaching. Vernacular homiliaries may well have been put to that purpose, but one would expect a lower survival rate, as such books would be likely to be discarded (or recycled) as changes in the language made them less useful. But I am also not convinced that the audience is unknowable. See the interesting comparison of Rochester manuscripts by Mary P. Richards, "Texts and their Traditions in the Medieval Library of Rochester Priory Cathedral," *Transactions of the American Philosophical Society* 78, pt. 3 (1988), pp. 2-3 and 85-120, especially pp. 87-94, 119. Richards suggests content differences between pre-conquest homiliaries, when Rochester was staffed by secular canons, and later manuscripts more suited to the needs of the Benedictines installed there after the Norman arrival.

[50]Clayton identifies it as *Transitus B²* in "The Assumption Homily in CCCC 41," *Notes and Queries* 234 (1989), pp. 293-95. The Latin has been published by M. Haibach-Reinische, *Ein neuer "Transitus Mariae" des Pseudo-Melito* (Rome: Pontificia Acadamia Mariana Internationalis, 1962).

reasonable to conclude that the "suspect" material was present when the bishop presented the book to the cathedral.[51] Apparently no one at the time found the text inappropriate for an episcopal library or at odds with the orthodox Bede.

In addition to the Old English versions, a Latin *Transitus* survives in Cambridge, Pembroke College MS 25.[52] This text belongs to the same family as the first part of the Blickling homily (a *Transitus C*), but is not closely related. The Blickling version seems to have been based on a text fairly close to the one printed by Wilmart.[53] Pembroke, by contrast, is a well-edited abbreviation. The redactor improved the Latin, substituting participles for the C texts' rambling subordinate clauses.[54] He excised repetitive passages — for instance, in other C texts, first John, then the other apostles describe their miraculous journey to Mary's bedside; in Pembroke, the two accounts are condensed

---

[51] Ker, no. 32 at p. 45, dates the marginalia to the first half or mid-eleventh century. Cf. Menner, *The Poetical Dialogues of Solomon and Saturn*, pp. 2-3. Menner suggests a later date, believing that the "ugly, insular" hand indicates a post-Conquest, even early twelfth-century scribe. That would associate the marginalia still more firmly with the cathedral community at Exeter, but would mean that the notice of donation was written in retrospect. Since the notice is given in the present tense (*Hunc librum dat Leofricus episcopus ęcclęsię . . . in Exonia ubi sedes epicopalis est*) and repeated in the present tense in Old English, this seems to me unlikely. For the notice of gift, see Max Förster, "Ae. Bam handum twam awriten," *Archiv für das Studium der neueren Sprachen* 62 (1932), p. 230.

[52] Gneuss (no. 131) dates it to the later eleventh century. The manuscript has occasioned much interest among scholars of Old English prose, as it seems to be a representative of a homiletic collection that served as a source for a number of Old English homilies. It is discussed by James E. Cross, *Cambridge Pembroke College MS. 25* (London: King's College, 1987). Cf. Cross, "Toward the Identification of Old English Literary Ideas — Old Workings and New Seams," *Sources of Anglo-Saxon Culture*, ed. Paul E. Szarmach, pp. 77-101, Studies in Medieval Culture 20 (Kalamazoo, MI: Medieval Institute Publications, 1986).

[53] Wilmart, pp. 325-57.

[54] To offer one example of many: Pembroke's "Oremus ad dominum ut ostendat nobis causam congregandi in unum" (fol. 114v, "Let us pray to the Lord that he reveal the reason for gathering us together") replaces the longer and more ungainly phrasing of C (Wilmart, p. 332): "ut notum faciat nobis quae sit causa quod nos hodie voluit in unum congregare" ("that he make known to

into one.[55] Other cuts make the Pembroke homily more dramatic: when John asks for the help of his fellow apostles, they arrive in an instant — "lo, suddenly, as he spoke." There is none of the intervening narrative that slows the pace of other Assumption accounts.[56]

J. E. Cross identified Pembroke 25 as a source book for preachers, but it may have been intended to supply readings for monks, for it has something of a monastic flavor.[57] There is, for example, a certain modesty in the way that the legend is presented that makes it seem especially appropriate for a celibate audience. Unlike C texts generally, this version does not permit John to enter Mary's bedroom by himself, and Mary withdraws to bathe herself *in secreto*.[58] Also unlike other C texts, this account opens with the statement that the angel announcing Mary's death came "ad sanctam Mariam *cum esset in templo dei diebus et noctis vigilans et orans in secretis locis cum ceteris sanctis virginibus*."[59] The phrases *in secretis locis*, "in a place of withdrawal," and *cum ceteris sanctis virginibus*, "with other holy virgins," suggest that Mary spent the

us what the reason is that he wished us to gather together"). Blickling closely follows the latter (Morris, p. 139): "Uton gebiddan us to urum Drihtne þæt he us þæt cuþ gedo þæt he us todæge wolde on ðisse tid gesomnian" ("Let us pray to our Lord that he make known to us why he wished for us to gather together at this time").

[55] Cf. Wilmart, pp. 334-37, and Pembroke fol. 115r.

[56] Cf Wilmart, pp. 331-32 (a C-text); Haibach-Reinische, p. 71 (a B-text); and Pembroke, fol.114v.

[57] Cross, *Pembroke*, p. 57. His remarks apply to the intended use of the original collection, which has several continental analogues, rather than this particular manuscript. But since the homilies are in Latin, they would have to be translated to be comprehensible to the faithful. Moreover, the collection includes several items on priests' duties (see Cross, *Pembroke*, pp. 41-42, 55), which seem an inappropriate subject for public preaching. On the monastic use of homiliaries for Night Offices and other readings required by the Benedictine Rule, see Henri Barré, *Les homéliares carolingiens de l'école d'Auxerre* (Vatican City: Biblioteca Apostolica Vaticana, 1962), pp. 1-4; Réginald Grégoire, *Les homéliares du Moyen Âge* (Rome: Casa Editrice Herder, 1966), pp. 5-6; Milton McC. Gatch, *Preaching and Theology in Anglo-Saxon England: Ælfric and Wulfstan* (Toronto and Buffalo: University of Toronto Press, 1977), pp. 27-30.

[58] Pembroke 25, fol. 114v, 114r; cf. Wilmart, pp. 331, 327.

[59] Pembroke 25, fol. 113v: "to St. Mary *while she was in the temple of God*,

years after the Passion in a convent. A further change suggests a redactor well accustomed to the liturgical round of prayers. As the apostles carry out the body for burial, they sing (in both C and B families) "Exiit Israhel de Egypto ALLELUIA;" in Pembroke only (so far as I know) is added "Alii dicebant qui convertit aridam [*vel solida* (*sic*) above the line] petram in stagnum aquae et rupem in fontes aquarum."[60] Inserted thus, it sounds like an automatic response to a familiar phrase from mass or office. Monastic liturgical use is also suggested by the manuscript's association with the community at Bury,[61] although again other purposes are possible. Cross notes that the items in this collection (and their vernacular analogues) emphasize basic moral themes, and that they draw on sources explicitly addressed to clerics charged with parish preaching, so he may be right to assume that some kind of concern for *ad populum* preaching underlies this collection.[62] Monastic connections need not preclude this: a later abbot of Bury acquired something of a reputation for popular preaching, and he may not have been unique in his interest.[63]

All in all, the surviving manuscripts suggest a full range of uses: private reading, monastic offices, and perhaps public preaching. In the multiple versions, representing two major Latin families and various permutations thereof, we have evidence of a vibrant and healthy tradition as well as broad acceptance of this apocryphal tale, not simply by the unlearned or credulous, but by those who would have contributed to orthodox consensus in the Anglo-Saxon church. And indeed, why should they doubt the truth of the legend? It had the "testimony of

keeping watch and praying day and night *in a place of withdrawal with other holy virgins.*" The italicized words do not appear in the manuscripts collated by Wilmart; see p. 325.

[60] Pembroke 25, fol. 116v. Psalms 113.8: "Qui convertit petram in stagna aquarum, Et rupem in fontes aquarum."

[61] Montague Rhodes James, *A Descriptive Catalogue of the Manuscripts in the Library of Pembroke College, Cambridge* (Cambridge: University Press, 1905), p. 25.

[62] Cross, pp. 57-58, 91-92.

[63] Frank Barlow, *The English Church, 1066-1154* (London and New York: Longman, 1979), p. 217.

antiquity,"[64] for it was recorded in holy books by pious men. As Pelikan notes, in the establishment of orthodoxy, ecclesiastical authority and long usage lent weight to any doctrine.[65] On both those grounds, the Assumption apocrypha pass muster.

If Ælfric's objections to the legend did not persuade his contemporaries, it makes little sense for modern scholars to speak as though he introduced a new standard of orthodoxy to the late Anglo-Saxon church. Nor should we take his remarks as an indication that a new, more critical spirit had entered the church with the reform movement. While Ælfric was undoubtedly anxious to avoid falling into theological error, he had not developed a set of critical principles that would enable him to distinguish untrustworthy apocrypha from the creditable miracles of hagiography or the New Testament, *dwollican béc* from *riht geleafa*. Unlike Bede, who applied scriptural and chronological criteria to sift the wheat from the chaff, or like Augustine, who based his condemnation of the apocryphal *Visio Pauli* on its discrepancy with the Pauline epistles, Ælfric relied on his authorities to tell him what should or should not be believed.[66] As Mary Clayton noted some time ago, he did not know what was wrong with the apocrypha he repudiated; he knew only that some saintly person had condemned them.[67]

In the case of the Assumption, Ælfric's objections were based on a work attributed to St. Jerome, but written (probably) by Paschasius

---

[64] The phrase is, of course, Archbishop Parker's, the title for his treatise using Ælfric's writings to defend Reformation doctrine on the Eucharist.

[65] Pelikan, *Growth of Medieval Theology*, pp. 16-17.

[66] See James, trans., *The Apocryphal New Testament* (Oxford: Clarendon Press, 1924), p. 525, and Clayton, *Cult*, p. 238. The premise of the *Visio Pauli* is contradicted by 2 Corinthians 12. 3-4: "And I know that this man was caught up into paradise . . . and he heard things that cannot be told, which man may not utter."

[67] Clayton, *Cult*, pp. 244-45. Ælfric was "unwilling to run the danger of heresy and chose to avoid all but the briefest mention, as he appears to have been unclear about the exact reason for their exclusion." John C. Pope notes Ælfric's willingness to believe "preposterous" legends in his review of *Preaching and Theology in Anglo-Saxon England* by Milton McC. Gatch, in *Speculum* 54 (1979), pp. 129-36 at p. 36.

Radbertus.[68] In fact, Ælfric did not compose the warning against heresy that Grant urges us to "bear in mind;" he took it over nearly whole-sale from Radbertus.[69] He certainly shared Radbertus's opinion — he would not have repeated it otherwise — but there is a subtle difference between what he was actually doing and how it has sometimes been perceived. He was a reporter, not a critic. He was mining the sources, repeating what he found, which is not quite the same thing as launch-ing a campaign to reform the belief system of the English church.[70]

Since Ælfric had not developed a set of objective critical stan-dards, he accepted most legends without hesitation, objecting to only a few, when he learned in the course of his reading that they had been condemned by some venerable authority. This is why he translated other apocrypha of sometimes dubious reputation, including the *Acts of Peter and Paul, James, John, Simon and Jude, Matthew*, and Bar-

[68] Clayton, *Cult*, p. 235. The Latin text is printed by A. Ripberger, ed., *Der Pseudo-Hieronymus-Brief IX "Cogitis me": Ein erster marianischer Traktat des Mittelalters von Paschasius Radbert*, Spicilegium Friburgense 9 (Fribourg: Universitätsverlag, 1962).

[69] This explains why the passage cited by Grant, *Three Homilies*, p. 14, includes an address to "eower mædenlica heap" — your virginal company — a peculiar expression for a sermon *ad populum*, but of course Ælfric is quoting here. See Clemoes, *Catholic Homilies*, p. 429. Clayton, *Cult*, p. 236, thinks that Ælfric's translation makes a more forceful condemnation of the story: he does translate *apocryphum* as "seo lease gesetnys, ðe þurh gedwollmen wide tosawen is" (Clemoes, *Catholic Homilies*, p. 430; "the false story that is widely disseminated through those in error [or heretics]"). Ælfric also omits the phrase "quod multi latinorum pietatis amore, studio legendi, carius amplectuntur, praecertim ex his cum nihil aliud experiri potest" ("which many of the Latins from love of piety and enthusiasm for reading embrace the more ardently, from these things above all when nothing else can be proved"), which is something of a justification of pious belief. Still, he comes down in favor of the doctrine of the Assumption, if not the narrative: "cwædon þeah gehwylce lareowas, þæt hyre sunu, se þe on þam þriddan dæge mihtlice of deaðe arás, þæt he eac his moder lichaman of deaðe arærde, and mid undeadlicum wuldre on heofonan rice gelogode" (Clemoes, *Catholic Homilies*, p. 431: "yet certain teachers say that her son, he who on the third day arose with power from the dead, that he also raised his mother's body from death and with undying glory established her in the kingdom of heaven.") The passage is taken from a later chapter of Radbertus.

[70] There is a comparable situation in the problem addressed by M. R. Godden, "Ælfric's Saints' Lives and the Problem of Miracles," *Sources and Relations:*

tholomew, all derived from the *Historia Apostolica* of pseudo-Abdias.[71]
The case of the *Acts of Peter*, in which the apostle confronts Simon
Magus and ultimately is martyred, is particularly interesting. It had
long been regarded by some churchmen as suspect: it was, for instance,
condemned by the so-called Gelasian decree, a sixth-century list of
apocrypha damnata that included the *Transitus Mariae*, the *Acts of Andrew*, and the *Acts of Matthew*.[72] According to Enid Raynes, Ælfric
knew the decree — at least, it appears in a manuscript associated with
him.[73] If so, he did not recognize his sources as those named on the
list, despite the fact that the decree includes not only the *Acts of Peter*,
but also names Simon Magus specifically.[74] Despite the earlier challenges to the legend, or perhaps unaware of them, Ælfric included it
in his first series of homilies. His version, however, is abbreviated: he
states that he will tell the tale *mid scortre race* because it has already
been fully rendered into English.[75] And in fact, another English ver-

---

Studies in Honour of J. E. Cross, ed. Marie Collins et al. (Leeds: University
of Leeds, 1985), pp. 83-100: Ælfric's assertion that miracles are no longer
necessary (a phrase taken from Gregory the Great) and his frequent recital of
contemporary miracle working in other homilies. Godden works to resolve
the contradiction, finally deciding that Ælfric questioned miracles on his own
account, but used them in his sermons as an aid to the faithful. I suspect the
answer is simpler: here again Ælfric is reporting the results of his research
and translating the words of venerable authority.

[71] Cf. M. R. James, *Apocryphal New Testament*, pp. 462-69 and Clemoes,
Catholic Homilies, pp. 391-99 (Peter and Paul), 513-19 (Andrew), 206-16
(John), 439-50 (Bartholomew); Godden, *Catholic Homilies*, pp. 241-47
(James), 280-87 (Simon and Jude), 275-79 (Matthew).

[72] PL 59:157-64; James, *New Testament Apocrypha*, p. 21, notes the date is in
dispute but suggests "not later than the sixth century."

[73] See Enid M. Raynes, "Ms. Boulogne-sur-Mer 63 and Ælfric," *Medium
Ævum* 26 (1957), pp. 65-73; cf. Clayton, *Cult*, p. 245.

[74] PL 59:162, 164. The decree lists titles only, which may explain why Ælfric
did not identify his version (reworked by pseudo-Abdias to include the
martyrdom of Paul) with the *Acts of Peter*; however, it is hard to understand
why he also overlooked the condemnation of the *Acts of Andrew* and the *Acts
of Matthew*. Perhaps he came across the list only late in his career, or perhaps
the Boulogne manuscript is not as closely associated with Ælfric as Raynes
believes.

[75] Clemoes, *Catholic Homilies*, p. 391.

sion still survives, in the "heterodox" Blickling homiliary. Was this the longer version that Ælfric had in mind? Certainly scholars have been quick to connect Ælfric's comments about "heretical books" to the Blickling homiliary when discussing the Assumption apocrypha; perhaps his approval of the "heretical" *Acts of Peter* should be connected to the Blickling book as well.

The case of the apocryphal *Acts of Peter* illustrates my point. Ælfric was not imposing a new orthodoxy on the late Saxon church and rejecting the "wild" narratives of pre-reform generations. From a modern perspective, there is little to distinguish the *Acts of Peter* from the *Transitus Mariae*. Both seem improbable; neither is supported by scripture. If anything, the tale of Peter's martyrdom appears somewhat more unseemly, since it portrays the apostles in a contest of sorcery with a diabolically-assisted magician. But the legend was accepted by the late Anglo-Saxon church and, here at least, Ælfric shared the beliefs of his contemporaries.

By translating such marvels into English, Ælfric showed his trust in tradition, a desire to make it accessible, not to overturn it. He had undoubtedly read more widely than many other clerics of his age, but, like them, he tended to believe what he read, whether it was apocryphal tales or criticism of them. Under the circumstances, it hardly seems proper to turn some of his judgments (the ones that most conform to modern rationalism) into the benchmark of Anglo-Saxon orthodoxy, using them to assess the theological merits of other surviving manuscripts.

Why have we given Ælfric such authority? In part, I think, it is because his name, like Wulfstan's, is one we know. When so much has been lost over the course of centuries, the survivors loom like giants. Moreover, Ælfric's works, especially his homilies, were very popular, and not only for their scholarship. He offered collections of homilies for almost every occasion. For those looking for readings for the liturgical year, no doubt some of the attraction lay in their comprehensiveness. But just because contemporaries drew on Ælfric's works, it does not mean they accepted his judgment on heretical books. In fact, the evidence suggests the opposite.

One of our witnesses to the Assumption legend comes from
CCCC 198, which contains mostly Ælfrician material.[76] The compilers clearly had access to a good-sized collection of Ælfric's work, since
they drew from both series of the *Catholic Homilies*. We must admit
the possibility — even probability — that this included an Ælfrician
homily for the Assumption, yet despite the warnings about false teaching and lying English works, the compilers opted for the traditional,
familiar (and in this case, garbled) account. Other collections also freely
mix Ælfric's work with apocrypha, showing the compilers' willingness
to adopt his works without adopting his views. For instance, Ælfric
had refused to say much about the early life of the Virgin Mary "þy
læs ðe we on ænigum gedwylde befeallon," but scribes inserted a sermon drawn from the Gospel of pseudo-Matthew into three otherwise largely Ælfrician collections: Oxford, Bodleian Library, Hatton
MS 114; Cambridge, Corpus Christi College MS 367; and Oxford,
Bodleian Library, Bodley MS 343.[77] Bodley 343 also includes a composite homily that draws on the *Visio Pauli*, another work criticized
by Ælfric.[78] In Cambridge, Corpus Christi College MS 162; London,
British Library, Cotton MS Tiberius A. iii; and London, Lambeth
Palace, MS 489, versions of the apocryphal "Sunday letter," supposed
to have fallen from heaven to enforce the day's observance, appear with

[76] On this manuscript, see above, n. 47.

[77] Ker, nos. 331 (Worcester, s. xi, 3rd quarter), 63 (s. xii), 310 (s. xii²); only
Hatton 114 is early enough to be included by Gneuss, *Handlist*, no. 638.
As witnesses to Ælfric's work, the manuscripts mentioned here are also
described by Godden, *Catholic Homilies*, pp. xxi-lxxiv, and John C. Pope,
Homilies of Ælfric: A Supplementary Collection, EETS, o.s. 259 (Oxford:
Oxford University Press, 1967), pp. 14-91. For the Old English sermon, see
Bruno Assmann, *Angelsächsische Homilien und Heiligenleben* (Kassel: Georg H.
Wigand, 1889), pp. 117-37. Interestingly, CCCC 367, though fragmented,
still includes Ælfric's first Assumption homily, suggesting that the compiler
was aware of Ælfric's views.

[78] Ker no. 310, item 64. The homily is collated with Homily 46 in Arthur
Napier, *Wulfstan: Sammelung der ihm zugeschriebenen Homilien* (Berlin:
Weidmannsche Buchhandlung, 1883), pp. 232-42. The section drawing on
the *Visio Pauli* begins at p. 235.

Ælfric's works.[79] CCCC 198 contains the Blickling version of the *Acts of Andrew*; and both Cambridge, Corpus Christi College, MS 303 and London, British Library, Cotton MS Vespasian D.xiv translate from the *Gospel of Nicodemus*.[80] These three are all manuscripts in which homilies by Ælfric predominate. In short, there is no indication that Ælfric's cautious attitude rubbed off onto his compatriots. Nor should this seem surprising — after all, we have the *Gospel of Nicodemus* bound up with the four New Testament Gospels in a late eleventh-century manuscript, Cambridge, University Library, MS Ii.2.11.[81]

The use of apocrypha is not the only case in which Ælfric's stricter standards were rejected by the Anglo-Saxon church: his assertion that the days between Good Friday and Easter are *swigdagum* (days on which no sermon should be delivered) also met resistence. As Paul E. Szarmach notes, later scribes looked to other sources for homilies for the occasion, since Ælfric did not supply them: hence the appearance of the Vercelli homily *De Parasceve* in four otherwise "heavily Ælfrician collections."[82] Indeed, Ælfric's claim drew a strong protest in one eleventh-century homiliary: one ought to preach at any time,

---

[79] Ker, nos. 38 (southeastern, s. xi in.), 186 (Christ Church, Canterbury, s. xi med.), 283 (Exeter, s. xi, 3rd quarter); Gneuss, *Handlist*, nos. 50, 363, 520. The sermon is printed by Napier, "An Old English Homily on the Observance of Sunday," *An English Miscellany Presented to Dr. Furnivall* (Oxford: Clarendon Press, 1901), pp. 357-62; Napier, *Wulfstan*, pp. 215-26, 291-99.

[80] Ker, nos. 48, item 64; 57, item 17 (Rochester, s. xii¹); 209, item 31 (Rochester or Christ Church, Canterbury, s. xii med.). William H. Hulme prints the Cotton version in "The Old English Gospel of Nicodemus," *Modern Philology* 1 (1903-04): pp. 579-614. CCCC 303 is a variant of the CCCC 41 *Nicodemus*, also printed by Hulme, p. 610.

[81] Ker, no. 20; Gneuss, *Handlist*, no. 15. On the near canonical authority of the *Gospel of Nicodemus*, see Antonette Di Paolo Healey, "Anglo-Saxon Use of the Apocryphal Gospel," *The Anglo-Saxons: Synthesis and Achievement*, ed. J. Douglas Woods and David A. E. Pelteret (Waterloo, Ont.: Wilfrid Laurier University Press, 1985), pp. 93-104 at p. 98. Cf. Jackson J. Campbell, "Latin Tradition and Literary Use of the 'Descensus ad Infernos' in Old English," *Viator* 13 (1982), pp. 107-58 at p. 113.

[82] Paul E. Szarmach, "The Earlier Homily: *De Parasceve*," *Studies in Earlier Old English Prose*, ed. Paul E. Szarmach (Albany: State University of New York Press, 1986), pp. 381-99 at p. 385, notes that "silence is a motif on Good Friday, witness the silent adoration of the cross and the suspension of

wrote Coleman, but especially on the days commemorating Christ's passion, in order to bring the people to repentance.[83]

If Ælfric was thus at times out of step with the consensus of the English church, his views cannot not be regarded as a standard of orthodoxy, at least not from a medieval perspective. But what about modern opinion? Adjectives such as "wild and extravagant" or "heterodox" suggest the present's negative judgment of the past, but is there any harm in using them? The problem is that in applying such labels we tend to build up a misleading view of the church, in which non-Ælfrician religious sensibilities seem to be the exception rather than the norm. By making Ælfric the herald of a new, more rigorous orthodoxy, we impose a false progress on the Anglo-Saxon church. Manuscripts such as CCCC 41 become "backsliding," even though the backsliding persists throughout the Anglo-Saxon period and beyond. We also use that standard to date surviving records. Milton McC. Gatch, for instance, gives an early date for the different vernacular versions of the *Apocalypse of Thomas*, despite the dating of the manuscripts:

> All four versions, however late the transcriptions, date from the middle or first half of the tenth century, and thus precede the rather more cautiously orthodox period of English sermon writing inaugurated by Ælfric of Eynsham in the final decade of the first millennium.[84]

Similarly, D. G. Scragg, in compiling the invaluable "Corpus of Vernacular Homilies and Prose Saints Lives before Ælfric," seems to sug-

---

singing, but neither the Latin homiliarists nor the old English ones extended the silence to preaching. Within this overall context Ælfric's reluctance to write a sermon for Good Friday is somewhat puzzling." Joyce Hill, "Ælfric's 'Silent Days,'" *Leeds Studies in English* 16 (1985), pp. 118-125, suggests that Ælfric adapted a monastic practice to a lay context.

[83] Neil Ker, "Old English Notes Signed 'Coleman,'" *Medium Ævum* 18 (1949), pp. 29-31 at p. 29. The manuscript is CCCC 178; a marginal objection also appears in Hatton 114 (Ker, no. 41, p. 63 and Ker, no. 331, p. 395).

[84] Milton McC. Gatch, "Two Uses of Apocrypha in Old English Homilies," *Church History* 33 (1964), p. 379. He cites, at p. 388n, John Earle's statement that the Blickling book is "plainly of the age before the great Church reform . . . when the line was very clearly drawn between canonical and uncanonical." But two of Gatch's witnesses to the *Apocalypse of Thomas* are eleventh century: CCCC 41 and CCCC 162 (which also has a variant in the twelfth-century Hatton 116).

gest that if a homily does not meet Ælfric's standards of orthodoxy, it must go back to a time before the reform.[85] Yet most of the witnesses to this "pre-reform" homiletic material do not predate Ælfric; they are from collections of the eleventh and twelfth centuries. Scragg recognizes that where homilies appear only in late manuscripts, their dating cannot be secure: "proof of the earlier composition of any of their items . . . must rest on stylistic and linguistic analysis, evidence for which is not yet very full."[86] Often, however, in deciding whether a piece is early or late, the presence of apocrypha appears to be a major criterion.[87]

Clearly there are cases in which homilies can be connected to the two earliest collections, the Blickling and Vercelli manuscripts — witness Scragg's recent demonstration that material from a composite homily in Cambridge, Corpus Christi College, MS 201 predates the Vercelli book, an exciting discovery.[88] But there are numerous other anonymous works surviving in unique copies (four of the six homilies in CCCC 41, for instance), and we should be cautious about assigning them to any particular period, recognizing that we cannot know their date by their content.[89] For the most part, we have no way of ascertaining whether they are copies of earlier works or texts freshly translated for the volume in which we find them. We know that the apocrypha continued to circulate; we know too that the compilers of composite homilies mixed attributed and anonymous materials, unconscious of

---

[85] D. G. Scragg, "The Corpus of Vernacular Homilies and Prose Saints' Lives before Ælfric," *Anglo-Saxon England* 8 (1979), pp. 223-77.

[86] Scragg, "Corpus of Vernacular Homilies," p. 224.

[87] See, e.g., Scragg, "Corpus of Vernacular Homilies," p. 261, for the commentary on Cotton Vespasian D.xiv, a twelfth-century manuscript; and p. 259 for the comment that the eleventh-century manuscript Cambridge, University Library, Ii.2.11 is "probably to be associated with the interest in apocryphal literature witnessed by many tenth-century homilies."

[88] Donald Scragg, *Dating and Style in Old English Composite Homilies*, H. M. Chadwick Memorial Lectures 9 (Cambridge: Department of Anglo-Saxon, Norse, and Celtic, 1999), pp. 4-5.

[89] Two homilies have Vercelli connections. The presence of Vercelli material does not, of itself, indicate an early date for other items in the manuscript, any more than the presence of the Blickling Assumption homily means an early date for (the mostly Ælfrician) CCCC 198.

the two "traditions" of modern scholarship. We should probably assume, absent evidence to the contrary, that apocrypha continued to be regarded as worth translating and that homilists whose names are now lost to us may have carried on the labor of rendering Latin texts into the vernacular. And even if they did not — even if all our translated apocrypha are in fact pre-reform — the evidence of manuscripts such as CCCC 41 suggests that apocryphal materials remained a vital part of Anglo-Saxon religiosity.

CCCC 41 *is* puzzling. We do not know who the scribe was, why he (or she) took the trouble to copy out these particular texts, and what, if anything, he intended to do with them. But we can say that he was not as far out of the mainstream as is sometimes supposed. Indeed, if we set aside questions of orthodoxy and look without prejudice at the kind of materials he brought together, we find a collection of devotional works that seem intended to enhance and strengthen religious faith. There, next to Bede's account of the successful progress of Christianity in England, the scribe recorded the *Solomon and Saturn*, in which the Pater Noster wins out over pagan learning. He listed useful "charms" or cures, which may not reflect modern rationalism about the way the world works, but must be considered essentially Christian, since they invoke the help of Christ and his saints.[90] He included prayers and other bits of liturgical material useful for a priest; and he wrote down the six homilies, which stress resurrection and salvation, Christianity's central theme. In that respect, the apocrypha are appropriate companion pieces to the Bede, as they show not only God's power, but his mercy, especially towards those who, like Mary, do his will.

Perhaps Ælfric (had he still been living) would not have approved of every item in the collection, but his views were not at issue for the scribe of the margins. Ælfric did not speak for the whole English church. When we characterize him as the author of a new standard of orthodoxy, contrasting his work with other homiletic remains, we do both him and the compiler of CCCC 41's homilies a disservice.

[90] CCCC 41: pp. 206, 272, 326, 329, and 350-53. The only "charm" that does not make reference to Christian belief is at p. 182, but this must be considered theologically neutral as no divine powers, either pagan or Christian, are named.

We misinterpret Ælfric's own religious world view, which left adequate room for many extra-scriptural materials handed down by tradition. We also diminish the significance of such fortunate survivals as CCCC 41, effectively silencing the anonymous Anglo-Saxon who, in filling the manuscript's margins, left us another perspective on eleventh-century Christianity.

Textual Appropriation and Scribal (Re)Performance in a Composite Homily: The Case for a New Edition of Wulfstan's *De Temporibus Anticristi*

JOYCE TALLY LIONARONS

THE FAMILIAR CONCEPT of the literary text, defined as an autonomous arrangement of words shaped by an individual writer and reflecting that writer's authorship, is taken for granted in most contemporary scholarship. In recent years, however, the applicability of the idea of the text to medieval literary works has been challenged by scholars studying the manuscript culture of the Middle Ages. Medievalists have argued convincingly that it was only "the development of printing with movable type"[1] that created the conditions that allowed the literary text as such to come into existence in the first place. Before the appearance of print technology, each occurrence of a written work was unique, the product of a specific, historically conditioned intersection between one or more authors, one or more scribes, and the material conditions of a particular manuscript's creation, which might include the state of the exemplar; the skill of the scribe or scribes in terms of calligraphy, illumination, and graphic design; and the proposed or *de facto* literary context, that is, which works were chosen or simply available to be copied and bound together to form a manuscript book. Only with the rise of print culture, with "the advent of vast replication of a literary work through mechanical means, [did] the concept of an autonomous 'text' controlling the form of all copies of that particular work become . . . inescapable."[2]

Nevertheless, the language scholars have traditionally used to describe manuscripts and their contents carries with it an assumption of textuality born in a print culture — we speak of textual "archetypes"

---

[1] Fred Robinson, *The Editing of Old English* (Oxford: Oxford University Press, 1994), p. 37.

[2] Robinson, p. 39.

and "variants;" we identify scribal "corruption" and "errors," just as if a separate, uncorrupted master text did in fact exist outside of and prior to the manuscript work. The labor of modern textual critics and editors has largely been devoted to writing the master texts lacking in the medieval witnesses by working backwards from the manuscripts to create "originary" or "authorial" versions of medieval works — in short, to textualizing the non-textual. The manuscript works themselves are then all too often regarded as debased and corrupted variants of the modern editor's recreated text, with the scribe or scribes who created those works seen as obstructions in the editor's path to the author's intentions and words. Medieval textual criticism as it has traditionally been practiced becomes, in John Dagenais's words, "the only discipline I can think of that takes as its first move the suppression of its evidence."[3] The end result of such editorial practice is that modern readers read a fundamentally different work from that encountered by medieval readers. The printed critical edition of a work, first stripped of its manuscript context as well as any identifiable errors, incoherencies, or interpolations, and then textualized, authorized, and provided with an extensive critical apparatus to clarify and explain any difficulties that remain, is generally the only version of the medieval work to which modern readers have access; by contrast, medieval readers read the work the scribe provided in whatever manuscript was available. The difference is not simply that the modern reader has a "better" text. Instead, the textualization of a medieval work alters the relationships among author, work, and reader in ways that can hinder rather than help our understanding of medieval literature.

One reason that the creation of a critical print edition makes such a significant difference is that the idea of the author in manuscript culture is as problematic as the idea of the text. Tim William Machan has suggested that even our modern assumption of a "distinction between authors, who creatively compose texts, and scribes, who transmit or corrupt them" presupposes an anachronistic model of literary composition that "views manuscript production as an (ineffective) prototype of . . . print culture."[4] Medieval ideas of authorship, as A. J.

---

[3] John Dagenais, *The Ethics of Reading in Manuscript Culture: Glossing the Libro de buen amor* (Princeton: Princeton University Press, 1994), p. xviii.

[4] Tim William Machan, "Editing, Orality, and Late Middle English Texts," *Vox Intexta*, ed. A. N. Doane and Carol Braun Pasternack (Madison: University of Wisconsin Press, 1991), p. 241.

Minnis has pointed out, had little to do with creativity or originality, and much to do with the establishment of a work's "authority" with regard to the writer's subject matter.[5] Writers gained *auctoritas* (both "authority" and the distinction of "authorship") by writing works that were considered authoritative because they were manifestly true; conversely, works were authoritative if they were written by *auctores* or "authors." The relationship between author and work in the Middle Ages did not resemble that between a parent and child, as modern metaphors describe it, but was instead circular, merging author with text to create an interdependent identity. Thus in manuscript culture, Dagenais asserts, "The *auctor* is his text."[6] Attributions of authorship might be omitted in manuscripts if they were deemed unnecessary to establish the *auctoritas* of a work, while in other manuscripts the attribution of works to known *auctores*, even if such attributions were false by modern standards, served to provide legitimizing credentials to works by unknown or unfamiliar writers.

But if manuscript works have neither textuality nor authorship in the modern sense of the terms, how can they be characterized? One increasingly popular answer is to regard the scribal copying of a manuscript work, not as the inevitably flawed transmission of an authorial text, but rather as a *performance* of the work by an individual writer in a manner analogous to a preliterate singer's rendition of an oral poem. This viewpoint shifts the critical focus away from manuscript works as textual objects differing from printed texts only in the technology of their (re)production and onto the medieval processes of composition. For as Dagenais points out, even though "[t]he handwritten text as product resembles the mechanically reproduced book; the process of its creation mimics the unique, occasional nature of oral tradition and oral performance."[7] Similarly, A. N. Doane, in a discussion of the manuscript transcription of traditionally oral poetry, postulates a practice of scribal "reperformance" of the poems, that is, a situation in which scribes "rehear [the works], 'mouth' them, 'reperform' them in the act

[5] A. J. Minnis, *The Medieval Theory of Authorship* (London: Scolar Press, 1984).

[6] Dagenais, p. 177.

[7] Dagenais, p. 17.

of writing in such a way that the text may change but remain authentic, just as a completely oral poet's text changed from performance to performance without losing authenticity."[8] Likewise, Fred Robinson asserts that a theory of scribal reperformance need not be limited to the transcription of traditionally oral literature, since any scribal copying from an exemplar could be equally performative and by necessity equally variable: "To expect a medieval copyist . . . to submit himself mindlessly to his exemplar and refrain from introducing anything of himself into his performance would have seemed as unreasonable as to expect that a minstrel should suppress his creative talents when giving an oral rendition of a ballad or romance. As in oral tradition, so in scribal tradition, medieval texts had to be protean and indeterminate if they were to survive at all."[9] Textual indeterminacy, summed up in Paul Zumthor's term *mouvance*, is a hallmark of manuscript culture. Rather than undergoing erasure in a modern critical edition, Zumthor asserts, *mouvance* should be considered an essential component of the manuscript work: "Each version, each 'state of the text' should in principle be considered not so much the result of an emendation as of a re-using, a re-creation."[10]

As this brief summary makes clear, the theoretical perspective of much recent scholarship requires medievalists to go back to the manuscripts in order to reconsider questions of textuality, authorship, and *mouvance*. However, many professional medievalists and almost all students have limited access to the original documents. The creation of digital facsimiles of medieval manuscripts may in future help to alleviate this problem, but the day when a scholar will be able to call up any medieval manuscript on a home computer is still many years away, if it comes at all. In addition most readers, especially beginning students, are glad for the help that the apparatus of a critical edition ide-

[8] A. N. Doane, "Oral Texts, Intertexts, and Intratexts: Editing Old English," *Influence and Intertextuality in Literary History*, ed. Jay Clayton and Eric Rothstein (Madison: University of Wisconsin Press, 1991), pp. 80-81.

[9] Robinson, p. 37.

[10] Paul Zumthor, *Essai de poétique médiéval* (Paris: Seuil, 1987), p. 10, cited in English by Dagenais, p. 22.

ally provides. The problem remains that editorial practice lags behind critical theory in providing scholars with accessible representations of manuscript culture adequate to the re-evaluation of medieval works that current theory requires.

Anglo-Saxon studies are no exception to this rule. Although Fred Robinson has provided several articles demonstrating the necessity to consider Anglo-Saxon works in their manuscript contexts,[11] and extensive discussions of the problems of editing Old English texts have appeared,[12] most Old English works are available only in editions prepared according to editorial practices that privilege reconstructed "authorial" texts over manuscript performances. Wulfstan's homilies in general and his *De Temporibus Anticristi* in particular provide an interesting case study of the issues involved. Dorothy Bethurum's critical edition of the homilies first appeared in 1957;[13] it has recently been reissued in unrevised form by Oxford University Press. Her edition is in the best tradition of the so-called "old philology": Bethurum offers only those texts she can confidently authenticate as Wulfstan's own, and she scrupulously edits the manuscripts to eliminate scribal errors and interpolations, providing a "best authorial text" version of twenty-six separate Old English homilies and four Latin works, as well as manuscript variants and an extensive critical apparatus. Upon publication Bethurum's edition was immediately hailed as an important advance over Arthur Napier's now hard-to-find 1883 collection[14] of sixty-two works, which included a large number of composite homilies as well as homilies once attributed to Wulfstan but now recognized as either Ælfrician or the work of Wulfstanian imitators, and today her edition provides not only the standard text of Wulfstan's work, but also often the only available text. When measured by traditional criteria her edition is an altogether admirable piece of scholarship; nonetheless, in

[11] The essays are collected in *The Editing of Old English*, see note 1.

[12] D. G. Scragg and Paul E. Szarmach, eds., *The Editing of Old English: Papers from the 1990 Manchester Conference* (Cambridge: D. S. Brewer, 1994).

[13] Dorothy Bethurum, ed., *The Homilies of Wulfstan* (Oxford: Clarendon Press, 1957, rpt. 1998).

[14] Arthur Napier, ed., *Wulfstan: Sammlung der ihm zugeschriebenen Homilien nebst Untersuchungen über ihre Echtheit* (Berlin: Weidmannsche, 1883).

its steadfast adherence to print culture models of authorship and textuality, Bethurum's edition unavoidably misrepresents the performative nature of Anglo-Saxon homiletic works.

In a recent discussion of editorial theory, Joyce Hill asserts that "modern concepts of authorship . . . are not applicable to the Anglo-Saxon period, *even when they appear to be present*."[15] Most often, of course, they are not present. The majority of Anglo-Saxon homiletic manuscripts give no indication of authorship at all, identifying homilies through rubrics indicating the particular date in the liturgical calendar for which they are appropriate or, in the case of sermons written for no specific occasion, by such all-purpose rubrics as "Item," "Sermo," or "Larspell." Where indications of authorship do appear, as in the rubric "Incipiunt sermones Lupi Episcopi," found in three of the four manuscripts containing the Wulfstanian sermon that Bethurum prints as Homily VI (Napier II), it is difficult if not impossible to determine which homilies beyond the immediate one the word "sermones" applies to. Even the *exceptio probat regulam* of Wulfstan's most famous sermon, identified in three out of five manuscripts as "Sermo Lupi ad Anglos Quando Dani Maxime Persecuti Sunt Eos," is in two manuscripts identified anonymously as "Larspell" (Cambridge, Corpus Christi College, MS 419) and as "Sermo" (Oxford, Bodleian Library, MS Bodley 343). In addition, the dually performative nature of sermons — which were presumably composed to be preached out loud to a congregation — further obscures authorial identification, which of necessity disappears in oral performance when, as Clare Lees puts it, "there are only speakers and listeners [and] all homilies are anonymous homilies . . . mediated through the trope of the voice of the preacher."[16]

Wulfstan's work in its manuscript context also provides examples of both *mouvance* and performativity. *Sermo Lupi ad Anglos* exists in

[15]Joyce Hill, "Ælfric, Authorial Identity, and the Changing Text," *The Editing of Old English*, ed. D. G. Scragg and Paul E. Szarmach (Cambridge: D. S. Brewer, 1994), p. 179, emphasis in the original.

[16]Clare Lees, "Working with Patristic Sources: Language and Context in Old English Homilies," *Speaking Two Languages: Traditional Disciplines and Contemporary Theory in Medieval Studies*, ed. Allen J. Frantzen (Albany: State University of New York Press, 1991), p. 166.

three distinct versions, perhaps made by Wulfstan himself for different occasions, but possibly examples of scribal reperformance. In addition, pieces of Wulfstan's work and imitations — reperformances — of his style occur in many of the anonymous homilies extant in Anglo-Saxon manuscripts but largely unavailable in print editions. Medieval users of homiletic manuscripts tended to revise the works they appropriated to fit their own individual purposes, and vernacular sermons in particular were "often cannibalized for use in making new composite homilies."[17] Wulfstan's distinctive rhetorical style is relatively easy to detect within the composite homilies, and a study of the ways in which scribes and preachers used his work could provide a great deal of useful information about both homiletic composition and preaching in Anglo-Saxon England. But because most scholarly energy has hitherto been devoted to differentiating Wulfstan's "authentic" homilies from the numerous "inauthentic" scribal reperformances, no extended study of the uses of his work has appeared.

Still, even within the accepted canon of Wulfstan's work the performative character of the homilies is apparent. Wulfstan himself consistently "reperforms" his own sermons, reiterating key phrases and formulaic "bywords"[18] verbatim throughout his homilies and even his law codes in a manner reminiscent of oral-formulaic poetry. In fact, as Andy Orchard has recently demonstrated, Wulfstan's sermons, with their rhythmic, almost poetic prose ornamented by alliteration, occasional rhyme, and frequent wordplay, can "be analyzed in precisely the same way as Old English verse," since they "demonstrably rely on the formulaic repetition of rhythmical phrasing."[19] In addition, of course, like all Anglo-Saxon homilists Wulfstan appropriates material from other works, both vernacular homilies and Latin texts, not quoting verbatim in the manner of a modern author citing a source, but reperforming his sources to make them his own.

De Temporibus Anticristi, printed as Homily IV in Bethurum's edition and as number XVI in Napier, is in large part a Wulfstanian

[17]Jonathan Wilcox, ed., *Ælfric's Prefaces* (Durham: Durham Medieval Texts, 1994), p. 34.

[18]Andy Orchard, "Oral Tradition," *Reading Old English Texts*, ed. Katherine O'Brien O'Keeffe (Cambridge: Cambridge University Press, 1997), p. 109.

[19]Orchard, p. 111.

reperformance of Ælfric's Old English *Preface* to the *Catholic Homilies*; in Bethurum's words, Wulfstan "reworked" the *Preface*, "enlarging and developing it."[20] The homily is extant in three manuscripts. Two, Cambridge, Corpus Christi College, MS 201[21] and Oxford, Bodleian Library, MS Hatton 113,[22] date from the latter part of the eleventh century, and each contains the majority of the homilies identified as Wulfstan's, while the third, Oxford, Bodleian Library, MS Bodley 343,[23] was written in the third quarter of the twelfth century and contains six authenticated Wulfstanian sermons, three more in Wulfstan's style, and fifty-four Ælfrician texts. Although this later manuscript contains a large number of Middle English forms and would seem to be the farthest removed from an original authorial text, Bethurum argues that it also "retains in many cases authoritative readings not found elsewhere."[24] In the case of *De Temporibus Anticristi*, its authority apparently rests on its omission of a long, most likely scribally interpolated, narrative passage concerning the apostles Peter and Paul that is contained in both of the earlier manuscripts. In order to understand precisely what has been lost by Bethurum's preference for a "best authorial text" over the performances of the homily contained in the earlier manuscripts, it will be necessary to look at both *De Temporibus Anticristi* and its Latin and Old English sources in detail.

Ælfric's major source for his Old English *Preface* to the *Catholic Homilies* is Adso of Montièr-en-Der's *De Ortu et Tempore Antichristi*,[25] a short treatise on the Antichrist written in 954 in the form of a letter to Queen Gerberga, wife of the Frankish King Louis d'Outremer, and extant in both Latin and Old English translation in Anglo-Saxon

---

[20]Bethurum, p. 288.

[21]Ker 49; Gneuss 65.

[22]Ker 331; Gneuss 637.

[23]Ker 310.

[24]Bethurum, p. 5.

[25]D. Verhelst, ed. *Adso Dervensis: De Ortu et Tempore Antichristi* (Turnholt: Brepols, 1976). All quotations from Adso are from this edition; page numbers are indicated within the text in parentheses.

homiletic manuscripts.[26] Wulfstan apparently knew and used both Adso and Ælfric, for although *De Temporibus Anticristi* is based primarily on Ælfric's *Preface*, it also contains material from Adso not found in Ælfric. As would be expected, the differences in the three works stem from the differing circumstances of the three writers. Adso is purportedly writing at the request of the queen, who has asked, as he tells us in the prologue to the work proper, *scire de Antichristi impietate et persecutione, necnon et potestate eius et generatione* (20), "to learn about the wickedness and persecution of the Antichrist, as well as of his power and origin." Adso accordingly provides a biography of the Antichrist in standard hagiographic format and style, with particular emphasis on the ways in which the life of the Antichrist, whom he labels *contrarius Christo* (26), "opposite to Christ," provides a perverse mirror image of the life of Jesus. Yet he is careful not to carry the parallels too far: he asserts that those who claim the Antichrist will be born of a virgin alone are wrong, and he emphasizes that the conception of the Antichrist will be the result of ordinary human sexual intercourse; his evil will stem not from the manner of his conception, but from the fact that the devil will enter his mother's womb to corrupt the child before it is born (23). Adso is also quick to reassure the queen that although the last days are approaching, they have not yet arrived: he interprets 2 Thessalonians 2:3 to mean that the Antichrist will not appear until all the kingdoms once subject to Rome have defected, and he patriotically declares that *quandiu reges Francorum durauerint, qui Romanum imperium tenere debent, Romani regni dignitas ex toto non peribit* (26), "as long as the Kings of the Franks who rightfully possess the Roman Empire shall last, the dignity of the Roman Empire will not completely perish." He goes on to predict the coming of a "Last Emperor," a Frankish king who will once again unite the Roman Empire. Not until that king has ended his reign will the coming of the Antichrist and the end of the world be at hand.

[26]The primary Old English translation of Adso is an anonymous homily found in two manuscripts connected with Wulfstan, CCCC 419 (Ker 68; Gneuss 108) and Oxford, Bodleian Library, MS Hatton 114 (Ker 331; Gneuss 638), and may have been used or even commissioned by him; it is printed by Napier as Homily XLII of his collection. The second, found only in the twelfth-century manuscript London, British Library, Cotton Vespasian D.xiv, is a brief summary of Adso that adds nothing to the first homily's narrative.

Ælfric translates material found in Adso's Latin *De Ortu et Tempore Antichristi* for his Old English *Preface*, but he reuses the material to suit his own needs. Ælfric's stated objective in writing the Catholic Homilies as a whole is to ensure that his English-speaking audience will have *god lar*, "good doctrine," because, he says, *ic geseah ⁊ gehyrde mycel gedwyld on manegum engliscum bocum* (174),[27] "I have seen and heard of great error/heresy in many English books." Ælfric emphasizes that the correction of such error assumes increasing importance as the advent of the Antichrist draws near: *menn behofiað godre lare swiðost on þisum timan þe is geendung þyssere worulde* (174), "men are especially in need of good doctrine in this time, which is the end of this world." Correct doctrine, as it is found in well-written books, can give human beings the courage and enduring faith necessary to withstand the Antichrist's temptations: *Gehwá mæg þe eaðelicor þa toweardan costnunge acuman ðurh godes fultum. gif hé bið þurh bóclice lare getrymmed. for ðan ðe ða beoð gehealdene þe oð ende on geleafan þurhwuniað* (175), "Each person may resist the coming temptation more easily, through God's help, if he is encouraged through book learning, because those who persevere in their belief until the end will be saved." Ælfric has no reason to want to reassure his audience that any time is left before the end, and he accordingly omits Adso's references to the Last Emperor in order to emphasize the nearness and horror of the final days. He also omits most of the narrative detail concerning the life of the Antichrist that Adso so carefully organizes and records, but he retains a few incidents and details that he can use to further his theme of the prevalence of error and the importance of correct doctrine to be able to recognize the truth.

Thus Ælfric reiterates and accentuates Adso's assertion that the Antichrist will be born of human parents, appropriating Adso's example that the Antichrist will be born of a virgin alone as an instance of the sort of error he intends to correct in his work. Moreover, whereas Adso enumerates the wonders the Antichrist will perform as counterparts to Christ's miracles, stating as one example that the Antichrist

[27]Quotations from Ælfric are from Peter Clemoes, ed., *Ælfric's Catholic Homilies: The First Series*, EETS s.s. 17 (Oxford: Oxford University Press, 1997), and are cited in the text by page number.

faciet ignem de celo terribiliter uenire (24), "will make fire come down from heaven in a terrifying way," Ælfric points out that sending fire from heaven is in fact beyond the power of the Antichrist, just as it was beyond the power of the devil when he sent fire from above to destroy Job's flocks:

> Ne sende se deofol ða fyr of heofenum. þeah ðe hit ufan come. for ðan ðe he sylf næs on heofonum. syððan he for his modignysse of aworpen wæs; Ne eac se wælhreowa antecrist næfð þa mihte þæt he heofenlic fyr asendan mæge. ðeah ðe hé þurh deofles cræft hit swa gehiwige. (176)
>
> The devil did not send the fire from heaven, although it came from above, because he himself was not in heaven after he was cast out for his pride. Nor also does the cruel Antichrist have the power to send heavenly fire, although through the devil's craft he may make it appear to do so.

Likewise, Ælfric believes Adso errs in asserting that the Antichrist *mortuos etiam in conspectu hominem suscitari* (24-25), "will raise the dead in the sight of men," because the power to raise the dead is God's alone. He corrects Adso's error by stating rather that *Hé ⁊ his gingran awyrdað manna lichaman digellice ðurh deofles cræft. ⁊ gehælað hi openlice on manna gesihðe. ac hé ne mæg nænne gehælan. þe god sylf ær geuntrumode* (175), "he and his followers will harm men's bodies secretly through the devil's power, and heal them openly in men's sight, but he may not heal any whom God himself has made ill."

Ælfric continues his theme of the correction of error by ending the *Preface* with a plea to those who copy his book to do so carefully and verbatim, lest through his reperformance a scribe *gebringe þa soðan lare to leasum gedwylde* (177), "turn true doctrine into lying heresy." His efforts to endow his work with the status of a master text were both exceptional and, as might be expected in a manuscript culture, unsuccessful. Lacking the textual stability and authority that mechanical reproduction in multiple copies provides, "his works were distributed extensively and repeatedly in the forms and contexts which he condemned."[28]

[28]Wilcox, p. 71.

In *De Temporibus Anticristi*, Wulfstan appropriates material from both Adso's letter and Ælfric's *Preface* to create a new homily emphasizing "the necessity for repentance and good works in view of the imminence of the Last Day."[29] His particular concern is that his readers/listeners be prepared to recognize and resist the deceptions of the Antichrist, and his (re)performance of the material he takes from the two earlier writers is consistently modified to emphasize the theme of deceit. Like Ælfric, Wulfstan omits virtually all of the narrative material from Adso's work, replacing it with moral exhortation and dire admonitions concerning the power of the Antichrist and the punishments awaiting those who succumb to him. Thus when he repeats the assertion that the Antichrist will make fire come from above, Wulfstan briefly acknowledges Ælfric's concerns with a concessionary clause, *swylce hit of heofonum cume* (131), "as if it comes from heaven," and goes on to state that if anyone worships the Antichrist for fear of that fire, *he sceal aa on helle on ecan bryne wunian* (131-32), "he shall dwell forever in hell in eternal fire." In the same manner Wulfstan appropriates Ælfric's point that the Antichrist can heal only those whom he himself has first injured, but Wulfstan is not concerned, as is Ælfric, that his audience might ascribe too much power to the Antichrist; rather he is anxious to make sure they understand just how evil and deceptive the Antichrist will be:

> He bið eal unwrenca full. Ðonne beswicð he swyðe fela manna þurh þæt, þæt he gebrocað mænige man dihlice ⁊ gehæleð eft ætforan mannum þær hy on lociað, þonne geseoð hy hwæt he þonne deð ⁊ nytan na hwæt he ær dyde. Ælc yfel he mæg don, ⁊ ælc he deð. (131)

> He is full of evil strategems. He will deceive very many men through the way that he injures many men secretly and heals them afterwards in front of men while they watch, when they see what he does then and not what he did before. He may do any evil thing, and he will do every evil thing.

To further emphasize the theme of the Antichrist's deception and the necessity for the faithful to recognize and resist him, Wulfstan

[29]Bethurum, p. 282.

turns to a passage in Adso's letter in which he enumerates the three ways in which the Antichrist will try to tempt the Elect — through bribery, through terror, and through signs and wonders:

> Quos vero non poterit muneribus corrumpere, superabit terrore. Quos autem terrore non poterit, signis et miraculis seducere temptabit. Quos nec signis poterit, in conspectu omnium miserabili morte cruciatos crudeliter necabit. (25)

> Those he cannot corrupt with gifts, he will overcome with terror. Those he cannot overcome with terror, he will try to seduce with signs and miracles. Those he cannot seduce with signs, he will torture cruelly and miserably put to death in the sight of all.

Wulfstan's translation/reperformance of these lines reorders the list to emphasize the Antichrist's deceptiveness: he omits Adso's references to gifts entirely, places deceitful signs and wonders first, and adds to the list the Antichrist's ultimate lie, that he himself is God.

> Se gesawenlica deofol wyrcð fela wundra ⁊ segð þæt he God sylfa beo, ⁊ mid his gedwimerum mæst ælcne man beswicð; ⁊ þa þe he elles beswican ne mæg, þa he wyle neadunga genydan, gyf he mæg, þæt hi Godes ætsacan ⁊ him to gebugan. Gyf hi ðonne þæt nellað, þonne sculan hi ehtnessa mycle ⁊ eac earmlicne deað geþolian. (130-31)

> The visible devil will work many miracles and say that he is God himself, and with his illusions deceive each man; and those whom he may not deceive otherwise, he will compel by force, if he may, so that they renounce God and worship him. If they will not do so, then they will suffer great persecution and miserable death.

One of the most striking details within Wulfstan's homily is his appropriation and use of a well-known patristic image for the purification of the soul found in Ælfric's *Preface,* an unusual rhetorical move for Wulfstan since, however standard the image might be, it results in one of the only similes in the entire corpus of his work. Ælfric asserts that the elect will be cleansed of sin through the ordeal of the Antichrist's persecutions, *swa swa gold bið on fyre afandod* (175), "just as gold is purified in the fire." Wulfstan characteristically transforms the assertion into an exhortation: *Beþence gehwa hine sylfne be ðam þe he wille, ne cymð ure æfre ænig to Godes rice ær we beon æfre ælcere synne swa clæne amerede swa æfre ænig gold mæg clænost amerod weorðan* (129-30), "Let him who will think to himself that none of us will come into God's kingdom before we have been purified of each and every sin as clean as any gold may be purified." Wulfstan's use of the simile is accentuated by its rhetorical placement within the homily as the end and culmination of an extended passage concerning the purification of sins, amplified from a brief mention in Ælfric's work to almost a full quarter of Wulfstan's sermon as printed in Bethurum's edition.

However, the sermon as printed in Bethurum's edition is not the entire sermon as it is found in the two earliest manuscripts, CCCC 201 and Hatton 113. These manuscripts each contain an *exemplum* concerning the life of Simon Magus and the martyrdom of Saints Peter and Paul as an illustration of the sort of wonders and crimes the Antichrist can be expected to perform and the ways in which the faithful can aspire to resist him. The *exemplum* comprises well over a third of the homily as it appears in the manuscripts, taking up 56 manuscript lines out of a total of 142 in CCCC 201, and 89 manuscript lines out of 245 in Hatton 113. It is most likely an example of scribal reperformance, as it is neither composed in Wulfstan's characteristic rhetorical style nor comprised of the type of material Wulfstan usually includes in his homilies, where *exempla* are as rare as similes. In a manuscript culture in which authorship in the modern sense is not privileged, the scribal addition of the *exemplum* would be considered an example of textual reperformance certainly as "authentic" and potentially as valuable as Ælfric's appropriation of Adso's work or Wulfstan's reperformance of Ælfric's simile. In a textualized print culture, however, the passage must be relegated to the status of an "inauthentic" interpolation, and Bethurum accordingly omits it as non-authorial in her edition of the homilies.

In doing so, Bethurum relies in part on the authority of Bodley 343, a late manuscript she admits is the farthest removed and least reliable of the three surviving witnesses. Bodley 343 gives a truncated version of the sermon, lacking the *exemplum* as well as one sentence preceding it and five following it, and then picking up again after the omissions with the final three sentences of the homily. Bethurum cuts and pastes between the manuscripts: using Hatton 113 as her base manuscript up to the point at which the *exemplum* begins, she includes one sentence omitted in Bodley 343, relies on Bodley 343 to justify her omission of the *exemplum,* and then returns to Hatton 113 for five more sentences omitted in Bodley 343 and the end of the homily. She thereby creates the master text privileging original authorship that print culture requires, but she does so at the expense of the manuscript record and the pre-print culture it represents, rendering the work as it was read by medieval readers almost inaccessible to the modern scholar.[30] For a re-evaluation of *De Temporibus Anticristi* in its manuscript context it is therefore necessary to restore the *exemplum* and to consider its place within the homily as whole.

Simon Magus, the magician of Acts 8:9-24, whose name became synonymous with the sale of church offices — simony — because of his attempt to buy the power of the Holy Ghost from the apostles Peter and John, was regarded in the Western Church from the fourth century onward as a precursor of the Antichrist. The identification stems primarily from Simon's use of magic to deceive the Samarians so that they esteemed him as a great man, saying in the Vulgate, *hic est virtus Dei quae vocatur Magna,* a passage translated in the Douai-Rheims version as "this man is the power of God, which is called great" (Acts 8:10). But by the late Anglo-Saxon period in England, the story of Simon Magus had grown far beyond its Biblical origins:[31] the extended legend makes Simon a sorcerer of Rome allied with the emperor Nero,

[30]Thus the version of the Peter and Paul story was inadvertently omitted from the listing of Old English texts using the Pseudo Marcellus *Passio Petri et Pauli* as a source in the SASLC Trial Version when it appeared [F. M. Biggs, T. D. Hill, and P. E. Szarmach, *Studies in Anglo-Saxon Literary Culture: A Trial Version* (Binghamton: Center for Medieval and Early Renaissance Studies, 1990), p. 59] . Some modern scholars have been aware of its existence: Bethurum notes the excision in her edition, and both John C. Pope [Review of *The Homilies of Wulfstan, Modern Language Notes* 74 (1959), pp. 338-39] and Karl Jost [*Wulfstanstudien* (Bern, 1959)] discuss the interpolation briefly. See Joyce Tally Lionarons, "Another Old English Version of the *Passio Petri et Pauli,*" *Notes and Queries,* n.s. 45 (1998), pp. 12-14.

[31]A good history of the Antichrist legend can be found in Bernard McGinn, *Antichrist: Two Thousand Years of the Human Fascination with Evil* (San Francisco: Harper, 1994).

himself often seen as a type of Antichrist. Simon's demonic magic is pitted against the apostolic miracles of Peter and Paul, and although he loses the contest, Simon's perfidy plays a large part in instigating the apostles' martyrdom at Nero's hands. The story is told in Old English three times: in *De Temporibus Anticristi*, in the anonymous Blickling Homily XV,[32] and in Ælfric's Catholic Homily XXVI, *Passio Apostolorum Petri et Pauli*.

Blickling Homily XV, entitled *Spel Be Petrus & Paulus* in the manuscript by a later hand than that of the main scribe, is a fairly faithful Old English translation of a large portion of the Pseudo-Marcellus *Passio sanctorum apostolorum Petri et Pauli*.[33] The legend is presented, we are told, in order to honor (*weorðian*, 171) the two apostles as examples for all Christians of steadfastness in the face of persecution, and it contains little in the way of direct homiletic instruction or exhortation. Simon Magus is presented throughout the sermon as a type of Antichrist who pretends to Christ's power and tries to persuade the Emperor to worship him as God. The homily is organized around a series of three increasingly direct confrontations between the two apostles, primarily Peter, and Simon. In the first, Simon makes *ærene næddran*, "brazen serpents" (172-73), that can move and fly in order to impress the populace with his power, while Peter performs actual miracles, healing the sick, casting out devils, and raising the dead. When the two apostles and Simon are summoned before Nero for the second of their confrontations, Simon transforms himself, first into a young child, then into an old man, as a demonstration of his powers, causing Nero to hail him as the Son of God. The apostles counter with an account of Christ's crucifixion and resurrection, and we learn that Simon has attempted to imitate Christ by arranging his own fraudulent execution and then returning from this mock "death" after three days. But when Peter challenges Simon to prove his divinity by anticipating the

---

[32]Richard Morris, ed. and trans., *The Blickling Homilies* (Oxford: EETS o.s. 58, 63, 73, 1874-80, rpt. 1967). All quotations and translations from Blickling XV are from this edition; page numbers are indicated within the text in parentheses.

[33]Lipsius, Ricardus Adelbertus and Maximillianus Bonnet, eds., "*Passio sanctorum apostolorum Petri et Pauli*," *Acta Apostolorum Apocrypha* (Lipsiae: Hermann Mendelsohn, 1901), pp. 120-77.

apostle's thoughts and actions, Simon fails. Peter has a piece of barley bread[34] brought to him secretly, blesses and breaks the bread into two pieces, and hides the pieces in his sleeves. Simon, enraged that he cannot guess what Peter is up to, summons two huge dogs to attack the apostle; when Peter shows them the bread, the dogs disappear into thin air.

The third and final confrontation occurs when Simon has a high tower built and leaps from the top in the sight of the assembled populace, having summoned invisible demons to keep him aloft and prove his divinity once and for all. Paul kneels and prays, and Peter abjures the demons in the name of God to desert Simon. They do, and when Simon falls to his death, he *tobærst on feower dælas,* "burst asunder into four parts" (188-89). Four stones are then placed where the pieces lay to commemorate the event. Nero holds steadfastly to his error, patiently waiting three days for Simon's resurrection, but when Simon remains dead, he kills the apostles in anger at their deeds.

Ælfric tells much the same story in his Homily XXVI, but the Simon Magus narrative comprises only about half of the homily proper. The first part is an explication of Christ's well-known words to Peter in Matthew 16, which Ælfric quotes in Old English:

> Ic ðe secge þæt ðu eart stænen. ꓶ ofer þysne stan ic getimbrie mine cyrcan. ꓶ hellegatu naht ne magon ongean hi; Ic betæce þe heofenan rices cæge. ꓶ swa hwæt swa þu bintst on eorþan. þæt bið gebunden on heofenum; ꓶ swa hwæt swa þu unbinst ofer eorþan. þæt bið unbunden on heofonum; (388)

> I say to you that you are a rock, and on this rock I will build my church, and the gates of hell may not avail against it. I commit to you the key of the kingdom of heaven, and whatever you bind on earth, that will be bound in heaven; and whatever you unbind on earth, that will be unbound in heaven.

Ælfric explains that Christ calls Peter a rock because of his faith in Christ, whom the apostle Paul had called a rock; the true foundation

---

[34]The origins of Peter's actions here are somewhat obscure. Albert Ferreiro discusses this incident in "Simon Magus: The Patristic-Medieval Traditions and Historiography," *Apocrypha* 7 (1996), pp. 147-65. On the subject of barley bread as an agent of exorcism, see Sarah Larratt Keefer, "*Ut in omnibus honorificetur Deus*: The Corsnæd Ordeal in Anglo-Saxon England," *The Community, the Family, and the Saint,* ed. Joyce Hill and Mary Swan (Turnhout: Brepols: 1998).

upon which the church is built is thus not Peter, but Christ himself:

> Eall godes gelaðung is ofer þam stane gebytlod þæt is ofer
> criste . . . seo is mid gecorenum mannum getimbrod. na mid
> deadum stanum. ⁊ eall seo bytlung þæra liflicra stana is ofer
> criste gelogod. for þan ðe we beoð þurh ðone geleafan his
> lima getealde ⁊ he ure ealra heafod; Se þe [ne] bytlað of þam
> grundwealle his weorc hryst to micclum lyre. (390)
>
> All of God's church is built on that rock, that is, upon Christ .
> . . [the foundation] is constructed of chosen men, not of dead
> rocks; and all the building of those living rocks is founded on
> Christ; therefore we, through that belief, are accounted his
> limbs, and he the head of us all. He who does not build from
> that foundation, his work falls to great perdition.

Ælfric uses this beginning to set up his narrative of the Simon Magus story as a direct comparison between Simon Peter and Simon Magus; the first Simon is part of the body of Christ, the second a limb of the devil's. The magician is thus presented in the homily as a sort of anti-apostle rather than Antichrist, and Ælfric carefully selects the material he uses from the Pseudo-Marcellus to emphasize the parallel opposition between the two men. He therefore omits the story of Simon Magus's fraudulent death and resurrection with its implicit comparison to Christ, and he replaces it with two further confrontations between Peter and Simon, also found in the Pseudo-Marcellus. In the first, Simon Magus pretends to raise a man from the dead by causing the corpse to move *mid deofles cræft*, "through the devil's craft" (392), and he tells the people to kill Peter, whom he calls a false prophet and *minne wiðerwinnan*, "my adversary" (392). But Peter challenges him: *gif he geedcucod sy sprece to us; astande. onbyrige metes ⁊ ham gecyrre* (392), "if he is restored to life, let him speak to us, and stand up; let him taste food, and go back home." When Simon is unable to accomplish this feat, Peter does so in God's name, and the resurrected man kneels before Peter and proclaims his faith in Christ. The crowd wants to kill Simon, but Peter restrains them: *cwæð ðæt se hælend him tæhte þone regol þæt hi sceoldon yfel mid gode forgyldan* (393), "he said that the Savior taught him the rule, that they should repay evil with good." In the second confrontation, Simon attempts to murder Peter by tying a huge mastiff in his dwelling, which he believes will devour the apostle. But Peter commands the dog to pursue Simon instead, again with the injunction not to harm him, merely to rip his garments to shreds. In each confrontation, Peter appears as much a magician as Simon; the difference lies simply in the source of their respective powers.

When at the end of the story Simon falls to his death and breaks into four pieces, Ælfric adds that *ða feower sticcu clifodon to feower stanum þa sind to gewitnysse þæs apostolican siges oð ðysne andweardan dæig* (396-97), "the four pieces cleaved to four rocks, which are witnesses of the apostolic victory to this day." If Simon Peter is the living rock on which Christ builds his church, Simon Magus, having built on the devil's foundation, quite literally *hryst to micclum lyre*, "falls to great perdition" and becomes dead, broken rock. The image of the rocks thus frames Ælfric's implicit contrast between the two men, underscoring the portrayal of Simon Magus as the obverse and anti-type of the apostle.

Ælfric's portrayal of Simon is unusual because, as stated above, Simon is most often seen as a type of Antichrist. Both Simon and the Antichrist are magicians who claim to be God and attempt to prove their divinity by working signs and wonders. Both are opposed by two holy men sent from God, Simon by Peter and Paul, the Antichrist by Enoch and Elias; in each case the magician's opponents defeat his magic but are nonetheless martyred. However, both their deeds while alive and the manner of their deaths assure Peter and Paul a place among the saved; Enoch and Elias rise from death after three days to ascend into heaven. Simon dies by falling from a great height at Peter's word; Adso tells us that the Antichrist will be killed by the word of God on the Mount of Olives, *in illo loco, contra quem ascendit Dominus ad celum* (29), "in the place opposite to where the Lord ascended to heaven." The Old English translation of Adso makes the comparison between Christ's ascension from the Mount of Olives and the Antichrist's fall from the same location even more explicit, saying that the Antichrist falls *niðer into helle to ðam ealdan deofle his fæder fram þære stowe, þe he swa modiglice mid woge him geahnode, forðan Crist Godes sunu astah ær*

þanon up to heofonum to his halgan fæder,[35] "down into hell to the old
devil his father, from that place where he so pridefully and wickedly
established himself, because Christ, God's son, rose from there up to
heaven to his holy father." The extended parallel to Simon Magus's
attempt to fly and subsequent fall suggests itself almost unavoidably.

Although clearly based on the work of the Pseudo-Marcellus,
the *exemplum* found in *De Temporibus Anticristi* owes nothing to the
Old English translation found in Blickling XV and Ælfric's homily,
and it includes only the first and last of the confrontations between the
apostles and Simon. Like the rest of Wulfstan's homily, the *exemplum*
focuses on the theme of deceit, and therefore pays greatest attention
to Simon's fraudulent assertions of divinity and the signs and wonders
he performs to prove them. All of Simon's wonders within the homily
consist of the creation of false appearances: he makes not only brass
serpents, but also stone idols seem to live and move; he transforms
himself three times instead of two in his attempt to impress the emperor, first into a child, then into a middle-aged man, and finally into
an old man; he appears to fly, but is actually held aloft by demons. By
contrast, Peter's miracles transform reality for the better: *gehælde mistlice gebrocode men, blinde ⁊ deafe ⁊ dumbe ⁊ mistlice gelewede*, "he healed
men afflicted in various ways, the blind and deaf and dumb as well as
those with other illnesses." Moreover, Peter's words reveal the truth of
Simon's deceptions when the saint charges the demons helping him to
fly to abandon him and he falls to his death. The passage ends with an
explicit comparison between Simon Magus and the Antichrist, both of
whose power stems from *se sylfa deofol*, "the devil himself."

The inclusion of the *exemplum* makes *De Temporibus Anticristi*
the only Old English work to combine the legend of the Antichrist
with the story of Simon Magus. The combination provides Wulfstan's
homily with a temporal depth and typological sophistication that is
not found either in his sources for the Antichrist legend or in the two
Old English analogues to the Simon Magus story. By joining the two
legends, the scribal reperformance of the homily compels its audience
to look backwards and forwards in time simultaneously, back to the
deceptions practiced by Simon Magus, and forward to those anticipated on the part of the Antichrist, thus underscoring the precarious

[35]Napier, p. 201.

position of human beings in the present, balanced delicately between past dangers and future threats, with only the *god lar* of the homilist as their guide. It also provides two sets of holy men as examples of steadfastness in Christian faith and opposition to the enemy, Peter and Paul against Simon Magus, and Enoch and Elias against the Antichrist, and the martyrdom of all four reminds the audience that true victory lies in salvation, not in a temporary public triumph over the devil's magic or in physically surviving persecution. Finally, the combination rounds out the lessons of sacred history by assuring the audience that surrounding all, preceding the advent of Simon Magus and following that of the Last Enemy, is Christ, in his first and second comings.

It is unfortunate and ironic that the homily in its entirety is not widely available for study by Anglo-Saxonists. Joyce Hill has recently suggested that we are not "doing justice to the literary and intellectual history of the period if we pay less attention" — or no attention at all — "to . . . non-authorial 'modifications'" of medieval works, and that therefore "editorial activity should properly be extended to revisions, derivatives, and composites."[36] A new edition of *De Temporibus Anticristi,* based on a single manuscript and regarded as an individual rendition of Wulfstan's homily by an anonymous scribe who chose to include the Simon Magus *exemplum* as part of his (re)performance of the work, is clearly necessary to allow the literary history of both the Antichrist legend and the Simon Magus story to be fully appreciated by modern scholars. Such an edition, however, is only a partial solution to the problem of editing manuscript works in a print culture that expects as part of its cultural norms both authorial authenticity and textual stability rather than scribal reperformance and manuscript *mouvance.*

The obvious first step towards finding a full solution is to re-conceptualize our view of manuscript works. Dagenais suggests we may begin to do this if we "suppress the idea that these manuscripts 'represent' an authentic literary text," and instead "view the various manuscript witnesses as part of a system of differences."[37] At this first level of interpretation of a manuscript work, the task of the editor is

[36]Hill, p. 179.

[37]Dagenais, "That Bothersome Residue: Towards a Theory of the Physical Text," *Vox Intexta,* ed. A. N. Doane and Carol Braun Pasternack (Madison: University of Wisconsin Press, 1991), p. 252.

primarily comparative, seeking to articulate the differences within the system rather than eliminating them in the presentation of a "best text." This activity would seem to require a new sort of scholarly edition, one which would include not only all surviving manuscript witnesses of a particular work, but also the works that the medieval scribes and authors have appropriated in the course of their performances, and a critical apparatus capable of guiding the modern reader through the complexities such a multiple presentation would engender. Obviously I would not be alone in suggesting that electronic media may provide a solution to the logistical problems such an edition would pose, nor would I be the first to reflect on the irony of post-print culture affording a means to represent pre-print works — but a theory of hypertext would take me far beyond the scope of this essay.[38]

At a second level, according to Dagenais, editors may "push beyond a theory which leaves the physical text freed of representation but still caught up in a system of differences" to one that contains only "concrete physical objects whose concrete and individual presence we must now attempt somehow to master."[39] At this level there could be no editions, merely facsimiles and manuscript descriptions designed to make the manuscripts accessible to modern readers. As I understand Dagenais, the second level is not designed to replace the first, but rather to ground it in the physical reality of individual manuscripts rather than in the abstract and anachronistic idea of literary textuality.

---

[38]For hypertext theory, see Richard J. Finneran, ed., *The Literary Text in the Digital Age* (Ann Arbor: University of Michigan Press, 1996); George P. Landow, *Hypertext: The Convergence of Contemporary Critical Theory and Technology* (Baltimore & London: Johns Hopkins University Press, 1992); Jerome McGann, "The Rationale of Hypertext," 1995, available online from http://jefferson.village.virginia.edu/public/jjm2f/rationale.html; and Peter L. Shillingsburg, *Scholarly Editing in the Computer Age* (Ann Arbor: University of Michigan Press, 1996). For an article dealing specifically with editing Old English in hypertext, see Patrick W. Conner, "Beyond the ASPR: Electronic Editions of Old English Poetry," *New Approaches to Editing Old English Verse*, ed. Sarah Laratt Keefer and Katharine O'Brien O'Keeffe (Cambridge: D. S. Brewer, 1998): 109-26.

[39]Dagenais, "That Bothersome Residue," p. 255.

My edition of *De Temporibus Anticristi*, appended to this essay, is an attempt to walk a fine line between a simple manuscript transcription and a version of the manuscript work edited for easy accessibility to the modern reader. The text is that of Hatton 113 throughout: italicized letters indicate expansions of standard manuscript abbreviations; letters in brackets are restored from illegible forms in the manuscript. Because I have not been concerned in this essay with a comparison of the various performances of the homily, I have not provided manuscript variants; they can be found in Bethurum and in Napier. I have, however, indicated where Bethurum's edition ends and begins again, as well as where Bodley 343 ends and begins.

De Temporibus Anticristi

Note on the manuscript: Oxford, Bodleian Library, Hatton MS 113 (Ker 331; Gneuss 637) dates from the third quarter of the eleventh century, measures 10 1/2 x 6 1/4", and contains 23 lines on each page. With Hatton 114, it is part of a two-volume set of homilies known as St. Wulfstan's Homiliary. The composite manuscript was copied by the Worcester scribe Wulfgeat and contains glosses written by the "tremulous" Worcester hand as well as other Worcester glosses. Hatton 113 contains twenty of Wulfstan's homilies, several by Ælfric, and others printed by Napier as Wulfstanian. *De Temporibus Anticristi* is contained on folios 52a–56b.

Leofan men us is mycel þearf þæt we wære beon. þæs egesli-
can timan þe towerd is. Nu bið swyðe raðe ante cristes tima þæs
ðe we wenan magan. ⁊ eac georne witan. ⁊ þæt bið se egeslicesta.
þe æfre gewearð syððan þeos woruld ærost gescapen wæs. he byð
5 sylf deofol ⁊ ðeah mennisc man geboren. Crist is soð god. ⁊ soð
mann; ⁊ ante crist bið soðlice deofol ⁊ mann. Ðurh crist com eallum middanearde help. ⁊ frofer. ⁊ ðurh antecrist se mæsta gryre.
⁊ seo mæsta earfoðnes. þe æfre ær on worulde geworden wearð. ⁊
eall. mancynn forwurde forðrihte; gif god his dagas ne gescyrte.
10 Ac god gescyrt his dagas for ðæra þingan þe him gecorene syn. ⁊
he gehealdan habban wile. ⁊ ðeah on þam fæce þe he bið. he gedeð

swa mycel to yfele swa næfre ær ne gewearð. Ælcne mann he wile
awendan of rihtan geleafan. ⁊ of cristendome. ⁊ bespannan to his
unlarum gif he mæg. ⁊ god hit geþafað [f. 52b] him sume hwile;
15 for twam þingum. An is ærest þæt men beoð þurh synna. swa forð
forworhte þæt hi beoð þæs wel wyrðe þæt deofol openlice þænne
fandige hwa him full. fyligean wille. Oðer is þæt god wile þæt ða þe
swa gesælige beoð. þæt hi on rihtan geleafan ðurhwuniað. ⁊ ðam
deofle anrædlice wiðstandað; he wile þæt þa beon raðe amerede.
20 ⁊ geclænsode of synnum. þurh ða myclan ehtnesse. ⁊ ðurh þæne
martirdom ðe hy þonne poliað. forðam nis nan man þæt ne sy
synful. ⁊ ælc man sceal sar ðolian oðþon her. oðþon elles hwær be
ðam þe he þurh synna geearnað; ⁊ ðy bið seo ehtnes þonne godum
mannum swa stið. forðam þe hy sculon beon raðe geclænsode ⁊
25 amerode. ær se mycle dom cume. Đa ðe wæron forðferede for
hund gearum. oððon gyt furðor. wel þa magan beon nu geclænsode. We motan nyde þæt stiðre þolian. gyf we clæne beon sceolan.
þonne se dom cymð; nu we þæne fyrst nabbað. þe þa hæfdon þe
wiðforan us wæron. Beþence gehwa hine sylfne be ðam [f. 53] þe
30 he wille. ne cymð ure æfre ænig to godes rice. ær we beon æfre
ælcere synne swa clæne amerede swa æfre ænig gold mæg clænost
amerod weorðan.

Leofan men, God geþafað þam deofle antecriste þæt he mot
ehtan godra manna. forðam þe hi sculon swa ic ær cwæð ðurh ða
35 ehtnesse beon geclænsode. ⁊ syððan clæne faran to heofona rice. þa
þonne þe his leasungum gelyfað. ⁊ him to gebugað. þam he byrhð
her for worulde ⁊ ða he weorþað her; ac hy sculon raþe æfter ðam
ecelice forweorðan. ⁊ aa wunian syððan mid him on þære sweartan
helle grunde. Se gesawenlica deofol wyrcð fela wundra; ⁊ segð þæt
40 he god sylfa beo; ⁊ mid his gedwimerum mæst ælcne man beswicð.
⁊ þa þe he elles beswican ne mæg; þa he wyle neadunga genydan
gyf he mæg, þæt hi godes ætsacan; ⁊ him to gebugan. Gyf hi ðonne
þæt nellað; þonne sculan hi ehtnessa mycle. ⁊ eac earmlicne deað
geðolian. Eala gesælig bið þeah se ðe to þam anræde bið. þæt he
45 forðam ne awacað; ac witodlice þæra bið ealles to lyt. þe he ne beswice. oðþon [f. 53b] þurh his searucræftas. oðþon ðurh þæne gryre
þe he on mancynn set. Vre drihten crist. gehælde fela þæra on life.
þe unhale wæron; ⁊ se deofol antecrist gebrocað ⁊ geuntrumað þa

ðe ær hale wæron. ⁊ he nænne gehælan ne mæg buton he hine

50 ærest awyrde. Ac syððan he þæne mann gebrocod hæfð. syðþan he
mæg don swylce he hine gehæle; gyf he geswicð þæs þe he ær þam
men to yfele dyde. He bið eal unwrenca full. Ðonne beswicð he
swyðe fela manna þurh þæt; þæt he gebrocað mænine man dihlice;
⁊ gehælð eft ætforan mannum þær hy onlociað; þonne geseoð hy

55 hwæt he þonne deð. ⁊ nytan na hwæt he ær dyde. Ælc yfel he mæg
don. ⁊ ælc he deð. He deð þæt fyr cymð ufene. swylce hit of heofonum cume. ⁊ he mid þam fela forbærnð ealswa he hwilum ær iobes
æhta dyde. Ac se ðe for þæs fyres ege him to gebihð. he sceal aa on
helle. on ecan bryne wunian.[1] Ne can ic ne æfre ænig man oðrum

60 asecgan for eallum þam egsan þe ðurh þæne deofol on worulde
geweorðan sceal; þonne age we [f. 54] mycle þearfe. þæt we god
ælmihtine georne biddan þæt he us gescylde wið þæne egesan. ⁊ us
gestrangie swa his willa sy.[2]

⁊ mycle ðearfe agan þa þe þæs timan. gebidað þæt hi wære

65 beon. ⁊ þæt hi gemyndige beon þæra þinga þe deofles menn oft ær
þurh drycræft drugon. Fela þinga dydan þa geogeleras on egypta
lande þurh drycræft. ongean þæt ðe moyses þurh godes mihta þær
fela wundra worhte. ⁊ swa we habbað be manegum geræd ðe ge-
hwar þurh drycræft. mid deofles fultume. menn mis[t]lice dwele

70 dan. Betere eac þæt we nu sum to bysne secgan. An deofles man
was hwilan on rome. simon hatte. se geswencte swyðe þearle twe-
gen mære godes ðegnas; þæt wæs SANCTUS PETRUS. ⁊ SANC-
TUS PAULUS. Hy bodedon on rome cristendom ærest; ac se
deofles man hy gedrehte. ⁊ þæt folc gelette wundorlice swiðe. He

75 sæde þæt hit eal leasung wære þæt ða godes þegnas bodedon; ⁊ he
worhte þurh drycræft fela wundra ðær men to locedon. he dyde æt
sumum sæle þæt an æren nædre hy styrede. eal swylce [f. 54b] heo
cucu wære. ⁊ man hæfde geworht þa on ðam dagum on rome an-
licnessa. ⁊ þæt hæþene folc þurh deofles lare weorðe don þa heom

80 for godas; þa he gemacode eac þurh drycræft. þæt hy agunnon

---

[1] Bodleian 343 omits the rest of the homily except the final three sentences, ll.
97-105 of this edition.

[2] Bethurum's edition stops here, picking up again at line 89 of this edition.

swylce hy cwice wæron. Ðonne dyde petrus þurh godes mihta
betere þing. Gehælde mistlice gebrocode m*en*. Blinde. ⁊ deafe. ⁊
dumbe. ⁊ mistlice gelewede; And þa wearð hit cuð æt nyhstan
þa*m* casere þe þa on þam dagum romware weold; eal hu hy hit
macedon; ⁊ mon
85 herede him ðearle swiðe þæne symon. Leton þa gedwolan men;
swylce he se simon godes sylfes sunu wære. ⁊ ða het æt nyhstan se
casere feccan þæne symon to him. ⁊ þa ða he him to com ⁊ him
ætforan stod. þa ablende he þurh deofles cræft swa þæs caseres ea-
gan. ⁊ ðæra þe him mid wæron. þæt heom ðuhte oðre hwile þa hy
90 hine beheoldon þæt he wære swylce hit cild wære þæt hy on locedon; oðre hwile eft swylce he medemre ylde man wære; ⁊ oðre
hwile swylce he eald geðungen man wære; ⁊ swa on mænige [f. 55]
wisan he hiwode þurh drycræft fela leasbregda ⁊ þa þa se casere eal
swylc geseah; þa wende he þæt hit godes agen bearn wære; ⁊ se
95 deofles man gealp þæt he eac swa wære. ⁊ þæt folc him to swyðe.
þæs gelyfde. Ða wunnan þa godan godes þegnas ongean þæt swyðe;
⁊ sædon þæt he luge; ⁊ hy eac þurh godes mihta mid manegum godum þingu*m* geswutelodon þæt hy riht hæfdon; ⁊ þæt hit eal leas
wæs þæt se þeodloga sæde. Da æt nyhstan cwæð se simon. þæt
100 he gecyðan wolde þæt he gode wære. Het þa aræran ænne stepel.
⁊ sæðe þæt he þyder upp stigan wolde. ⁊ englas hine þær underfon
scoldan. ⁊ to heofonu*m* ferian. ⁊ ðær eall þæt folc on locode, he
stah up to ðam stepele. ⁊ of ðam stepele hof upp on lyfte swylce he
wolde wið þæs heofonas weard. Ða clypode se casere. ⁊ cwæð þæt
105 ða swytol wære. þæt hit eal soð wæs þæt he ær sæde; ⁊ þæt hit
eal leasung wære. þæt petrus ⁊ paulus. þæt folc mid bregdan. Da
abædan hy uneaðe þæt man geðyldgode sume hwile. oð man wiste
to hwam se ende gehwurfe. [f. 55b] ⁊ clypedon þa to gode swiðe
georne. hwæt þa s*anctu*s petrus beseah raðe æfter þam up to þam
110 lyfte. ⁊ clypode hludre stefne. ⁊ ðus cwæð. Ic halsige eow deofles
gastas. þe þæne deofles mann gynd þa lyft feriað ⁊ ðurh þæt menn
bepæcað. þæt ge þurh godes ælmihtiges bebod hine nu ða forlætan.
þæt he næfre leng mid his mane menn ne beswice. Sona swa he hit
gecweden hæfde. þa forleton hy hine. ⁊ he hreas nyðer. feoll þæt
115 he eall tobærst. Da wæs swytol godes miht. þeah he þæs deofles
gedwyld lange ær þafode. Eac we habbað on bocum geræd þæt fela

oðra deofles manna wide wæran þe godes ðegnas oft þurh deofles
cræft swyðe geswencton. ⁊ folc swyðe gedwealdon. ac hit þincð us
to langsum nu to gereccanne. Ge magan þeah be þissum anum
120 gecnawan. þa he ðurh deofol. swilcne cræft hæfde ongean swylce
godes þegnas. swylce wæs *sanctus* petrus ⁊ *sanctus* paulus. æthweg
hit bið þonne se deofol sylf cymð þe ana cann eall *þæt* yfel. ⁊ ealle
þa drycræftas þe æfre ænig man æfre geleornode. ⁊ eall he hit cyð
þonne [f. 56] openlice þurh hine sylfne. þæt he oft ær dyde. þurh
125 þa ungesæligan þe his larum fyligdon.

Se sylfa deofol þe on helle is *þæt* is se þe þonne wyrð on þam
earmsceapenan men antecriste. ⁊ bið soðlice ægðer ge deofol ge
man. ⁊ he eall mancyn þonne openlice swyðor gedrecð ⁊ gedwelað.
þonne hit æfre ær wurde. We agan þy swyðe mycle þearfe. *þæt* we
130 wið swylcne ege wære beon. ⁊ eac þa warnian þe swylc nyton swylc towerd is. Forðam þe hit is nyr þam timan þonne ungelærede
men gelyfan willan. ⁊ þæt is gesyne þy is ðeos woruld. fra*m* dæge
to dæge wyrse ⁊ wyrse. Eac ic secge to soðe þæt deofol wyle ælces
mannes geðanc gyf he mæg swyðe gelettan. þæt he hit na ne un
135 derstande. þeah hit him man secge. ne hine wið *þæt* ne warnige. ⁊
ðurh *þæt* wyrð mæst manna beswicen. þe hy ne beoð swa wære. ne
swa wel gewarnode ær. swa hy beðorfton. La hwæt is se man on
life buton hine god ælmihtig gehealde. ⁊ he ær gewarnod þe bet sy;
þæt he þonne ðurh deofol beswicen ne wyrðe. Ac utan warnian
140 us georne. ⁊ ge[f. 56b]earnian to gode. þæt he us gescylde swa his
willa sy. Uton habban anrædne geleafan ⁊ fæstræde geþanc to urum
drihtne. þonn*e* þeah hit gebyrige þæt we þære yrmðe gebidan sculon. ⁊ on þisum life earfoða adreogan; þeah gif we ne awaciað. ac
þurhwuniað on rihtan geleafan. god us forsceawað ece reste. On
145 godes naman ic bidde; þæt *cristenra* manna gehwylc hine sylfne
georne beþence. ⁊ geornlice to gode gebuge ⁊ fram synnum gecyrre. ⁊ geearnige. þæt he gemanan habban mote on heofona rice
mid þam þe leofað. ⁊ rixað a butan ende. amen.

Multilingual Glosses, Bilingual Text:
English, Anglo-Norman, and Latin
in Three Manuscripts of Ælfric's Grammar

Melinda J. Menzer

I N HIS ENCYCLOPEDIC WORK *Teaching and Learning Latin in Thirteenth-Century England*, Tony Hunt prints the Anglo-Norman glosses that appear in three manuscripts of Ælfric's *Grammar* and *Glossary*: Cambridge, Trinity College, MS R.9.17, Cambridge, Cambridge University Library, MS Hh.1.10, and London, British Library, Cotton MS Faustina A.x.[1] He discusses these in the context of vernacular glosses on Latin grammatical texts, including the *Doctrinale* of Alexander of Villa Dei, the *Graecismus* of Eberhard of Bethune, and the works of John of Garland. Hunt argues that Anglo-Norman glosses on the *Grammar*, like those on Latin school-texts, show us that medieval teachers used French in their teaching: "[Ælfric's] exposition of the parts of speech in Latin was sufficiently practical to attract the attention of several teachers who used his Latin text to elaborate the Anglo-Norman equivalents of the various paradigms, especially verb conjugations."[2]

While Hunt's conclusions about Anglo-Norman glosses on Latin school-texts are sound, his presentation of the glosses on Ælfric's *Grammar* is somewhat misleading. In spite of the fact that the *Grammar* contains English and Latin, Hunt includes only the Latin text with the glosses, even when the glosses appear over English text. In addition, Hunt's presentation of the glosses in CUL Hh.1.10 does not make clear that two Anglo-Norman hands are present in the section on verbs and that one of those hands is also responsible for numer-

---

[1] Tony Hunt, *Teaching and Learning Latin in Thirteenth-Century England*, 3 vols. (Cambridge: D. S. Brewer, 1991). Hunt describes the glosses in the Trinity manuscript (Ker no. 89, Gneuss no. 182) on p. 26, the glosses in the Cotton Faustina manuscript (Ker no. 154A, Gneuss no. 331) on pp. 23-26 and 99-111, and the glosses in the CUL manuscript (Ker no. 17, Gneuss no. 13) on pp. 111-13, all in volume 1.

[2] Hunt, p. 100.

ous Latin and English glosses throughout the manuscript. Although Hunt's focus on Latin and Anglo-Norman is understandable given his project, pulling the Latin text and Anglo-Norman glosses out of their manuscript contexts creates an inaccurate picture of what is going on in these manuscripts.

To understand fully what these glossators were doing with the *Grammar*, we must recognize the multilingual nature of the text and its unique appeal to Anglo-Norman glossators. But looking at this English and Latin text and its Anglo-Norman glosses will not only teach us about how medieval readers used Ælfric's *Grammar*, it also will give us a unique perspective on the interaction among these three languages in post-Conquest England. In this paper, I will briefly discuss Ælfric's *Grammar*, showing how it functions as a grammar of both Latin and English; then I will look at glosses on each of the three manuscripts, discussing how they used English, Latin, and Anglo-Norman French in their work with the text.[3] The glosses show that the boundaries between the languages were fluid: some scribes and glossators easily moved among the languages, and others gave both vernaculars the kind of scholarly attention usually accorded to Latin.

Ælfric's *Grammar* attracted Anglo-Norman glosses like no other Old English text. In his *Catalogue of Manuscripts Containing Anglo-Saxon*, Ker lists sixteen manuscripts that also contain French; of those sixteen, three contain copies of Ælfric's *Grammar*. No other English-language text has French glosses; in the rest of the manuscripts, the French appears independently, as glosses on Latin text (sometimes with English glosses), or as part of a trilingual formula.[4] The question

---

[3] For more information on the relationship among these three languages in England after the Conquest, see M. T. Clanchy, *From Memory to Written Record: England 1066-1307*, 2nd ed. (Oxford: Oxford University Press, 1993), especially Ch. 6, "Languages of Record," pp. 197-223.

[4] The thirteen remaining manuscripts divide roughly into three categories. First, four of the manuscripts Ker lists have French glosses that have little to do with the Old English also contained in the manuscript. These include Oxford, Bodleian Library, Laud Misc. 567 (Ker, no. 346; not included in Gneuss); London, British Library, Harley 585 (Ker, no. 231; Gneuss, no. 421); Oxford, Bodleian Library, Hatton 76 (Ker, no. 328B; Gneuss, no. 633); and Cambridge, University Library Ii.1.33 (Ker, no. 18; not included in Gneuss). A similar manuscript is London, British Library, Cotton Titus

about the three copies of Ælfric's *Grammar* that contain Anglo-Norman glosses is whether the glossators are interested in English or if they are interested only in the *Grammar*'s Latin text.

Although Ælfric's work is often called his *Latin Grammar*, the majority of the explanatory text of the *Grammar* is in English. The *Grammar* resembles a commentary on Ælfric's source text, the *Excerptiones de Prisciano*: a Latin lemma is followed by a longer English explanation, usually including but not limited to a translation of the Latin.[5] For example, the text begins:

A.iv, containing a copy of the Old English Rule of Saint Benedict, as well as a Latin version of chapter 49 and part of chapter 48 of the Rule followed by a French translation of those excerpts (Ker, pp. 262-3, no. 200; Gneuss, no. 379). Second, there are two examples of short texts that appear in one language and are then repeated in the two others: Oxford, Bodleian Library, Rawlinson C. 641 (Ker, no. 348; not included in Gneuss) and London, British Library, Cotton Titus D.xxiv (Ker, no. 201; not included in Gneuss). These show us little about the interaction of English and French, although they do show us that people like to write proverbs and formulas in multiple languages. Third, there are six manuscripts that contain both English glosses and French glosses on Latin text. Two are Cambridge, Trinity College O.2.31 (Ker, no. 95; Gneuss, no. 190) and Cambridge, Corpus Christi College 23 (Ker, no. 31; Gneuss, no. 38). A third manuscript, Oxford, Jesus College 26 (Ker, no. 355; not included in Gneuss), is the only example of French and English glosses translating the same Latin text; Ker describes it: "F. 170v contains a table of the degrees of consanguinity within which marriage is forbidden, illustrating ch. 90 of bk. 7 of a mid-twelfth-century copy of the Panormia of Ivo of Chartres (Patr. Lat. clxiii. 1303). The French and English names of relationship are entered in a contemporary hand above the table, in columns on the left and right sides respectively" (p. 433). Similarly, there are three examples of trilingual glossaries: London, British Library, Royal 7 D.ii (Ker, no. 258; not included in Gneuss); Oxford, Bodleian Library, Bodley 730 (Ker, no.317; not included in Gneuss); and London, British Library, Stowe 57 (Ker, no.272; not included in Gneuss). I have seen these three glossaries *in situ*. They also contain English and French mediated by the presence of Latin; both the vernacular languages are there to translate the Latin, not each other. Hunt also lists other examples of trilingual glossaries in "The Trilingual Glosses in MS London, British Library, Sloane 146, ff. 69v-72r," concentrating mainly on herbal glossaries. These glossaries are not listed by Ker or Gneuss because they contain Middle English, not Old.

[5] See David W. Porter, *Excerptiones de Prisciano, Excerpts from Priscian: The Source for Ælfric's Latin-Old English Grammar* (Woodbridge: Boydell and Brewer, 2002).

SECVNDVM DONATVM OMNIS VOX AVT ARTICV-
LATA EST AVT CONFVSA. ARTICVLATA EST,
QVAE LITTERIS CONPREHENDI POTEST; CONFV-
SA, QVAE SCRIBI NON POTEST. stemn is geslagen lyft
gefredendlic on hlyste, swa micel swa on ðære heorcnunge is.
ic secge nu gewislicor, þæt ælc stemn byð geworden of ðæs
muðes clypunge and of ðære lyfte cnyssunge. se muð drifð
ut ða clypunge, and seo lyft byð geslagen mid ðære clypunge
and gewyrð to stemne. ælc stemn is oððe andgytfullic oððe
gemenged. andgytfullic stemn is, þe mid andgyte bið gecly-
pod, swaswa ys *arma virumque cano* ic herige þa wæpnu and
ðone wer. gemenged stemn is, þe bið butan andgyte, swylc
swa is hryðera gehlow and horsa hnægung, hunda gebeorc,
treowa brastlung ET CETERA.[6]

Ælfric translates the Latin lemma in the course of his explanation, but
he also offers additional information that appears only in English. The
text is not in Latin with English translations; on the contrary, it is an
English-language text liberally sprinkled with Latin quotations and
examples.

But not only is Ælfric's *Grammar* written in English, it is also
about English. Ælfric sets out in the very first sentence of his Latin
preface that this grammar teaches both Latin and English to its read-

---

[6] Quotations from the text are from Julius Zupitza, *Ælfrics Grammatik und
Glossar* (Berlin: Weidmann, 1880), here p. 4. Unless otherwise noted,
translations are mine. "According to Donatus, all *sound* is either articulate
or confused. Articulate is that which can be rendered in letters; confused
that which cannot be written. Sound is beaten air perceptible by the sense
of hearing so much so as there is listening. I say now more certainly that all
sound is made from the crying of the mouth and the striking of the air. The
mouth drives out the cry, and the air is struck with the crying and made into
sound. All sound is either meaningful or mixed. Meaningful sound is that
which is spoken with understanding, as is *arma virumque cano* I sing of the
weapons and the man. Mixed sound is that which is without understanding,
such as the mooing of cows and neighing of horses, the barking of dogs,
rustling of trees, etc."

ers: ". . . quatinus perlectis octo partibus Donati in isto libello potestis *utramque linguam, uidelicet latinam et anglicam,* uestrae teneritudini inserere interim, usque quo ad perfectiora perueniatis studia" (emphasis mine).[7] Similarly, he describes the text in the English preface as providing "sum angyn to ægŏrum gereorde,"[8] that is, to Latin and English.

Modern readers of the *Grammar* often hold that, in spite of these statements of purpose, Ælfric could not have meant that he intended to teach English grammar as well as Latin grammar. For example, Vivien Law, one of the few who has discussed this issue in depth, writes in "Anglo-Saxon England: Ælfric's Excerptiones de arte grammatica anglice," "No description of Old English is to be found in [Ælfric's *Grammar*]: the vernacular forms presented alongside the Latin paradigms only serve to illustrate the latter." She continues, "He does not claim that Old English had five declensions or four conjugations, nor did he attribute to it the complex Latin system of moods and tenses. The sole purpose of the vernacular forms which accompany the Latin paradigms is to make plain the meaning of the Latin."[9]

Law's argument, however, is based on a incomplete picture of what an English grammar would look like, a picture drawn from analogies to what we know about teaching Latin. Law focuses on the para-

---

[7] Zupitza, p. 1. ". . . having read through Donatus's eight parts of speech, you may in this book apply to your tenderness both languages, namely Latin and English, in the time until you reach more perfect studies." Translation by Jonathan Wilcox, ed., *Ælfric's Prefaces*, Durham Medieval Texts 9 (Durham, 1995), p. 130. All of Ælfric's longer works are introduced by a Latin preface followed by an English preface.

[8] Zupitza, p. 3: "some introduction to both languages."

[9] Vivien Law, "Anglo-Saxon England: Ælfric's *Excerptiones de arte grammatica anglice*," *Histoire Épistémologie Langage* 9 (1987), pp. 47, 60. Scholars who believe that the *Grammar* has something to do with English usually see that aspect of the text as secondary or even accidental. Peter Clemoes describes the text as "a Latin grammar — the first grammar written in English and having some interesting things to say about English usage as well as Latin" ("Ælfric," *Continuations and Beginnings*, ed. Eric G. Stanley (London: Nelson, 1966), p. 182. C. P. Wormald notes, "[Ælfric's] educational works were designed to teach Latin, not English, though, as he recognized, his *Grammar* was

digms of conjugations and declensions, seeing those as the important part of the *Grammar*. But English speakers reading the *Grammar* do not need to memorize paradigms; they already know how to speak their language. What they need — and what Ælfric provides — is an understanding of how English can be analyzed systematically, using the tools of the Latin grammarians. To make an analogy, I do not teach my Modern English Grammar students how to conjugate verbs in English — they already know how. Instead, I make them aware that there is a category of words in English called verbs, and verbs do particular things and behave in particular ways. Ælfric's *Grammar* teaches English grammar in the same way.

Ælfric's discussion of pronouns in the introduction to the parts of speech provides one of the clearest examples of his English grammar:

> PRONOMEN is ðæs naman speljend, se spelað þone naman,
> þæt ðu ne ðurfe tuwa hine nemnan. gif ðu cwest nu: hwa
> lærde ðe?, þonne cweðe ic: Dunstan. hwa hadode ðe? he me
> hadode: þonne stent se he on his naman stede and spelað
> hine. eft, gif ðu axast: *quis hoc fecit?* hwa dyde ðis?, þonne
> cwest ðu: *ego hoc feci* ic dyde ðis: þonne stent se ic on ðines
> naman stede. . . .[10]

The description of the concept "pronoun" is completely in English: a pronoun is a word that replaces a noun. We get an example of how pronouns work in English first, before any discussion of Latin. Even

bound to be important for English also . . . . The truth is that Ælfric and his contemporaries were overwhelmingly concerned with the education of the clergy. In a passage from the English preface to his *Grammar*, Ælfric seems almost to echo Alfred's preface [suggesting that English should be taught], but it is the supply of clergy with Latin skills that preoccupies him" ("The Uses of Literacy in Anglo-Saxon England and Its Neighbours," *Transactions of the Royal Historical Society* 5th ser. 27 (1977), pp. 108-09.

[10] Zupitza, pp. 8-9. "The pronoun is the noun's replacement, which replaces the noun so that you do not have to name it twice. If you say now: who taught you?, then I say: Dunstan. Who made you a monk? He made me a monk: then the *he* stands in the place of his name and replaces it. Again, if you ask: *quis hoc fecit?* who made this?, then you say: *ego hoc feci* I made this: then the *ic* stands in the noun's place."

after the Latin example, Ælfric writes, "þonne stent se *ic* on ðines naman stede": *ic*, not *ego*. English is the primary subject here, and Latin is taught by comparison to English. At the end of his introduction to the parts of speech, Ælfric again explicitly states that he has been addressing English grammar as well as Latin grammar: "witodlice on ðisum eahta dælum is eal ledenspræc belocen, and ðæt englisc geðwærlæcð to eallum ðam dælum, swaswa we nu sceortlice trahtnodon."[11]

In comparison to Ælfric's English grammar, Latin instruction in the Middle Ages, especially the later Middle Ages, focused on grammatical information non-native speakers require, like information about noun declensions and verb conjugations. One of the difficulties for medieval students, in fact, was that many of the grammatical works that were popular in the time period were originally intended for native speakers of Latin and, as a result, were not perfectly suited to the needs of non-native speakers. In another article, "The Study of Latin Grammar in Eighth-Century Southumbria," Law describes Donatus's paradigms in the *Ars minor*, a text written in the fifth century and used for over thousand years: "Even the renowned *Ars minor* of Donatus offered an incomplete selection of paradigms — for the noun, the words *magister, musa, scamnum, sacerdos* and *felix*, all chosen to exemplify gender, not declension; and for the verb, just *legere*."[12] But, as Law explains, Donatus does not need to conjugate verbs since his fifth-century audience, native speakers of Latin, already know how to conjugate verbs in Latin. Donatus also does not give examples of each of the five declensions of nouns; he knows that his readers know how to decline nouns. Like Donatus's work, Ælfric's *Grammar* was written to teach grammar to people who spoke the language they were studying; the difference is that Ælfric teaches English grammar, alongside the Latin grammar.

Did the *Grammar's* readers recognize this work as an English grammar as well as a Latin grammar, or did they use it solely as a Latin grammar? One way of answering this question is by looking at the

[11] Zupitza, p. 11. "Truly all Latin is enclosed in these eight parts [of speech], and English conforms to all these parts, as we just said a moment ago." Ælfric also discusses English semantics and English derivational morphology in the *Grammar*.

[12] Vivien Law, "The Study of Latin Grammar in Eighth-Century Southumbria," *Anglo-Saxon England* 12 (1983), p. 58.

glosses on the text. The Anglo-Norman glosses in the three manuscripts indicate that readers engaged with the text in a variety of ways. While the Trinity scribe was interested in Ælfric's work as a Latin grammar, one of the Cambridge University Library glossators shows interest in Latin, English, *and* Anglo-Norman. And, while they have very different agendas, two primary glossators in Cotton Faustina A.x recognize that Ælfric's *Grammar* teaches English as well as Latin.

Cambridge, Trinity College R.9.17

Cambridge, Trinity College R.9.17 contains an abbreviated and modified form of Ælfric's *Grammar* without the *Glossary*.[13] It is one of the later copies of the *Grammar*, dating, Ker suggests, from the late eleventh or early twelfth century.[14] Much of the English text present in other copies has been omitted, and that which remains has almost all been moved to the gloss: Ælfric's Latin text, with some abbreviations, forms the main text, while Ælfric's English text is interlined. The overall effect of the scribe's alterations is to take away the focus on English and to turn the work into a more conventional Latin grammar with some vernacular glosses. The scribe's motivation for this revision is unclear: why would he bother with the considerable project of transforming Ælfric's *Grammar* into a more conventional grammar when he could simply have used any of the other Latin grammars?[15]

---

[13] Seven copies of the *Grammar* are accompanied by the *Glossary*; four, including Cambridge, Trinity College R.9.17, are not. The other three manuscripts are fragmentary and may or may not have had the *Glossary* with them.

[14] Ker, p. 134, no. 89. We know little of the provenance of this manuscript. M. R. James notes that it was owned by John Parker and corrected by a Parkerian scribe. See James's description in *The Western Manuscripts in the Library of Trinity College, Cambridge*. 4 vols. (Cambridge: Cambridge University Press, 1900-4).

[15] Of course, the scribe of Trinity College R.9.17 may be copying someone else's abbreviation of Ælfric's text. But, as Ker notes, some of the interlined English text appears only in this copy of the *Grammar* (p. 134). In addition, it is clear that the scribe had an exemplar containing the introductory material but deliberately left it off: he begins to add it to the end of the manuscript on the same page that he ends his abbreviated text, although he then changes his mind and adds a translation of the Distichs of Cato instead. Since the Distichs of Cato were widely used in medieval schools, the text's presence suggests that this manuscript may have been used as a school text as well.

Perhaps he was working in a library lacking basic resources; he may have used Ælfric's *Grammar* because that was all he had. In any case, this manuscript is definitely a working, rather than a display, text; the vellum contains large holes, up to five in a page, which the scribe has carefully written around.

Hunt provides a list of the Anglo-Norman glosses in this manuscript.[16] He believes that the glosses are "slightly later" than the text; Ker, however, believes that the text and the glosses — both French and English — are in the same hand, and from looking at the manuscript, I agree.[17]

The Anglo-Norman glosses appear as occasional replacements for English words. For example, in the list of third-declension words that end in short *a*, three French words appear:

calur
eal swa gað þas. hoc cauma .

mæiriē   hiw   nama   cliða   imagine   rædels gesceaft
thema . scema . onoma . malagma . agalma . Enigma . plasma .

geflit
Baptisma . dogma. scisma . et similia . (fol. 8v, lines 24-26)[18]

Compare the text as Julius Zupitza presents it: "ealswa gað ðas naman: *hoc cauma* swoloð, *thema* antimber, *scema* hiw, *onoma* nama, *malagma* cliða, *agalma* anlicness, *aenigma* rædels, *plasma* gesceaft, *baptisma* fulluht, *dogma* lar, *scisma* geflit ET HIS SIMILIA and þisum gelice."[19] The scribe has replaced *swoloð* with *calur*, *antimber* with *mæiriē* (perhaps *mætriē*), and *anlicness* with *imagine*. In addition, he has omitt ed

---

[16] Hunt omits the glosses that appear on fol. 8v, which I transcribe below. Two other glosses that seem to be French appear on fol. 8r and 8v: pirus [perier], ficus [fier]. Zupitza also includes the Anglo-Norman glosses in the apparatus of his edition of the *Grammar* and *Glossary*.

[17] See Ker, pp. 134-35, for his discussion of the manuscript.

[18] I have marked expanded abbreviations with underlining throughout this article.

[19] Zupitza, p. 33. "These nouns decline the same way: *hoc cauma* heat, *thema* theme, *scema* hue, *onoma* name, *malagma* poultice, *agalma* likeness, *aenigma* riddle, *plasma* creation, *baptisma* baptism, *dogma* dogma, *scisma* strife *et his similia* and the like."

translations of words that are probably familiar to him: *baptisma* and *dogma*. Throughout the manuscript, the scribe provides equivalents to the Latin vocabulary when he needs them using whatever word is most familiar to him, whether that word is of English or French descent. This modification suggests that the scribe was either comfortably bilingual or, perhaps, that his English already contained some French vocabulary, even at this very early date. The scribe does use some French words that are in Modern English today; for example, in the next line of fol. 8v, the scribe replaces the now-defunct Old English word *hleda* with the French word we regularly use in Modern English, *ceaire*, or "chair."[20]

The scribe of Trinity R.9.17 is not using Ælfric's text as an English grammar; on the contrary, he has deliberately converted the work into a Latin grammar. In his interlineations, the scribe treats English and Anglo-Norman as basically interchangeable; he does not choose one language or another to translate but instead uses whichever words are most familiar to him. The scribe is making deliberate choices in modifying Ælfric's text; he decides every step of the way whether to keep, omit, or change Ælfric's words. The fact that he easily adds French to the text, without any kind of sign to distinguish it from the English, suggests that in his mind the boundary between the two languages was fluid.

Cambridge University Library Hh.1.10

Cambridge University Library Hh.1.10 is a copy of Ælfric's *Grammar* and *Glossary* from the second half of the eleventh century. The text has been glossed in three languages: Latin, Anglo-Norman, and English.[21] All but two of the glosses in Anglo-Norman are by one glossator, who conjugates the verb *aimer* in all its active and passive forms above the conjugation of the verb *amo*. The second hand is responsible not only for the remaining two French glosses, which appear later in the section on verbs, but also for extensive Latin glosses and some English glosses throughout the manuscript.

---

[20] *Ceaire* is used to gloss *hoc sedile*.

[21] Along with the Old English glosses, there are marginalia in Modern English by Robert Talbot and John Joscelyn.

The first hand's glossing consists simply of Anglo-Norman glosses on Latin text: the glossator seemingly ignores Ælfric's English-language explanations. Certainly, the glossator may have been influenced by Ælfric's English verb paradigms to add French paradigms to the manuscript, but there is no clear evidence of his interest in anything but Latin verbs.[22] For that reason, it is the second, trilingual glossator who concerns me here. Although the numerous glosses in the text are cramped and quite small, it is clear that one glossator is responsible for this group: the ascenders on his letters have a curve that distinguishes his glosses from the others.[23] Why would one person gloss this text in three different languages? Or, to consider this question from another direction, why does Ælfric's *Grammar* evoke this trilingual response?

Only one folio of the manuscript contains all three languages, fol. 67r, in Ælfric's section on "defective" or impersonal verbs:[24]

[22] See, however, my discussion of Hand 2's glossing on London, British Library, Cotton Faustina A.x below. The decisive difference between this glossator and Hand 2 is that Hand 2 also glosses grammatical terminology, indicating an interest in grammatical concepts as well as in the paradigms.

[23] I would like to thank Timothy Graham, who very kindly looked at these glosses for me and agreed that they are all by the same hand.

[24] The section is titled "De Verbis Defectivis"; it appears in Zupitza's edition on pp. 206-08. Folio 67r begins and breaks off in mid-sentence: "[I will say what they all] have and how they are conjugated. Sometimes they take the nominative case: *restat* is to remain and Joseph said, *ad huc restant anni quinque* there still remains five years. *Iuuat me* it is pleasing to me. Here it is accusative. Also *delectat*, it is pleasing *me, te, illum*. Dative *uacat mihi* I am unoccupied, *uacat nobis*. *Uacate lectioni* make leisure time for reading. *Licet mihi bibere* I may drink, *mihi licuit*, I must, *tibi licet, nobis licet. si nobis liceret*, if we must. Infinitive *licere*, to be allowed and *licuisse* and *licitum esse*. *Licentia* is permission. *Placet mihi* it pleases me. *Libet mihi* it pleases me, *placuit, libuit. Libens*, pleasant. Also *liquet* is clear. *Conuenit*, it is fitting. *Euenit* it becomes. *Accidit* it happens. *Expedit* it supports *mihi, tibi, nobis, et cetera*. Accustive. *te det animam meam uite mee* [my soul is weary of my life], Job said. *Decet* it befits, *me decet, nos decet. Decuit* it befits. Also *oportet* it befits, *oportuit. Penitet me* it displeases me, *penituit. Penitere* to repent. *Penitentia* repentance or atonement. *Me pudet* it shames me, *puduit. Pudere. Me pigit.* it does not please me, *piguit, pigere. Pigritia* sloth. *Miseret me* I pity, *misertum est. Miseria* misery. *Latet* is hidden, *me, te, nos. Liquet* is clear, *nobis*, to us, *et omnibus* and all. But this verb and the like do not have . . . ."

habbað . ꝺ hu hig beoð ge þeodde . Sume hi teoð no | min-
atiuum casum . restat . to lafe . ys . ꝺ ioseph cwæð . ad huc |
restant anni quinque gyt þær synd fif gear to lafe . | iuuat me .
me ge lustfullaþ . her is accusatiuus . Eall | swa delectat . ge

lustfallað . me . te . illum . Datiuus uacat | mihi ic eom æmtig
ego sum paratus vel deliberatus . vel

impeditus nos otiamus preparate uos adlegendum
. uacat nobis . Uacate lectioni . æm | tigað eow to rædinge
. licet mihi . bibere . mot ic druncan . | mihi licuit . ic moste
. tibi licet nobis licet . si nobis liceret . gif we moston . In
finitiuum licere . beon | alyfed . ꝺ licuisse ꝺ licitum esse . li-
centia . is ge leaf | placet mihi . me ge licað . libet mihi . me

ge lustfal | lað . placuit . libuit . libens. lustbære . eall swa li
et

| quet . swutol ys . Conuenit . ge rist . euenit . be com . |
apparet   auient   aueneit

accidit. ge limpð . expedit . fremað . mihi tibi . | nobis . et
cetera . Accusatiuo . te det animam meam uite mee . cwæð

iob . decet . ge dafe | nað . me decet . nos decet . decuit . ge
oportet

dafenode . | Eall swa oportet . ge dafenað . oportuit . penitet
| me . me ofþingð . penituit. penitere . be hreowsian . | peni-
tentia . be hreowsung . oþþe dæd bot . me þu | det . me

sceamað . puduit . pudere . me piget . me | ne listð . piguit .
me ofþincð

pigere . pigritia slæpð | miseret me . | me ofriwð . misertum
est . miseria . yrmð . latet | digle is . me . te. nos . liquet .
swutel ys . nobis . us . | et omnibus ꝺ eallum . ac þas word ꝺ
þillice nabbað

The two Anglo-Norman glosses written by the trilingual hand
are in some ways the most intriguing because they indicate that the
glossator was interested in etymologies and ambiguities in French. The
glosses appear over two compounds of *venio* on line 14: "Conuenit . ge
rist . euenit . be com." Over *Conuenit* the glossator has written *auient*;
over *euenit* he has written *aueneit*. The glossator knows that the AN
verb *avenir* has two meanings — "befall, come to" or, used impersonal-

ly, "be fitting for" — and therefore uses different forms of the one verb to gloss the two related Latin verbs. It is unclear (at least to me) why he uses the present tense to represent the impersonal *avenir* (*auient*) and the imperfect to represent the regular use of the verb (*aueneit*). But in any case, this is a clever little move: the glossator makes the point that one French verb can mean the same thing as two related Latin verbs. Even though these glosses are the only French words he writes in the manuscript, they show that the trilingual hand is interested in this kind of French semantic detail or wordplay.

The glossator's few Old English glosses show that he is interested in improving or updating Ælfric's English-language text and perhaps in providing additional English-language vocabulary. On fol. 67r, one OE gloss appears. Ælfric's text reads, "me piget . me ne listð." The glossator writes *me offincð* above *me piget*, introducing a synonym where Ælfric has used a negated antonym. Since Ælfric usually uses synonyms, this change makes a pair of Latin/OE synonyms parallel to the others. On fol. 55r, the glossator has written two OE glosses over equivalent OE terms: *geomrige* is glossed *sicige*; *bifige* is glossed *cwacige*. On fol. 26r, he has written *galnisse* in the margin just above line 17 next to Ælfric's "luxus . lust oððe gælsa," offering a third English translation. Either the glossator found these English words unclear and decided to provide better ones, or he is interested in adding to the English vocabulary provided by the text.

The glossator's Latin glosses show a similar interest in vocabulary, adding alternative Latin above Latin text. Some of these are simple: *uacat nobis* [nos otiamus],[25] *liquet* [apparet]; *decet* [oportet]. Other glosses offer many alternatives, including antonyms: *uacat mihi* [ego sum paratus vel deliberatus . vel impeditus]. These glosses do not necessarily clarify the meaning of a word or group of words; instead, they provide more vocabulary.[26] Similarly, on fol. 55r, the trilingual

---

[25] Zupitza prints this gloss as "nos ociamus" (p. 206).

[26] Wieland notes in his study of the glosses on Prudentius and Arator in CUL Gg.5.35 that a lexical gloss "only provides that particular meaning which is required by the context of the lemma." But, of course, Ælfric's *Grammar* offers no context for these words, so the glossator is free to offer many possible meanings. See Gernot R. Wieland, *The Latin Glosses on Arator and Prudentius in Cambridge University Library, MS Gg.5.35.* (Toronto, Pontifical Institute of Medieval Studies, 1983) p. 30.

glossator provides related vocabulary above Ælfric's third conjugation verbs: *texo . ic wefe* [unde textrinum opus]; *pecto . ic cembe* [unde pecten]; *messui . messum* [unde messor]; *rapio . ic ge lœcce* [unde raptor]; *alo . ic fede* [unde altor ⁊ altrix]. In each case, the trilingual glossator adds nouns that are related to Ælfric's Latin verbs. This interest in adding vocabulary suggests that the glossator may be a teacher who is trying to build up his students' vocabularies: the multiple glosses in English and Latin and the additional nouns augment rather than clarify Ælfric's text.

In other places in the manuscript, the glossator shows interest in Latin grammatical terminology as well. Throughout the manuscript, he glosses Ælfric's English-language terms with their more usual Latin equivalents and adds terminology when Ælfric leaves it out. For example, he glosses Ælfric's discussion of adverbs of time:[27]

Sume ge tacniað ma tida þus . Quando | eram iuuenis . þa þa
ic wæs iung . ⁊ axung . quando | uenisti . - hwænne come þu
futuro
. - to werdre tide . quan | do ueniam adte doce me . þonne
praeteritum
ic come to þe tæc | me . [eal swa] aliquando feci sic . hwilon
futuro
ic dide swa . Si ali | quando faciam sic . gyf ic æfre do swa .
et cetera . Eall | swa dudum . ge firn . Quondam . hwilon . ⁊
praeteritum praesens
olim . ge | tacniað . þreo tyda forð ge witene . ⁊ and werde. | ⁊
futurum
to werde .   (fol. 72r, lines 10-18)[28]

---

[27]Ælfric begins the section of the meaning of adverbs, "SIGNIFICATIO is getacnung, and ðes dæl hæfð fela getacnunga. TEMPORALIA synd, ða ðe tida getacnjað . . ." (p. 223). "Significatio is signification, and this part of speech has many meanings. *Temporalia* are those that signify time." He then gives examples in Latin and English.

[28] This passage can be found on p. 224 of Zupitza's edition: "Some signify more tenses in this way: *Quando eram iuuenis* When I was young; and asking: *quando uenisti* when do you come? Future tense: *quando ueniam ad te, doce me*, when I come to you, teach me. Also *aliquando feci sic*, while I did so; *si aliquando faciam sic*, if I ever do so, et cetera. Also *dudum*, once. *Quondam*, while, and *olim* signifies three tenses: past and present and future."

These glosses suggest that he is comfortable with Latin terminology.[29] Most interesting, the trilingual glossator glosses the name
Eadgarus (used as an example of a proper noun) with the Latin term
proprium nomen twice, on fol. 3v and 4v. Ælfric never uses the term
proprium nomen in his *Grammar,* choosing only to use his English
term, *agene naman.* The glossator must have known the term from
other grammatical texts or teachings and added it into the *Grammar.*

What does the trilingual glossator teach us, both about the
Grammar and about his attitude toward the three languages of post-
Conquest England? This hand seems to use the text as a framework in
which he can elaborate on Latin, English, and Anglo-Norman French.
He is familiar with Latin grammatical terminology and adds additional
vocabulary, which suggests that he may be a Latin teacher, glossing the
text in preparation for later explication to students. But his vernacular
glosses, especially the two French glosses, which can serve no purpose
but to make an interesting point about one French verb, show that
Latin is not his sole interest. While these glosses do not show that the
trilingual hand is interested in Ælfric's English grammar, they do show
that he is interested in the meanings of French and possibly English
words.

British Library, Cotton Faustina A.x

The Anglo-Norman glosses in the copy of the *Grammar* found
in Cotton Faustina A.x appear predominantly in two places, the section
on verbs and the glossary.[30] Hunt treats the two groups of glosses separately, and I will discuss only the glosses appearing in the verb section,
that is fol. 44-66v. I make this choice because the glossators of the

---

[29] Similar glosses appear in the following section, which describes adverbs of
place: "Sume synd localia . þæt synd stowlice . | for þan þe hig ge tacniað
stowa huc [in loco] . hyder . | illuc [ad locum] . þider . ueni [de loco] huc .
gan hyder" (fol. 72r, lines 18-20). "Some are *localia,* that is, adverbs of place,
because they signify places: *huc [in loco],* here; *illuc [ad locum],* there; *ueni
[de loco] huc,* come here." Here the glossator clarifies these adverbs with
prepositions.

[30] Some French glosses also appear in the copy of the Old English Rule of St.
Benedict following the *Grammar* and *Glossary;* Hunt prints these glosses
with the others from this manuscript.

glossary focus on the collection of Latin words.[31] The Anglo-Norman glosses on the verb section in this manuscript are far more extensive than the glosses in Cambridge University Library Hh.1.10.

The section of the text focusing on verbs begins, like most of Ælfric's sections, with a short passage of Latin followed by English explanation:

> CONIVGATIONES VERBORVM QVATTVOR SVNT SECVNDVM PRISCIANVM. CONIVGATIO VER-
> BORVM ys worda geðeodnys, and þæra sind feower æfter Priscianes tæcinge. naman habbað fif DECLENSIONES, and word habbað feower CONIVGATIONES.[32]

Ælfric describes the verb, tense, mode, person, and number and then explains the four conjugations. The explanatory text is in English, and Ælfric introduces both Latin and English grammatical terminology. When he delineates the verb paradigms, he begins by giving the word first in Latin, then in English: "amo ic lufige, amas ðu lufast," and so on. Later, he stops translating every form into English and translates the first person form only. At the end of each conjugation, Ælfric lists several Latin verbs in that conjugation with their English equivalents. Hunt publishes these glosses in his text, yet as I noted above, he does not include the English text or show whether glosses appear over the Latin or English text.[33] To give a short example of how the text and

---

[31] Hunt describes these glosses: "The composition and elaboration of medieval glossaries form a complex subject on which much work remains to be done. In England a practical and ready-made wordbook lay to hand in the work of Ælfric. In seven of the fifteen MSS of his *Grammar* there is appended a vocabulary of several hundred words arranged in eight sections by topics . . ." (p. 23). Hunt prints these glosses separately from the ones in the verb section (pp. 24-6).

[32] Zupitza, pp. 129-30. "*Coniugationes verborum quattor sunt secundum Priscianum. Coniugation verborum* is the conjugation of verbs, and there are four according to Priscian's teaching. Nouns have five *declensiones* and verbs have four *coniugationes*."

[33] In addition, there are four glosses on fol. 51v, three on the main text and one on the marginal text added by a hand that resembles Hand 2, omitted by Hunt. Zupitza includes these in his apparatus. The three on the main text appear over line 8; *docendi* [de enseinner]; *docendo* [enseinnant]; *docendum* [a enseinner]. The letters or word [fut] appear over *doctum fuit* in the marginal text.

manuscript appear, here is the beginning of the discussion of the first conjugation:

> Seo forme coniuga | tio is . þe maciað þone oðerne had . on
>   io aim   tu aimes   cil
> langne . as . | amo . ic lufige . amas ðu lufast . amat . he
>   aimet   nus amuns   vus
> lufað . | et pluraliter . amamus . we lufiað . amatis . ge
> amez   cil aiment
> lufiað . a | mant . hi lufiað .[34]

There are at least four hands glossing this section of the *Grammar* in French, but two hands predominate. Only 12 of 505 total glosses[35] occur in hands other than Hand 1 or Hand 2. Of the 493 glosses under consideration, 29% appear over Old English text, while 71% appear over Latin. These numbers are not especially illuminating until we break them down into Hand 1 and Hand 2. Hand 2 glosses almost exclusively over the Latin text: only one of 258 glosses appears over English. Hand 1, however, glosses 58% over English and 41% over Latin. [See page 112, Table 1]

Hand 1 very rarely glosses text, Latin or English, where there is no English translation. For instance, Ælfric stops giving complete English translations of the paradigms after his discussion of the active forms of the second conjugation. Hand 1 stops glossing in those places, reappearing when Ælfric starts a new verb with an English equivalent. For instance, Hand 1 disappears from fol. 54rv, reappearing when English text appears again on fol. 55r. Later in the text Hand 1 skips over fol. 63rv, where there is no English, but reappears with the English text on fol. 64r.[36] This indicates that while Hand 2 was probably read-

---

[34] This passage is found on fol. 43v, line 28 and fol. 44r, lines 1-4 (Zupitza, p. 130): "The first conjugation is the one that has the second person in long *as*: *amo*, I love *amas*. you love; *amat*, he loves; and plural *amamus*, we love; *amatis*, you love; *amant*, they love." As Hunt notes, the first three glosses appear in a hand that does not recur in the manuscript. The rest are in Hand 1 (see below).

[35] This number of total glosses does not include the glosses on the large text added in the margins on fol. 45v and 51v by a hand that greatly resembles Hand 2. Hand 2 (if it is he) also adds text on fol. 56r, but there are no French glosses on that marginalia. Hunt assumes these marginal additions are of parts of Ælfric's work that have been left out, but they don't seem to be.

[36] On fol. 64r, Hand 1 glosses over Latin twice and Old English once.

ing the Latin (although he may have been reading the English as well), Hand 1 was following the English text.

Table 1: Glosses by Language over Which Gloss Appears, British Library, Cotton Faustina A.x (fol. 44-66v)

	Total	*Hand 1*	*Hand 2*	*Other*
Number of glosses:	505*	239	258	12
Over OE:	144	139	1	4
Over Latin:	358*	98†	257	8
In margins:	3	3	0	0

*Four glosses over Latin text are begun by Hand 1 and finished by Hand 2; they are counted in each category but only once in the total.

†One gloss by Hand 1 appears over English and Latin text and is counted in each category.

Hand 1 and Hand 2 gloss different kinds of text as well. Ælfric's text in the verb section can be divided into three categories: the verb paradigms, the lists of verbs appearing at the end of each conjugation, and grammatical terminology. Both hands gloss the first kind of text, the paradigms, but they appear in a particular pattern. Hand 1 usually appears over the first person singular in a paradigm: for example, over *ic lufode* in "amabam ic lufode" is written *io amoe* (fol. 44r). Ælfric always includes the English equivalent for that form. Hand 2 fills in the rest of the paradigm, indicating that Hand 2 is glossing after 1.[37] Both of the glossators gloss the paradigms, Hand 1 concentrating on English text, Hand 2 more extensively glossing Latin text.

Hand 1 is especially interested in the second kind of text, the lists of verbs. This glossator adds French equivalents to the lists: ninety-seven glosses total. In the first set, Ælfric lists first conjugation verbs that make their preterit perfects ending in *-avi*. He begins with *amo* and continues:

[37] In addition, Hand 2 finishes up glosses started by Hand 1 four times. All four are examples of terminology glosses.

eall swa gað þas . beo ic weligie . beaui . ic welegode | beatum
         io dessir   io be
. gewelegod . lanio . ic toterre ; hio ic | gynige . inchoo . ic

ongynne . inchoaui . uacuo . | ic æmtige . turbo . ic gedrefe .
io su   io nag   io uenc
sudo . ic swæte . | Nauigo . ic rowe . triumpho . ic si[ge]rige

. flo . ic blawe . | flaui . armo ic ge wæpnige . orno . ic ge

frætwige . |no . ic swymme . naui . nato . ic swymme . palpo .
io tast   io apai
| ic grapige . sedo . ic [ge]stille . tenuo . ic gewanige . oððe .

ic do sumþing þinre . laboro ic swince . aro . ic | erige . cribro
io criblæ io esquaz
. ic syfte . quasso . ic to cwyse . calco . | ic trede . ambulo .
                         io traual
ic gange . precipito . ic scufe . uexo . ic drecce . euangelizo .
 io pree
ic godspellige . | (fol. 46v, lines 2-12)[38]

These bilingual lists become trilingual with the addition of Anglo-Norman translations.

    If we consider the glosses by Hand 1 as just another example of French on a Latin text, they do not seem all that interesting or unusual. Hunt notes that in Latin works glossators often turn areas of text that contain many different words into glossaries by adding vernacular glosses.[39] Unlike the glosses in Hunt's Latin texts or the

---

[38] This text appears on p. 137 of Zupitza's edition. "These also conjugate this way: *beo* I enrich. *beavi* I enriched. *beatum* blessed. *lanio* I tear up. *hio* I yawn. *inchoo* I begin. *inchoavi. vacuo* I empty. *turbo* I stir up. *sudo* I sweat. *Navigo* I sail. *triumpho* I win. *flo* I blow. *flavi. armo* I arm. *orno* I ornament. *no* I swim. *navi. nato* I swim. *palpo* I touch. *sedo* I am still. *tenuo* I wane or I make something thinner. *laboro* I work. *aro* I plough. *cribro* I sift. *quasso* I grind to pieces. *calco* I tread. *ambulo* I go. *precipito* I push. *vexo* I vex. *evangelizo* I preach the gospel."

[39] He notes specifically that Bernard Silvestris's *Cosmographia* contains such passages: "Whilst philosophical texts, such as Macrobius, rarely receive vernacular glosses, those which contained passages devoted to the natural world were viewed as providing ready-made word lists. The beautiful copy (s. xiii in.) of Bernard Silvestris's *Cosmographia* (c. 1147-1148) in Oxford, Bodleian Library, Laud Misc. 515, fol. 182r-219r has most of the vernacular glosses in the third section which includes many names of plants" (Hunt, p. 51).

glosses in Trinity R.9.17, however, Hand 1's glosses create a trilingual glossary. And indeed, these glosses on the verbs form true trilingual glossaries; unlike most "trilingual" glossaries listed by Ker, the Latin text is accompanied by English *and* French, not English *or* French.[40]

More important, however, Hand 1's pattern of glossing leads us to a very unusual conclusion: his glosses seem to indicate that he is a speaker of Anglo-Norman who is actually teaching himself English verbs. First, it seems reasonable to assume that a reader glosses a foreign-language text in his or her native tongue, not the other way around. That is, a French speaker would gloss a Latin or English text in French, while an English speaker would gloss a French text in English.[41] Hand 1, then, is probably fluent in French. Second, if Latin were his only concern, he would gloss Latin text indiscriminately, whether accompanied by English translation or not.[42] Yet, Hand 1, unlike Hand 2, only glosses where there is English text.[43] And Hand 1's glosses ap-

[40] Ker lists three manuscripts containing trilingual glossaries: London, British Library, Royal 7 D.ii; Oxford, Bodleian Library, Bodley 730; and London, British Library, Stowe 57. In the first two glossaries, Latin is glossed by either French or English. In the glossary in Stowe 57, on the other hand, some Latin words are glossed in both vernacular languages. In fact, space has been left for both French and English after every Latin word, but many words are missing one or the other. R. M. Garrett prints this glossary, which he dates c. 1200, in "Middle English and French Glosses Found from MS Stowe 57," *Archiv für das Studium der neueren Sprachen und Literaturen* 121 (1908), pp. 411-12.

[41] For example, Walter of Bibbesworth's *Tretiz*, designed to teach French to English speakers, is a rhyming French vocabulary with English interlined glosses. The language being learned forms the main text; the readers' native language forms the gloss. See M. T. Clanchy's description of the *Tretiz* on pp. 197-200.

[42] It is possible that Hand 1 is interested in the Latin, using English to translate the Latin, but if Hand 1's English is that good, why would he be glossing the text in Anglo-Norman? Of course, Hand 1 may be interested in English *and* Latin, just as Ælfric is. The unusual thing is, however, that a Anglo-Norman speaker would be interested in English at all.

[43] Ronald Buckalew notes that in the sixteenth century Robert Talbot learned Old English in the same way: "By using the Latin examples as glosses to their Old English translations, thereby reversing the original purpose of the *Grammar* from teaching Latin to learning Old English, Talbot could make

114

pear over English text slightly more than half the time. This pattern of glossing shows that while Hand 1 may well be interested in Latin vocabulary, he is reading the English, picking up the basics of English verb inflections and learning new vocabulary.

Why would a Anglo-Norman speaker want to learn English? The question reverses our usual assumptions about the interaction between French and English in post-Conquest England. We know that English speakers wanted to learn French: M. T. Clanchy notes that Walter of Bibbesworth wrote his *Tretiz* to help mothers teach French to their English-speaking children, and Ian Short discusses saints' lives in which knowledge of French is miraculously bestowed upon holy English speakers.[44] But the glosses made by Hand 1 show that at least one Anglo-Norman speaker wanted to learn or improve his English. Hand 1 might have good reason for being interested in English. Douglas Kibbee suggests that at least in the early part of the twelfth century, and to some extent later in the century, French-speaking priests were encouraged to use English in order to make their preaching accessible to more people; in addition, he notes that English was used, albeit rarely, in the courts.[45] It is also possible that this reader wanted access to English texts. Hand 1 may have wanted to read contemporary as well as older English-language works — charters, law codes, maybe

---

the *Grammar* his basic Old English textbook, as a number of others did after him" ["Nowell, Lambarde, and Leland: The Significance of Laurence Nowell's Transcript of Ælfric's *Grammar* and *Glossary*," *Anglo-Saxon Scholarship: The First Three Centuries*, ed. Carl T. Berkhout and Milton McC. Gatch (Boston: G. K. Hall and Co., 1982) p. 20]. Christine Franzen argues that the Tremulous Hand of Worcester, who copied the *Grammar* in the thirteenth century, was also teaching himself Old English [*The Tremulous Hand of Worcester: A Study of Old English in the Thirteenth Century* (Oxford: Clarendon, 1991), pp. 116-17].

[44] See Ian Short, "On Bilingualism in Anglo-Norman England," *Romance Philology* 33 (1980), pp. 467-79; and M. T. Clanchy, *From Memory to Written Record*, pp. 197-223.

[45] Douglas A. Kibbee, *For to Speke Frenche Trewely*, Studies in the History of the Language Sciences 60 (Amsterdam: John Benjamins, 1991), pp. 6-7.

even literature — and found Ælfric's *Grammar* a useful introduction.[46] For whatever reason, this twelfth-century Anglo-Norman speaker was using the *Grammar* to learn English.[47]

While Hand 1 of Cotton Faustina A.x is concerned with translating the English and creating glossaries from the verb lists, Hand 2 focuses on two types of text. First, he glosses the verb paradigms extensively, providing Anglo-Norman equivalents above the Latin like those found in CUL Hh.1.10. This might seem to indicate that Hand 2 is a French-speaker learning Latin. Hand 2, however, has a second interest: the grammatical terminology. Of the 24 terminology glosses, five are by Hand 1, fifteen are by Hand 2, and four more are begun by 1 and finished by 2.[48]

---

[46] French had not yet become the language of literature in the twelfth century: R. M. Wilson notes that while "during the thirteenth century French became the principal literary language in this country . . . . It is quite clear that during the twelfth century the chief competitor of English as a written language was Latin, not French" ["English and French in England 1100-1300," *History* 28 (1943), p. 40]. Wilson also notes, "Until the middle of the twelfth century this [English] literature is written almost entirely in the old West Saxon literary dialect" (p. 38); Gneuss points out that Ælfric uses standard Old English in the *Grammar* ["The Origin of Standard Old English and Æthelwold's School at Winchester," *Anglo-Saxon England* 1 (1972), p. 75].

[47] This analysis leaves open the question of why Hand 1 chooses to gloss the verb section of the *Grammar* rather than any other section. This section may have been especially appealing or useful to Hand 1 because it provided access to a large collection of verbs, whereas many contemporary glossaries are confined to nouns. Ælfric's own *Glossary* at the end of the *Grammar* is exclusively made up of nouns (London, British Library, Cotton Faustina A.x's glossary is also glossed in French). The verb section in the *Grammar*, then, provides a useful supplementary collection of verbs. It is interesting to note that many of the late twelfth-century or early thirteenth-century Latin wordbooks glossed by French speakers in search of Latin vocabulary are collections of nouns. For example, Hunt notes that Alexander Nequam's *De Nominibus Utensilium* "is . . . almost entirely concerned with nouns" (p. 181). In general, perhaps, nouns are the focus of word-lists.

[48] For example, one gloss reads "par la [Hand 1] imperatif met [Hand 2]" (fol. 44r). Perhaps Hand 1 only wanted to indicate that the examples were "for the" imperative (or optative, or whatever) mode; Hand 2 was interested in rendering the terms in French. Or course, these glosses confirm that Hand 2 is glossing after Hand 1.

Hand 2's grammatical glosses, unlike both hands' glosses of paradigms and lists, are not true translations.[49] Instead, they are examples of what Brian Merrilees calls "gallicization;"[50] instead of translating the words into French equivalents, the glossator assimilates them into French vocabulary by making them look French. For example, *imperativo modo* is transformed into *par la imperatif mot*. In another place, he glosses *ad secundam et tertiam personam* as *a la secunda et a la terce persona* (fol. 44r). Jacques Julien notes that this kind of terminology is characteristic of early French grammars; he writes of medieval French texts: "Du strict point de vue de la terminologie, les termes non assumés restent en latin . . . le reste est calqué."[51]

In contrast, Ælfric does translate the terms using native English morphemes. His terminology attempts to recreate a term's meaning in an English word. For example *imperativo modo* becomes *on bebeodendlicum gemete*, literally, "in ordering mode."[52] While Ælfric creates English terminology that explains grammatical concepts to an English-speaking audience, Hand 2's terms are of no immediately obvious use to a Anglo-Norman-speaking student; they do not explain the meaning of the concepts beyond what a reader could glean from the Latin itself. Why, then, does this glossator bother glossing the Latin terms in this way? Why create terminology that no one who does not already know Latin can understand?

I believe the only possible answer is that Hand 2 creates French-language terminology because he is creating a French grammar. His

---

[49] The few grammatical glosses by Hand 1 are more like "true" translations than Hand 2's: "PRESENTI TEMPORE," for example, is glossed "par la tens present" (fol. 44r). Ælfric translates the term into "on andwerdre tide" (Zupitza, p. 131).

[50] Brian Merrilees, "An Aspect of Grammatical Terminology in Insular French," *Cahiers de Lexicologie* 51 (1987), p. 194.

[51] Jacques Julien, "La Terminologie Française des Parties du Discours et de Leurs Sous-Classes au XVIe Siècle," *Langages* 92 (1988), p. 67.

[52] Zupitza, p. 131. For discussions of how Ælfric translates grammatical terminology into English, see Laurence Kennedy Shook, "A Technical Construction in Old English: Translation Loans in *-lic*," *Mediaeval Studies* 2 (1940), pp. 253-57; and Edna Rees Williams, "Ælfric's Grammatical Terminology," *PMLA* 73 (1958), pp. 453-62.

grammatical terminology does not have to mean anything in French if its purpose is to create French grammar as a field of study. Hand 2 emulates Ælfric's vernacular grammar with a vernacular grammar of his own. There is, however, one difference between Ælfric's English grammar and Hand 2's French one: Hand 2's grammar works as a grammar for non-native speakers rather than native speakers. His grammatical terminology is useless for French speakers, and he extensively glosses the paradigms, even where Ælfric does not bother to give English equivalents. These glosses make the Cotton Faustina A.x text a grammar more suitable for English speakers learning French inflectional morphology (readers who would still have the English grammatical terminology and Ælfric's English text to help them) than for French speakers seeking insight into grammatical concepts. Yet while Hand 2 writes a grammar for a different kind of audience, he has made the same leap of logic that Ælfric makes in writing an English grammar for native speakers: the tools that grammarians use to study and teach Latin can be used to describe vernacular languages as well.[53]

There is one small piece of evidence which suggests that Hand 2 might have been paying attention to specifics in the *Grammar* as well as copying the idea of a vernacular grammar. Hand 2 was influenced by Ælfric in one of the terms he created. Merrilees briefly mentions the Cotton Faustina A.x glosses in a note and comments, "It is interesting to note that MS. Cotton Faustina offers two forms to render *modus*, *met*, which may have been influenced by the English form *(ge)mete*, and *mot*."[54] Hand 2 may have been following both the Latin terminology and the English terminology in his glosses.

Both Hand 1 and Hand 2 saw that Ælfric's *Grammar* is a work about English as well as about Latin. Hand 1 uses it to learn English verbs; Hand 2 uses it to teach French ones. Hand 1 uses the text to

---

[53] These glosses form the first French grammar, predating the next by a century. See Brian Merrilees, "L'Art Mineur Français et le Curriculum Grammatical," *Histoire Épistémologie Langage* 12.2 (1990), pp. 12-29; and "Le Débuts de la Terminologie Grammaticale en Français: À Propos Desquelques Travaux Récents," *Romania* 109 (1988), pp. 397-411. Professor Merrilees kindly sent me these articles.

[54] Brian Merrilees, "An Aspect of Grammatical Terminology in Insular French," *Cahiers de Lexicologie* 51 (1987), p. 200.

learn English as a second language, a purpose for which the *Grammar* is not perfectly suited, but one that is possible given Ælfric's explanations and examples in English. Hand 2, recognizing that Ælfric has applied grammatical concepts to English as well as French, emulates his work, creating his own French grammatical terminology and explicating the inflectional morphology of French verbs.

The Anglo-Norman glosses on these three manuscripts of Ælfric's *Grammar* show that the medieval readers used the text in different ways, adapting the work to their own interests and needs. The glossator of Trinity College R.9.17 used the text as a grammar of Latin; the glossators of CUL Hh.1.10 and Cotton Faustina A.x had varying degrees of interest in English (and French) as well. All of these manuscripts, however, show that twelfth-century English readers did not necessarily treat English, Anglo-Norman, and Latin in different ways in spite of the languages' varying degrees of prestige. For the Trinity glossator, French and English are interchangeable. For the CUL Hh.1.10 glossator, all three languages are the object of linguistic interest. And for the two hands in the Cotton Faustina manuscript, vernacular languages can be studied in the same way as Latin. By looking at these glosses on the *Grammar* in their multilingual manuscript contexts, we see them as more than Anglo-Norman gloss and Latin text; they are evidence that the linguistic and social boundaries among the three languages of post-Conquest England were porous and fluid.

Three Tables of Contents,
One Old English Homiliary in
Cambridge, Corpus Christi College, MS 178

PAUL ACKER

C AMBRIDGE, CORPUS CHRISTI COLLEGE, MS 178, part A,[1] contains an early eleventh-century collection of Old English homilies, mainly by Ælfric.[2] In order to find their separate ways around this collection, three early users of the manuscript each provided a table of contents. The first table is written (between two "books" of homilies) by the late Old English scribe; the second is added by the remarkable early Middle English student of Old English texts, the "tremulous Worcester scribe;" and the third is added by the equally remarkable early modern English student of Old English texts, Archbishop Parker. These and other traces in the manuscript provide a record of its use: how three discrete readers attempted to make sense of their religious and linguistic heritage. Further, by comparing these three tables of contents, one can recover evidence of items now lost and even determine when, how, and where some of those items were relocated.

[1] Part B, pp. 287-457, was originally a different manuscript or booklet. Both parts were in Worcester (although still not necessarily bound together) by the mid-eleventh century, when additions made to each were incorporated into Oxford, Bodleian Library, Hatton MSS 113-114. Later in the century marginal notations were entered by Coleman [see N. R. Ker, "Old English Notes Signed 'Coleman,'" *Medium Ævum* 18 (1949), pp. 28-31] on pp. 229 and 97 (Ker misses another unsigned heading on p. 91). By the early thirteenth century the two parts were more certainly bound together (see below, re MS, pp. vii-viii) and were then both glossed by the tremulous Worcester scribe [on whom generally see Christine Franzen, *The Tremulous Hand of Worcester: A Study of Old English in the Thirteenth Century* (Oxford: Clarendon Press, 1991)].

[2] Peter Clemoes points to a few passages and small pieces that he thinks may not be by Ælfric; see *Ælfric's Catholic Homilies: The First Series. I: Text*, EETS s.s. 17 (Oxford: Oxford University Press, 1997), pp. 38-39.

The Old English Colophon and Anglo-Latin Table of Contents

On page 163 of the manuscript, the first of two scribes[3] wrote a colophon to what had been copied up to that point, the "first book" of the homiliary, and a Latin table of contents to what was to follow, the "second book."[4] The text of the colophon, previously transcribed in Wanley and Ker,[5] reads thus (I append a modern English translation):

(Her) geendað seo forme boc. & her æfter onginð seo oðer boc. on ægðer þara boca synd twelf spell. unleaslice;

(Ð)as spell þe stondað on þissere forman bec. þa man mæg secgan loca hwænne man wylle. ac þa spell þe standað on þissere æfteran bec. þa man sceal secgan on þam dagum þe hy to gesette synd; Ða twa & twentig spell synd be fullan gesette swa swa hi æt fruman wæron on þære ealdan .æ. bysne. ac twa spel of þisum. an be þam heafodleahtrum. & oþer be þam wiglungum synd geeacnode of oðrum spellum; Nu bidde ic on godes naman loca hwa þas boc hæbbe on his anwealde þæt heo nytt beo oðrum mannum. þæt he nan pleoh næbbe gif heo unnytt byð;

(I)n hoc codicello continentur duodecim sermones anglice. quos accepimus de libris quos ælfricus abbas anglice transtulit; .I. De adnuntiatione sancte marie. .II. De natiui-

---

[3] According to Ker, part A of the manuscript is copied by one scribe from pp. 1-169 (including the section transferred to CCCC 162, pp. 139-60; see below), then by a second scribe from pp. 170-270. The change occurs in the middle of Ker's Item 20, the first homily in the "second book." See N. R. Ker, *Catalogue of Manuscripts Contain Anglo-Saxon* (Oxford: Clarendon Press, 1957; rpt. with Supplement, 1990), p. 64.

[4] CCCC 178 is Ker no. 41, Gneuss no. 54, and has been described recently in John C. Pope, ed., *The Homilies of Ælfric: A Supplementary Collection*, EETS o.s. 259-60 (London: Oxford University Press, 1967, 1968), vol.1, pp. 62-67; Malcolm Godden, ed., *Ælfric's Catholic Homilies: The Second Series. Text*, EETS s.s. 5 (London: Oxford University Press, 1979), pp. lxviii-lxx; Franzen, pp. 49-51; and Clemoes, pp. 37-40.

[5] Humphrey Wanley, *Librorum Veterum Septentrionalium*, Vol. 2 of George Hickes, *Linguarum Veterum Sepentrionalium Thesaurus* (Oxford: Sheldonian Theatre, 1705), p. 121; Ker, *Catalogue*, p. 62.

tate *christi*. .III. De circumcisione *christi*. .IIII. De baptismo
christi; .V. De purificatione s*anctae* marie. VI. De quadrages-
sima. VII. De passione *christi*. VIII. De resurrectione *christi*.
IX. De octauis pasce. X. De uigilia ascen[s]is do*m*ini. XI De
ascensione do*m*ini. XII. De pentecosten.[6]

Here ends the first book & hereafter begins the second
book. In each of these books are twelve homilies, truly.
Those homilies that are in this first book one may say when-
ever one wants [i.e., *quando volueris*, homilies for unspecified
occasions]. But the homilies that are in this following book
one must say on the days for which they are set [i.e., homilies
for specified occasions]. Twenty-two homilies are set down
in full just as they originally were in the old exemplar.[7] But
two of these homilies, one concerning the cardinal sins and
the other concerning auguries, have been augmented from
other homilies.[8] Now I pray in God's name that whoever has
this book in his keeping should make it useful to other men
so that he bear no responsibility for its being unuseful.

---

[6] Initials that I enclose in parentheses are written (or filled) in red in the
manuscript; the Roman numerals are also in red. The scribe begins a new
line at these initials; I have started a new paragraph. I expand abbreviations
via italics; where I write *christi*, the scribe has the Greek-based abbreviation
xpi.

[7] The DOE, which calls this text "Scrib [Directions to Readers] 24 (Ker),"
does not quote this passage under *æ* or *bysen* and has no entry for *æ-bysen*
(Pope, vol 1, p. 63, renders *æ-bysne* here, but simply translates "exemplar;"
since *æ* usually means "law" an *æ-bysen* might mean an exemplar with the force
of law, i.e., an authorized copy). The DOE concordance places commas for
the points around *æ* in this quotation, but the scribe's points do not appear to
indicate pauses; rather they must be a form of expunction. I suggest the scribe
had begun to write *on þære ealde æ*, "in the old law (or 'Old Testament')," ·
a common phrase in Old English religious writings (it occurs, e.g., in the
beginning of the *Hexameron* earlier on in the manuscript). He then went
on to write the correct word *bysne*, then signaled his error via expunction
— an unfortunate error in a passage purporting to transcriptional accuracy.
(The scribe apparently also erased an error, probably *sceal* plus the beginning
of a wrong word, just before *sceal gesecgan* above; these errors are another
indication that the scribe is copying the colophon from an exemplar.)

[8] See Pope, vol. 1, pp. 63-64.

In this little book [i.e., the second book] are contained
twelve sermons in English, which we have taken from books
that abbot Ælfric translated into English. 1. On the annun-
ciation of the blessed Mary; 2. On the nativity of Christ; 3.
On the circumcision of Christ; 4. On the baptism of Christ;
5. On the purification of the blessed Mary; 6. On quadragesima; 7. On the passion of Christ; 8. On the resurrection
of Christ; 9. On the octave of Easter; 10. On the vigil of the
ascension of the Lord; 11. On the ascension of the Lord; 12.
On Pentecost.

This colophon yields some unique evidence for the early reception and transmission of Ælfric. It claims that most of the homilies
have been copied faithfully according to an old, perhaps authorized, exemplar (*be fullan gesette swa swa hi æt fruman wæron on þære ealde bysne*),[9]
but acknowledges that two homilies were augmented by supplementary
material from other homilies (*geeacnode of oðrum spellum*). This claim
and acknowledgment read like a direct reply to the closing admonitory
passages in a number of Ælfric's prefaces, including the preface to his
homilies on the lives of saints (a source for the homilies in "book one"
of this collection).[10] The end of this preface reads:

> Ic bidde nu on Godes naman, gif hwa þas boc awritan wille,
> þæt he hi wel gerihte be þære bysne, and þær na mare betwux
> ne sette þonne we awendon.[11]

[9] The MS collection contains material from the second recension of CH2,
completed after 1005 (Godden, p. xciv). Since CCCC 178 is copied c.
1025 (Ker, *Catalogue*, p. 60), its exemplar can hardly be "ancient;" perhaps
what is meant is that the text was copied not from the latest in a line of
multiple copies being made in the Worcester area but rather by returning
to an "old" (and perhaps authorized) exemplar. Hatton 113, by contrast, is
copied in part directly from CCCC 178 (Godden, pp. lxix-lxx; Pope, vol. 1,
pp. 76-77; Clemoes, pp. 154-56), and so could not make a similar claim to
authenticity.

[10] Items 3 (the *Interrogationes Sigewulfi*), 18 (*De falsis diis*), and the second part
of item 7 (*De duodecim abusivis*) are taken from the three works that were
added to the end of the Lives of Saints in London, British Library, Cotton
Julius E.vii, Skeat's base MS (see further below). Item 8 (*De auguriis*) is
compiled from LS homilies 17 and 21, with additions, and item 14 (*De tribus
ordinibus saeculi*) is an excerpt from LS 25.

[11] Jonathan Wilcox, ed., *Ælfric's Prefaces*, Durham Medieval Texts 9 (Durham:
Durham Medieval Texts, 1994), p. 121.

I pray now in God's name, if any man desire to transcribe this book, that he correct it well according to the copy [i.e., exemplar]; and set down therein no more than we have translated.[12]

The closing words of Ælfric's preface to Genesis sound a similar theme, but then go on to add an anathema that the CCCC 178 colophon also echoes:

Ic bidde nu on Godes naman, gif hwa þas boc awritan wylle, þæt he hig gewrite wel be þære bysne, for þan þe ic nah ge-weald, þeah þe hig hwa to woge bringe þurh lease writeras, and hit byð þonne his pleoh na min.[13]

I pray now in God's name that whoever copies this book should correct it well according to the exemplar, for I cannot prevent someone from introducing error through unreliable scribes, and it will then be his responsibility, not mine.[14]

Both versions employ the unusual word "pleoh," which seems to mean both responsibility (for correctness) and blame (for error).[15] The CCCC 178 anathema thus continues Ælfric's game of "passing the *pleoh*," sending the responsibility for error onto the next supervisor, scribe, or reader.

---

[12] Walter W. Skeat, ed., *Ælfric's Lives of Saints*, EETS o.s. 76, 82, 94, 114 (London: N. Trübner, 1881-1900), pp. 6-7. See also, in addition to the passages quoted, the prefaces to the first and second series of Catholic Homilies (Wilcox, pp. 110, 112) and the Old English letter to Sigeweard (Wilcox, p. 125). For a discussion of these passages, see Wilcox, pp. 70-71; and Joyce Hill, "Ælfric, Authorial Identity, and the Changing Text," in *The Editing of Old English: Papers from the 1990 Manchester Conference*, ed. D. G. Scragg and Paul E. Szarmach (Cambridge: D. S. Brewer, 1994), pp. 177-89.

[13] Wilcox, p. 119.

[14] The closing passage in the preface to Ælfric's *Grammar* (Wilcox, p. 116) is nearly identical. The *Grammar* (to judge by its current survival) did not circulate in homiliaries. The preface to Genesis survives in two Heptateuch manuscripts and as the first item in one homiliary, Cambridge, University Library, Ii.1.33 (see Wilcox, pp. 78-79). If either of these prefaces were in the exemplar from which the colophon author culled his material, the Preface to Genesis would thus be the more likely candidate of the two.

[15] The tremulous Worcester hand first glossed "pleoh" with *damnum*, then at a later time wrote *periculum*; see below for his other glosses to the colophon.

Earlier in the colophon, the use of the word "spell," clearly equivalent to "sermones" (in the Latin table of contents)[16] to refer to all the items in the manuscript, provides clues as to Anglo-Saxon generic distinctions (or non-distinctions) of texts within the Ælfrician corpus. One must first acknowledge, however, that this colophon and list of homily titles — the first of three tables of contents in the manuscript (and the only one original to it) — do not match up with the individual rubrics of the items as readily as one would like. Ker's catalogue records eighteen such rubrics before the colophon, not twelve. Pope leads the way toward resolving this difficulty, however; he notes that there are twelve "full homilies," namely Ker items 1-11 and 18.[17] One of these, the *Interrogationes Sigewulfi*, is no longer contained in the manuscript. Wanley suspected and Mac Lean argued in detail that Matthew Parker in one of his proprietary moods removed this piece from CCCC 178 and placed it in Cambridge, Corpus Christi College, MS 162.[18] Pope felt that the remaining six "short pieces" (Ker items 12-17) constituted "a significant deviation from the announcement of the colophon,"[19] but there is evidence from manuscript *ordinatio* that

---

[16] Ælfric in the Latin preface to CH1 claims to have included forty "sententias" (Wilcox, p. 107.18; and again after the Old English preface, p. 110.93); in the Latin preface to CH2 he claims forty "sermones" for CH1 and no less a number of "sententiarum" in CH2 (Wilcox, p. 111.16). In the Old English preface to CH2 he claims forty "cwyda" in each series (many of which bear the rubric "sermo"). In a passage quoted later in this essay, Ælfric distinguishes between the "spell" of his Catholic Homilies (CH2) and an added "cwyde," *De temporibus anni.* "Spell" and "sermo" thus appear to be his generic terms for homilies, which he can also however refer to less strictly as "cwydas" or "sententias."

[17] Pope, vol 1; p. 64. See also Clemoes, pp. 37-38.

[18] Wanley, p. 120; George Edwin Mac Lean, *Ælfric's Anglo-Saxon Version of Alcuini Interrogationes Sigewulfi Presbyteri in Genesin*, Ph.D. Dissertation, University of Leipzig (Halle: E. Karras, 1883), pp. 14-18. R. I. Page (*Matthew Parker and His Books*, Kalamazoo, MI: Medieval Institute Publications, 1993) and Timothy Graham ("The Beginnings of Old English Studies: Evidence from the Manuscripts of Matthew Parker," *Back to the Manuscripts*, ed. Shuji Sato, Tokyo: Center for Medieval English Studies, 1997, pp. 29-50) have discussed this transferral in light of other such rearrangements Parker made among his manuscripts; see further below.

[19] Pope, vol 1, p. 66.

these pieces should be regarded as subsidiary items and thus do not affect the numbering made in the colophon. The rubrics to items 3-11 and 18 are written in hybrid rustic capitals usually ranging across a whole line,[20] whereas the titles of items 12-17 are written in smaller and more compact rustic capitals, occupying only a part of the line, in brown ink with red infilling.[21]

We may compare a distinction made elsewhere by Ælfric. After the last homily and closing prayer in the Catholic Homilies, second series (CH2) in Cambridge, University Library, MS Gg.3.28, Ælfric writes of his *De temporibus anni*: "Her æfter fyligð an lytel cwyde be gearlicum tidum, þæt nis to spelle geteald" (Hereafter follows a little discourse, which is not to be reckoned as a sermon).[22] Ker's items 12-17 (or, if we wish, 11a-f) are thus also not to be reckoned, i.e. counted, among the sermons.[23]

[20] The red ink has oxidized to a muddy brown and thus is often difficult to distinguish from the text ink; under oblique light it appears shinier, even silvery.

[21] Item one originally had no rubric; its initial letter is massive and its first five words are arranged in oversized majuscules ([A]N ANGIN IS ALLRA ÐINGA) to the right of the initial. Subsequently one of Parker's sixteenth-century scribes provided a rubric in majuscules at the top of the page, "De initio creaturæ, Sermo," likely taken from the rubric to the same item in CCCC 162 (its item one). Item two, the *Hexameron*, has a title in brown rustic capitals and a red oversized initial. The rubrics to items three and four are now in CCCC 162, pp. 139 and [160]. Parker had pasted a vellum half-sheet over the rubric and beginning of item four when transferring item three (see further below), but this half-sheet was removed in 1970 (Graham, p. 44; the uncovered portion is reproduced in Page, plate 39) and tipped in at the end (after pp. 569-[570]; the reverse of the sheet was a document that has left some offset on p. [160]). Item four's rubric and opening in CCCC 178, p. [130] are a Parkerian pastiche, since pp. 129-30 are a supply sheet.

[22] Benjamin Thorpe, ed., *The Homilies of the Anglo-Saxon Church*, 2 vols. (London: The Ælfric Society, 1844, 1846; rpt. New York: Johnson Reprint Corp., 1971), p. vii. See also Ker, p. 20.

[23] The detailed Latin table of contents for the "second book" matches up with the manuscript contents rather better. The twelve titles given therein correspond, with minor changes in wording, to the rubrics of Ker items 20-26 and 28-32. Ker's item 27 is brief and begins with an oversized initial rather than a rubric. Pope calls this item a "pendant to the Palm Sunday homily [item 26] . . . a mere paragraph excerpted from *CH* I. xiv, and followed by Ælfric's injunction against preaching on the three still days before Easter" (vol. 1, p. 66).

Items two and three, the *Hexameron* and *Interrogationes Sigewul-fi*, we note, are counted among the twelve homilies. These pieces are lengthy (although no longer than the first homily, *De initio creaturae*) and modern editorial practice has singled them out in individual editions rather than in collections of homilies. Generically the *Interrogationes* would otherwise seem to be a catechism, providing Sigewulf's questions and Alcuin's answers (as translated by Ælfric) for the interpretation of Genesis. But the manuscript context here and elsewhere indicates that these pieces, too, counted as homilies.[24]

A consideration of the other surviving manuscript contexts of these first three "sermones" might help clarify their status within the Ælfrician canon. Item one, a homily on creation,[25] also occurs first in the Catholic Homilies, first series (CH1), in CUL Gg.3.28 (after the Latin and Old English preface), the base manuscript for Thorpe's edition. Here it is called *De initio creature ad populum quando volueris,* i.e., for general rather than fixed occasions (and hence potentially more flexible in its manuscript contexts). The *De initio creaturae* likewise initiates CH1 in London, British Library, Royal MS 7 C.xii and Cotton Vitellius MS C.v (although a preceding homily was added by a later hand).[26] Cambridge, Corpus Christi College, MS 188 represents an "expanded" version of CH1;[27] it probably also began with the *De*

---

[24] Mac Lean insisted that the *Interrogationes* be called a homily because of its inclusion in the Lives of Saints collection in London, British Library, Cotton Julius E.vii. Ker, doubtless also thinking of manuscript contexts, indexes the *Hexameron* and *Interrogationes* under "Homilies for unspecified occasions, including short pieces of a homiletic nature" (*Catalogue*, p. 532). Pope classifies the *Interrogationes* among "Tracts allied to the homilies and treated as such in certain manuscripts" (vol. 1, p. 142). Clemoes suggests that the *Hexameron* was composed to furnish a prefatory homily for an expanded series (pp. 74-75).

[25] The homily goes on to narrate the Fall and Christ's passion, thus effectively bringing Christian history from the creation up to the life of Christ, on which was based the proper of the season and thus Ælfric's homilies for the liturgical year.

[26] The *De initio creaturae* also leads off London, British Library, Cotton Vespasian D.xiv, a late "collection of theological pieces" (Ker, *Catalogue*, p. 271), although it may be on an added quire.

[27] Pope, vol. 1, p. 61.

initio creaturae (before its first quire was lost). The next item (now surviving acephalously) in CCCC 188 is the *Hexameron*, which also treats creation; the evidence of this manuscript thus suggests Ælfric himself regarded the *Hexameron* as a homily, suitable for incorporation into CH1. But since both the *De initio creaturae* and the *Hexameron* functioned well as introductions, we also find them in sequence leading off a different collection of Ælfric's homilies, The Lives of the Saints, in London, British Library, Cotton Otho B.x.[28] It is thus not surprising to see these two creation homilies leading off a more eclectic collection, the "twelf spell" for unspecified occasions in CCCC 178, nor to see the *De initio creaturae* alone inaugurating a different selection of homilies[29] for unspecified occasions in Cambridge, Corpus Christi College MS 162 (the manuscript into which Parker shifted the *Interrogationes* from CCCC 178, where it had originally occupied the third position). The *Interrogationes*, as a set of theological questions and answers relating to the Book of Genesis, follows upon the two homilies for creation suitably enough. Evidence that the *Interrogationes*, like the *Hexameron*, could be counted as a homily comes mainly from London, British Library, Cotton Julius E.vii, Skeat's "one good manuscript" of Ælfric's Lives of the Saints. After the run of saints' lives, that manuscript preserves an "appendix" consisting of the *Interrogationes*, the *De falsis diis*, and the *De xii abusivis*.[30] With homilies to the left of it and homilies to the right of it, the *Interrogationes* thus seems also to be counted a homily in the Cotton Julius manuscript, as well as in CCCC 178.

---

[28] The MS was badly burned in the Cotton fire and much of its contents has to be reconstructed from Wanley's catalogue; see Ker, *Catalogue*, p. 224.

[29] The *Hexameron* is used to initiate the homiliary in CCCC 302; see Clemoes, pp. 74-75.

[30] This last homily was lost from the manuscript but is still listed in the original table of contents (Skeat elected not to print these homilies in his edition). This appendix proved a good source of homilies for unspecified occasions; the other two items are likewise included in the "first book" of CCCC 178 and in similar runs in CCCC 303 and in Oxford, Bodleian Library, Hatton 115 (which omits *De falsis diis*) and 116 (these last two MSS were in Worcester, like CCCC 178, and bear a close relation to it; see Ker, *Catalogue*, pp. 399, 403).

Why Parker would move the *Interrogationes* from its likely spot in CCCC 178 to an unlikely one in CCCC 162 has seemed puzzling. Page, after describing the move, adds, "Why, I have not the slightest idea."[31] I suspect Parker's primary aim was to supply the Latin preface from Alcuin's original. The *Interrogationes* began midway down its page, so Parker was able to have Alcuin's preface copied on a half-sheet and then pasted in above the *Interrogationes*. But in so doing he covered over the end of the *Hexameron*, rendering it imperfect, a condition Parker abhorred (to judge by his treatment of other MSS). His solution was physically to remove the *Interrogationes*, turning it into a discrete copy by further pasting over the beginning of the homily that followed it. Before pasting over these half-pages of text preceding and following the *Interrogationes*, however, he made a copy of them; he then transcribed these copies on a supply sheet in CCCC 178, which would thus run smoothly across the gap caused by the removal of the leaves containing the *Interrogationes*.[32] Why move this text into CCCC 162 in particular? With two Genesis-based homilies starting off CCCC 178, Parker may have felt the *Interrogationes* could suitably move into a different manuscript that only had the one creation homily (the *De initio creaturae*). But the main reason for transferring the piece, I think, is that he could — that is, because the two manuscripts were being rebound at the same time[33] and because Parker could find a suitable physical location for the *Interrogationes* in CCCC 162. Had he moved it anywhere into the run of homilies for unspecified occasions in CCCC 162 (Ker articles 1-8), Parker would have at least been following medieval precedent. But he moved it instead into the run for the proper of the season. Articles 9 and 10 in CCCC 162 are homilies for the second Sunday after Epiphany, from CH2, then for the third

---

[31] Page, p. 54. See also Graham, who characterizes the transfer as "[o]ne of Parker's more inexplicable deeds"(p. 44).

[32] The two sides of the supply sheet are reproduced as plates 57 and 40 in Page, who suggests the hand is Parker's own.

[33] See Page, p. 55. CCCC 162 was Parker's "Primus liber homiliarum"and 178 his "Secundus liber homiliarum" (Ker, *Catalogue*, pp. 51, 60). The two are listed in Parker's register from about 1574 (Page, p. 3 and plate 5).

Sunday, from CH1.[34] Ker tells us three folios are removed here;[35] one might add that the next item should have been the homily on the Purification of Mary, the next item in CH1 (IX; the sequence continues, after the insertion of the *Interrogationes*, with Sundays in Septuagesima and Sexagesima from CH2 and Quinquagesima from CH1). Item ten in CCCC 162 nearly concludes at the bottom of page [136] with "Se ðe leofað & rixað on ealra worulda woruld abutan"; one of Parker's scribes has added in the line below "ende Amen."[36] (These words would have begun p. 137, followed by the rubric for *In purificatione Sanctae Mariae*.)[37] Having thus arranged for item ten to end at the bottom of page 136 (the verso of a leaf), Parker could then remove three leaves, add a blank leaf (pp. 137-[138]), and then insert the *Interrogationes*, which, once he had pasted in Alcuin's Latin preface, would begin at the top of the next page.

The Thirteenth-Century Table of Contents

In the early thirteenth century the so-called tremulous Worcester scribe supplied a second table of contents on an added parchment leaf, p. vii.[38] Since this second table of contents has not been reproduced, I provide a transcription here:

> i exameron
> ii De .iiij. post pentecosten. Erant apropinquantes ad ihesum

---

[34] The manuscript combines homilies from CH1 and CH2 into one yearly sequence, an arrangement that Ælfric specifically authorized in his Latin preface to CH1 (Wilcox, p. 107).

[35] Ker, p. 52.

[36] The CCCC 162 version has a slightly different ending from the one printed in Thorpe; see Clemoes, p. 248 (variants).

[37] Here I differ from Scragg, who suggests the next three leaves were blank. See D. G. Scragg, "Cambridge, Corpus Christi College 162," *Anglo-Saxon Manuscripts and their Heritage*, ed. Phillip Pulsiano and Elaine M. Treharne (Aldershot: Ashgate, 1998), pp. 71-83.

[38] None of the prefatory leaves are numbered in the manuscript; Ker refers to this one as p. vii, counting the folded sheet inserted by the printer in 1953 as pp. I-iv, then the document added presumably by Parker (with his number S.6 on its blank recto) as v-vi, then the next leaf as vii-viii. Ker, judging by the ruling, suggested this leaf was a spare one taken from part B

iii De dominica orationee
iiii Sermo ad populum in viii. pentecosten
v De viiito. viciis .ed. de duodecim abusiuis gradibus
vi De auguriis
viij [sic] Sermo de die judicii
viij Sermo ad populum quando volueris
ix Vnius confessoris
x De tribus ordinibus seculi
xj De infantibus non baptizandus
xij De Vaniloquio et neggligencia
xiii De auaricia
xiiii De falsis diis
xv annunciatio beate marie
xvi De Natiuitate domini
xvij Circumsisio domini
xviij Epiffania
xix purificatio
xx Dominica .j. in quadragesima
xxl Dominica palmarum
xxij Die pasce
xxiij Dominica .j. post pasca
xxiiij Vigilia ascensionis
xxv In ascensione domini
xxvj In die pentecosten
xxvij De septiformi spiritu

In his contents for the "first book" (nos. I-xiiii), the tremulous Worcester scribe misses out some items. He provides no rubric for the first homily in the manuscript, which indeed had none until Parker

of the manuscript (p. 64); William Schipper ["A Worksheet of the Worcester 'Tremulous' Glossator," *Anglia* 105 (1987), pp. 28-49] confirmed this supposition in noticing that the verso of the leaf (p. viii) contains a worksheet on which the tremulous Worcester scribe organized glosses from part B (and elsewhere; see also Franzen, pp. 50-51, 125-27). Leaf vii-viii is followed by a paper leaf with the Parkerian table of contents on its verso, which should thus be ix-x, but Ker places Parker's contents on p. xii. Page, disregarding the paper sheet and foliating instead of paginating, places Parker's contents on fol. iii v. (plate 38). Since Parker paginated the rest of the manuscript, paginating the prefatory leaves also would appear preferable.

had one copied in (*De initio creaturae. Sermo.*). More surprisingly, the tremulous Worcester scribe overlooks the *Interrogationes Sigewulfi*, although he certainly read through and glossed it. In attempting to record the many, closely occurring smaller rubrics of subsidiary items 12-17, he overlooks the first two: "De antichristo" and "De sanguine prohibito," which would thus occur between his items viii and ix. On page 137 he wrote "De sanguine prohibito" in the margin opposite the rubric, the only place where he does so, possibly indicating he realized his mistake at a later time. Leaving out two homilies and adding in four of the six subsidiary items, his list thus records fourteen items instead of twelve for the "first book" of homilies for unspecified occasions.[39]

From differences in wording, we can see that the tremulous Worcester scribe took his titles for the "second book" not from the original contents list on page 163 (the second half of the colophon, transcribed above, where titles for the second twelve homilies are given), but directly from the rubrics to the individual items. For instance, the table's item xviij, "Epiffania," is "Sermo in epiha[n]ia domini" in the rubric on page [190], but "De baptismo christi" in the list of titles on page 163.[40] We know the tremulous Worcester scribe read the original table of contents page (163) since he provides glosses for it, as he does for virtually the entire manuscript (parts A and B).[41] But in

---

[39] In his table of contents for CCCC 198, the Tremulous Worcester Hand recorded some items out of order. His items lvij, lviii, lviiij and lx are *sancti martini, Genesis an angin is* (the first homily he failed to record in CCCC 178), *Sancti johannis et de paradiso,* and *Sancti andree.* Parker has had folio numbers written in, which run 378, 367, 374[v], and 387 [for 386]; i.e., the order of items runs not 57, 58, 59, 60, but rather 59, 57, 58, 60.

[40] So also xxj "dominica palmarum" beside "Dominica palmarum de passione domini" vs. "de passione christi"; xxij "Die pasce" beside "Die dominica paschae" vs. "De resurrectione christi"; xxiij "Dominica .j. post pasca" beside "Dominica prima post pascha" vs. "de octauis pasce."

[41] His Latin glosses (and one Middle English gloss) for Old English words in the colophon, not previously recorded, are as follows: gesette: *statuti;* twa twentig: *ii xx;* æt fruman: *in primis;* æ: *vel* [l]awe; an: *vnum;* heafodleahtrum: *viii capitalia siinna;* geeacnode: *aug[m]entur;* gedo: *agat;* nytt: *valis;* pleoh: *damnum* [& later gloss] *periculum;* unnytt: *invtilis.* He also rewrites "ælfricus abbas" in the margin beside the same words in the Latin table of contents. He supplies added punctuation and writes the ME prefix *i-* above the OE prefix *ge-*.

his table of contents for the "second book," he records thirteen instead of twelve homilies (xv-xxvii). The additional item is his final one, "De septiformi spiritu," which has since been lost or removed from the end of the manuscript (part A), together with the end of the preceding item, "In die sancto pentecosten." Ælfric's *De septiformi spiritu*,[42] however, would likely not have been counted as a homily, but rather as what Pope calls a "pendant" to the Pentecost homily; it is thus treated in a number of other manuscripts, among them the "carefully arranged" Cambridge, Trinity College, MS B.15.34.[43]

After the last visible item in the contents list compiled by the tremulous Worcester scribe, the "De septiformi spiritu," one can clearly see that at least one and as many as three or four additional items have been erased. Even under ultraviolet and fiber optic lights virtually none of this erasure is recoverable, but one can just about see that a next item began with Roman numeral xxviii and an ascender. Pope worried that these erased items might likewise have compromised the total of twelve homilies for the "second book" itemized in the original colophon and contents list. Recovering these items may now be physically impossible, but we can turn to a third table of contents for additional evidence.

Parker's Early Modern Table of Contents

On page xii (or fol. iii v) Parker had one of his scribes write in another (now third) table of contents, as he did for many other of his manuscripts.[44] The first item in this table is the *De initio creaturae*, which as we have seen does not occur in the extant portion of the table

---

[42] Napier no. 8, preceded by the Latin summary that Napier (for the sake of convenience) printed before his no. 7, a longer adaptation by Wulfstan. See Arthur Napier, ed., *Wulfstan: Sammlung der ihm zugeschriebenen Homilien nebst Untersuchungen über ihre Echtheit* (Berlin: Weidmann, 1883). Ker's description of CCCC 178 mentions both *De septiformi spiritu* homilies without opting for either, but surely the version by Ælfric was the one lost from this Ælfrician collection. For a comparison of the two versions, see A. P. McD. Orchard, "Crying Wolf: Oral Style and the *Sermones Lupi*," *Anglo-Saxon England* 21 (1992), pp. 239-64.

[43] Pope, vol. 1, p. 142.

[44] See Ker, *Catalogue*, p. liii, for a list. Parker's table in CCCC 178 is reproduced in Page, plate 38.

made by the tremulous Worcester scribe. But since Parker had a rubric copied in for this item (as noted above), it is no surprise that he thus also includes it at the beginning of his table of contents. His item two is the *Hexameron*. An X has been placed on either side of item 3, the *Interrogationes*, and no page number has been entered for it, one of the many indications that Parker was responsible for removing the *Interrogationes* and transferring it to CCCC 162.[45] His list then runs much the same as that of the tremulous Worcester hand, which it is clear he is copying,[46] even to the extent of leaving out "De antichristo" and "De sanguine prohibito." These however are then added at the end of the list with their appropriate page numbers. The item just above them, "De septiformi spiritu," is recorded as starting on page 274, but an X after it indicates that Parker had it removed also. About three lines are skipped, after which the Rule of St. Benedict is recorded as beginning on page 237, leaving a gap of thirteen pages, presumably the remainder of the excised quire 19, after "De septiformi spiritu" had begun.[47] If the remainder of quire 19 had originally contained any more full homilies, it would have invalidated the count of twelve homilies for Book Two given in the (original) table of contents on page 163; it is thus more

---

[45] To Mac Lean's list of evidentiary points for this transferral one may add the fact that William L'Isle underlined Biblical quotations from the *Interrogationes* on pp. 152, 155, and 158 of CCCC 162, just as he did for items on either side (e.g., on pp. 136 and 173). He was culling material for a compendium of Old English translations from scripture, during the 1620s (according to Timothy Graham, "Early Modern Users of Claudius B.iv: Robert Talbot and William L'Isle," *The Old English Hexateuch: Aspects and Approaches,* Rebecca Barnhouse and Benjamin C. Withers [Kalamazoo: Medieval Institute, 2000], pp. 271-313); the *Interrogationes* must have been transferred by that time, since L'Isle did not thus underline items in CCCC 178. Parker's main years of manuscript collecting (and rearranging) were between 1568 and 1575 (Page, p. 2).

[46] Although his scribe copied the tremulous hand's table of contents rather than (for the second book) the original table on p. 163, Parker was certainly familiar with the original table; he underlined in his usual red crayon the words "hoc codicello continentur" and "ælfricus abbas;" he added his maniculus pointing to the same passage; and he had a vellum index tab attached to the edge of the leaf. (Parker's red crayon or pencil is mentioned by e.g. Ker, *Catalogue*, p. liii; Page, pp. 53-54, 125; and Graham, p. 37. I thank Graham for identifying the latter two pieces of Parkerian evidence.)

[47] Quires 1-18 (counting leaves transferred to CCCC 162) are all in quires of 8 folios, or 16 pages; presumably quire 19 would also have been 16 pages long.

likely that the quire contained either nothing beyond "De septiformi spiritu," or else "pendants" or "subsidiary items" such as were contained in Book One. If there were additional items following "De septiformi spiritu," however, one would have expected Parker's scribe to record them, since he records all the other items, including the two items later removed by Parker.

What, then, might the tremulous Worcester hand have written as its items number xxviij and following, and why were they later erased? We might first suspect that the Worcester scribe had, like Parker's scribe, realized his omission and added the rubrics for the first two subsidiary items in Book One, "De antichristo" and "De sanguine prohibito." But the trace of an ascender, in the way it was drawn, does not accord well with the first letter's being the D of "De antichristo," and there would have been no pressing need for either him or Parker to excise these rubrics later. It is more likely the Worcester scribe first added the two other rubrics he had omitted, "De initio creature" (or perhaps its opening words, "An angin"), and "Interrogationes Sigewulfi"[48] (perhaps then followed by the two subsidiary rubrics). Since Parker's scribe had placed these rubrics at the beginning where they belonged, he may then have gone back and excised them where they did not belong in the Worcester scribe's table of contents — especially once Parker had decided to move the *Interrogationes* to (the current) CCCC 162.

Whatever these absences may tell us, the presence of the three tables of contents as a whole provides a valuable record of three stages in the reception of Ælfric's work. The late Anglo-Saxon scribe (or more likely, that of his immediate exemplar) penned a response to Ælfric's authoritative urgings (as expressed in prefaces elsewhere) and conveyed some of his own organizational principles, his own desires for the work. Attempting to decode his numbering system of two balanced books of "twelf spell" each leads us to a better understanding of the manuscript's *ordinatio* as well as its conception of genres and subgenres in Ælfric's writings. A couple of centuries later, the tremulous Worcester scribe leafed his way through the collection, adding interlinear glosses and then copying rubrics on a single sheet for ease

[48] The trace ascender would better suit a majuscule A or I.

of reference. He left a record of the mistakes he made along the way as well as tantalizing traces of items now lost from the manuscript. On the reverse of that table of contents, he began to organize his glosses; here as elsewhere he was trying to interpret and preserve a linguistic heritage that was becoming opaque to him and his early Middle English colleagues. Matthew Parker was his spiritual heir, using the Worcester scribe's Latin glosses as well as the conveniently bilingual copy of the Benedictine Rule in part B of the manuscript to help recover, as he expressed it elsewhere, the "testimonie of antiquitie." His marginal comment to the Rule, written at the foot of the manuscript page (291)[49] boldly in red crayon, may serve as a summation: "In hoc libro facilius discitur Lingua Saxonica;" "in this book one may easily learn the Saxon language," and, we might add, something about how the recovery of that language progressed through the generations.

---

[49] Reproduced in Page, plate 60; Graham, plate 7.

The Boundaries Between Verse and Prose in Old English Literature

Thomas A. Bredehoft

D.G. Scragg's recent essay, "Towards a New Anglo-Saxon Poetic Records," explores some *desiderata* for a new edition of the Old English poetic corpus, discussing editorial concerns that range from titles and textual boundaries to issues of layout and editorial emendation.[1] But nowhere does Scragg address the possibility that the list of works making up the poetic corpus might need to be revised. This seems to be a tacit assertion that the boundaries of the corpus are secure, that the principles of exclusion and inclusion employed by Krapp and Dobbie need not be reconsidered.

Yet the basis for Krapp and Dobbie's corpus-defining decisions are not always as clear as we might like. While a metrical definition of Old English verse (based on Eduard Sievers's groundbreaking metrical analysis) generally underlies the *ASPR*, some texts are included that only marginally fit into a Sieversian metrical perspective. The *Metrical Psalms*, for example, are described as having a "very general metrical irregularity,"[2] and the following comment in the Preface to the final volume of the *ASPR* stands as the clearest statement of the collective edition's selectional principles:

> As a general rule, only those poems have been admitted which are written in the regular alliterative verse, but the *The Death of Alfred*, which has rime instead of alliteration, is included with the five other Chronicle poems, following the practice of earlier editors, and the metrical charms

[1] D. G. Scragg, "Towards a New Anglo-Saxon Poetic Records," *New Approaches to Editing Old English Verse*, ed. Sarah Larratt Keefer and Katherine O'Brien O'Keeffe (Cambridge: D. S. Brewer, 1998), pp. 67-77.

[2] George Philip Krapp and Elliot V. K. Dobbie, eds., *The Anglo-Saxon Poetic Records*. 6 vols. (New York: Columbia University Press, 1931-53), vol. 5, p. xvii.

[3] Krapp and Dobbie, vol. 6, p. v.

are printed in their entirety, though most of them are only
partly in verse and their metrical structure is often very far
from regular.[3]

As this passage suggests, the *ASPR* includes at least some "irregular"
poems, and it includes *The Death of Alfred* only because earlier editors
(i.e. Wülker and Sedgefield) had printed it with other *Chronicle* poems. The *ASPR*'s exclusion of a number of other passages of "irregular" verse from the *Chronicle* is justified by the following claim: "Since
these texts are all to be found in Plummer's edition of the Chronicle,
their omission here will be no hardship to scholars."[4] Yet the *ASPR*'s
canon-forming power has seemed to lead scholars in precisely the opposite direction: to treat the *Chronicle* as if it included exactly six poems, as in the books by O'Keeffe and Schrader, for example.[5]

As we can see, then, the *ASPR*'s use of meter as a definitional
tool has had serious consequences for students of Old English literature, and in a recent book Haruko Momma has seriously questioned
the efficacy of current understandings of Old English meter for defining a corpus of Old English verse:

When based on more than one poem, Old English metre no
longer seems homogeneous; and it ceases to seem unique
when compared to other alliterative composition. Unfortunately, no previous metrical theories have offered criteria with
which to describe Old English poetry as a whole or to separate Old English poetry from other alliterative composition.[6]

[4] Krapp and Dobbie, vol. 6, p. xxxiii.

[5] Katherine O'Brien O'Keeffe, *Visible Song: Transitional Literacy in Old English
Verse* (Cambridge: Cambridge University Press, 1990); and Richard Schrader,
Old English Poetry and the Genealogy of Events (East Lansing: Colleagues Press,
1993). Note also that Mildred Budny, "Old English Poetry in Its Material
Context," *Companion to Old English Poetry*, ed. H. Aertsen and Rolf H.
Bremmer (Amsterdam: VU University Press, 1994), pp. 19-44, suggests on p.
21 that the *Chronicle* "contains seven poems among its annals." Presumably,
this number includes the six poems printed in the *ASPR* as well as the 1086
poem on William the Conqueror.

[6] H. Momma, *The Composition of Old English Poetry* (Cambridge: Cambridge
University Press, 1997), p. 21.

[7] References in Table 1 are to the following invaluable (and I hope familiar)

What is important to understand about this state of affairs is that Sieversian metrics, while capable of being used to label some poems as "regular" and other poems as "irregular," may not be sufficient for defining the corpus of Old English verse. To put it another way, it is not clear that Anglo-Saxon poets or readers would have always agreed with our assessment of individual poems as "regular" or "irregular," and while such analytical metrical uncertainty remains in our minds, we should be hesitant to construct our corpus of Old English verse on purely metrical grounds.

In this essay, I will explore the evidence of manuscript presentation, which has previously been undervalued for what it can tell us about which texts belong within the canon of Old English verse. In particular, I examine the boundaries between verse and prose in surviving Old English manuscripts in an attempt to determine if and how such boundaries were negotiated by Anglo-Saxon readers and scribes. Since the nature of my study concerns texts that usefully juxtapose verse and prose, most of the longer and better-known poems are excluded as stand-alone texts, but of those that remain [see Table 1, p. 142], there are examples of both "regular" and "irregular" poems.[7] By examining such works from a viewpoint that itself takes no account of the quality of their meter, this study can offer a valuable perspective on the generic identity of works that have generally been excluded from both considerations of Old English verse and the published corpus of Old English verse.

resources: N. R. Ker, *Catalogue of Manuscripts Containing Anglo-Saxon* (Oxford: Clarendon Press, 1957; rpt. with Supplement, 1990); Helmut Gneuss, *Handlist of Anglo-Saxon Manuscripts* (Tempe, AZ: Arizona Center for Medieval and Renaissance Studies, 2001); and Elisabeth Okasha, *Hand-List of Anglo-Saxon Non-Runic Inscriptions* (Cambridge: Cambridge University Press, 1971). Although I have been fortunate enough to consult almost all of the manuscripts listed in Table 1 personally, the existence of facsimile editions, especially Fred C. Robinson and E. G. Stanley's *Old English Verse Texts from Many Sources,* EEMF 23 (Copenhagen: Rosenkilde and Bagger, 1991), has also been enormously helpful. Practical considerations have precluded the inclusion of facsimile images in this essay; many of these passages, however, can be examined in Robinson and Stanley's volume or in other published facsimiles.

141

VERSE TEXT	MANUSCRIPT OR OBJECT	REFERENCE*	
		KER	GN
Cædmon's Hymn	Cambridge, Univ. Lib., Kk.3.18	23	22
	Cambridge, Corpus Christi Coll., 41	32	39
	Oxford, Bodl. Lib., Tanner 10	351	668
	Oxford, Corpus Christi Coll., 279	354	673
The Meters of Boethius	London, Brit. Lib., Cott. Otho A.vi	167	347
Verse Charms	Cambridge, Corpus Christi Coll., 41	32	39
	London, Brit. Lib., Harley 585	231	421
	London, Brit. Lib., Royal 12 D.xvii	264	479
	London, Brit. Lib., Cott. Caligula A.iii	137	308
The Chronicle Poems	Cambridge, Corpus Christi Coll., 173	39	52
	London, Brit. Lib., Cott. Tiberius A.vi	188	364
	London, Brit. Lib., Cott. Tiberius B.i	191	370
	London, Brit. Lib., Cott. Tiberius B.iv	192	372
	Oxford, Bodleian Library, Laud misc. 636	346	
The Brussels Cross	Inscription: The Brussels Cross	Okasha 17	
Solomon and Saturn	Cambridge, Corpus Christi Coll., 422	70	110
Epilogue to CCCC 41	Cambridge, Corpus Christi Coll., 41	39	32

Table 1:
Texts and Manuscripts Containing Prose-Poetry Juxtapositions

*Sources for the reference numbers are fully cited in note 7. "Ker" refers to Ker's *Catalogue of Manuscripts Containing Anglo-Saxon*, and "Gn" to Gneuss's *Handlist of Anglo-Saxon Manuscripts*.

The conclusions of my study are notable: both "regular" and "irregular" examples of verse are distinguished from surrounding prose by precisely the same sorts of markers used to indicate other textual boundaries: the use of textual space or of visually prominent letters. Such boundary markers are not used in every case, however, and the bulk of my essay will consist of a simple survey of the manuscript evidence, with the relevant texts gathered into two broad groups: those whose verse-texts are explicitly identified as such, and those not so identified. Ideally, the scribal treatment of poems in the former group can help to interpret the record of those in the latter. Significantly, of course, the texts under consideration here include only those that have already been widely accepted as poetic, whether or not they fit the standards of Sieversian metrics; the scribal evidence that even "irregular" poems were treated as verse by Anglo-Saxon scribes provides a powerful argument for a broader, more inclusive canon of Old English verse than that of the *ASPR*.

Old English Verse Passages Identified as Verse in Context

The description of the Exeter Book in the book-list of Bishop Leofric's eleventh-century bequest to Exeter Cathedral (".*i. micel englisc boc be gehwilcum þingum on leoðwisan geworht*") might well be taken as a starting point for a modern understanding of Old English verse, for here a nearly contemporary Anglo-Saxon witness specifically identifies the texts of the Exeter Book as poetic.[8] It is worth pointing out that no such identifying comment is associated with any of the other three great poetic codices. Indeed, in both the Vercelli Book and the Nowell codex, prose and verse texts stand side by side, with no visual cues to indicate whether a particular text is prose or poetry: the identification, it seems, is left to the reader. Anglo-Saxon readers such as Leofric were clearly up to such a task, and modern attempts to understand the nature of Old English verse might usefully begin by considering poems specifically identified as verse.

---

[8] "One great English book of diverse things, wrought in the manner of songs" (Krapp and Dobbie, *ASPR*, vol. 3, p. ix). Unless noted otherwise, all translations from Old English are my own.

But where the identification of the Exeter Book texts as poetic stems from evidence originally external to it, the evidence of poems that are identified as poems *within* their original contexts is even more obviously important: the points at which a single scribe made the transition from prose to poetry (or *vice versa*) and where the content of the text itself highlighted the transition should be of enormous value in determining how the Anglo-Saxons distinguished between the two. Surely the most familiar passage of poetry that is identified as verse in nearby prose material is Cædmon's *Hymn*, especially as it appears in the Old English translation of Bede's *Historia ecclesiastica*. Within the Cædmon narrative in Book iv, chapter 25, the translator's repeated use of the verb "*singan*" (and, indeed, the entire narrative impact of the story) focuses the reader's attention on the *Hymn* as a song. And since the *Hymn* is recorded in four surviving copies of the Old English Bede, it provides a useful opportunity to examine how a number of scribes responded to this short piece of poetry as it was embedded in its prose context.

Oxford, Bodleian Library, MS Tanner 10, the earliest surviving manuscript of the Old English Bede, dates from the tenth century ("s. x¹"),[9] and Cædmon's *Hymn* is barely (if at all) distinguished from the prose that surrounds it; manuscript points both precede and follow the *Hymn*, but nothing we might describe as metrical pointing is in evidence. Katherine O'Brien O'Keeffe characterizes the pointing of this version of the *Hymn* as purely grammatical.[10] The only clues to the reader that the *Hymn* is poetic lie in the context of the narrative: the text immediately preceding the *Hymn* reads "*þa fers ꝝ þa word þe he næfre gehyrde, þære endebyrdnesse þis is.*"[11] Other than a point following "*is*," however, there is no other visible indication of a transition in the Tanner text. Likewise, the point following the final line of the *Hymn* is not visually different from any other points on the page (including

---

[9] Ker, *Catalogue*, p. 428.

[10] O'Keeffe, *Visible Song*, p. 44.

[11] Thomas Miller, ed. *The Old English Version of Bede's Ecclesiastical History.* 4 vols. EETS o.s. 95-96, 110-11 (Oxford: Oxford University Press, 1890-98), at vol. I, bk. ii, p. 344; "the verses and the words that he had never heard, of which this is the order."

the two within the *Hymn* itself), and so there is little to suggest that the Tanner scribe was attempting to present the *Hymn* as visually distinct from the surrounding prose at all.

In Oxford, Corpus Christi College MS 279, which Ker dates to the early eleventh century ("s xi in."),[12] there are no internal points within the *Hymn*, although there is a point after its final word. The first word of the *Hymn* is clearly capitalized, however, and the point after line 9b is followed by a "lower case" "ð," but one that may be large enough to be counted as a capital.[13] Cambridge, University Library, MS Kk.3.18, which is probably a copy of OCCC 279 (or of its exemplar), has three points within the *Hymn* (after lines 3a, 4a, and 6b), but is more striking for following OCCC 279 in capitalizing both the *Hymn*'s first word and the first word of the prose that follows, this time using the form of the letter ("Ð") that is explicitly a capital. In these two manuscripts, it seems likely that capital letters (in conjunction with points) are used to indicate the transition points from poetry to prose and back again.[14]

In many ways, however, the record of Cædmon's *Hymn* in Cambridge, Corpus Christi College MS 41 ("s. xi¹")[15] is the most interesting example of the *Hymn* in the Old English Bede. Like the record in CUL Kk.3.18 and OCCC 279, the copy of the *Hymn* in CCCC 41 begins with a capital "N," in this case a very large and prominent one.

---

[12] Ker, *Catalogue*, p. 432.

[13] In the discussion and analysis that follows, I use the term "capital" to refer not to a letter written in a script belonging to the family "Capitalis," but in the simpler sense of a letter larger and more visually prominent than the surrounding letters.

[14] Even such evidence as this must be weighed carefully, however. In CUL Kk.3.18, for example, there are at least 18 capitals in chapter 25 of Book iv of the Old English Bede, three of which (besides the one beginning the chapter) stand in the left-hand margin, and thus might seem to be more prominent than those beginning and following the *Hymn*. The scribe of this book, however, seems to regularly put capitals in the margin if they begin a line of writing, rather than using marginal capitals as markers for important textual divisions; the marginal capitals in Kk.3.18, then, do not appear to be significant, although it is important to note that the sheer number of capitals in this book would lessen the impact of the capitals bracketing the *Hymn*.

[15] Ker, *Catalogue*, p. 43.

And although no capital letter follows the end of the *Hymn*, we do see the end of the poem marked by the heavy punctuation normally used for chapter endings in this manuscript. Significantly, the space devoted to this mark of punctuation would have more than accommodated a regular point and the following word "*þa*" (four lines above this, for example, the scribe has squeezed "*bear*" of "*bearnum*" into considerably less space). Thus, although the copy of the *Hymn* in CCCC 41 has no internal points,[16] the poem is nevertheless visually set apart from the prose that surrounds it; indeed, the version of Cædmon's *Hymn* in CCCC 41 is probably more clearly defined visually than that in any other of the Old English Bede manuscripts.[17]

In view of the prominence of the visual cues marking the beginning and end of Cædmon's *Hymn* in CCCC 41, it is interesting to note that the contextual cues regarding the beginning of the poem are less effective in this manuscript than in the others. Apart from orthographic differences, OCCC 279 and CUL Kk.3.18 generally agree with the Tanner lead-in to the *Hymn*, part of which I cited above:

> þa ongan he sona singan in herenesse Godes Scyppendes þa fers
> ⁊ þa word þe he næfre gehyrde, þære endebyrdnesse þis is[18]

CCCC 41, in contrast, has a text with a very different effect:

> þa ongan
> he sona singan on hergunge godes scyp
> pendes ða uers ⁊ þa word godes þe he
> næfre ær ne gehyrde ne heora ende
> byrdnesse.[19]

---

[16] O'Keeffe, *Visible Song*, p. 43 reports a point after 7b, but I was unable to see one. As I hope is clear, this essay owes a great intellectual debt to O'Keeffe's book, and although I sometimes disagree with her conclusions, this work would not have been possible without her example.

[17] The capital letter in CCCC 41 that begins Cædmon's *Hymn* is the first capital used since the beginning of the chapter; two other capitals are used near the end of the chapter on page 326, but neither is as large and prominent as the capital "N" at the beginning of the *Hymn*.

[18] Miller, *Old English Bede*, vol. I, bk. ii, p. 344. "Then he immediately began to sing in praise of God the Creator the verses and the words that he had never heard, of which this is the order."

[19] CCCC 41, p. 322; "Then he immediately began to sing in praise of God the Creator the verses and the words of God that he had never heard before, nor

The prominent capital "N" and the heavy punctuation that mark the boundaries of the *Hymn*, then, are even more crucial in the *Hymn*'s "immediate context" in CCCC 41, since (unlike the other texts of the Old English Bede) the prose lead-in to the *Hymn* in CCCC 41 does not specifically alert readers to the point at which the verse begins.[20]

Taken as a group, the texts of Cædmon's *Hymn* in manuscripts of the Old English Bede suggest that scribes did often find it useful or valuable to mark the transition from prose to verse and back, at the least with a point (as in Tanner 10), or later with capitals and points in combination. In all four texts, pointing within the *Hymn* itself is sparse, and metrical pointing does not seem to have been one of the tools used to indicate the poetic nature of the *Hymn*. But a consideration of the tenth-century Tanner 10 manuscript, with its relative lack of separational markers between the *Hymn* and the surrounding prose, and of the eleventh-century records in the other three surviving copies of the Old English Bede, where the boundary is marked more clearly, does suggest that (at least in the eleventh century) the boundary between verse and prose was frequently seen by scribes as a transition point significant enough to be marked with a capital letter or other visual markers.

their order." In citing Old English texts from the manuscripts, I use several conventions of presentation that may be in need of explanation. Words or letters surrounded by slanting brackets indicate insertions after the first writing, and I mark expansions of abbreviations with underlining. Pointing and capitalization follow manuscript usage. In some cases I will relineate verse passages according to modern conventions of layout in order to facilitate examination of the relation between form and (non-spatial) presentational features such as capitals and pointing.

[20] Interestingly, the record of the *Hymn* in CCCC 41 includes three unique readings ("*Nu we herigan sculan,*" "*wuldorgodes,*" and "*wundra fela*"). A fourth unique reading ("*þe*" for "*þa*") is a less clear example of lexical substitution, although it does seem to replace a temporal adverb with a relative pronoun. Though not within the scope of the present study, the collocation of these variants in CCCC 41 might be profitably investigated in terms of O'Keeffe's notion of formulaic reading. Notably, the ordering of "*herigan*" and "*sculan*" in the first line appears to involve a metrical shift; the significance of this change in the context of the obvious verse nature of the passage should also be of great interest.

Like Cædmon's *Hymn*, the *Meters of Boethius* are also particularly interesting when considering the relation between poetry and prose.
Existing within an Old English translation of a culturally-important
Latin original, the *Meters* as they are found in British Library, Cotton
MS Otho A.vi largely correspond with the poetic *Metra* in the Latin Boethius. Any reader familiar with the format of Boethius's Latin
Consolation of Philosophy would probably have recognized the similar
alternation between poetry and prose in the Otho A.vi manuscript of
the Old English Boethius.[21] But for those readers not familiar with the
Latin original, the *Proem* to the *Meters* (now destroyed, but preserved
in Oxford, Bodleian Library MS Junius 12, which contains Junius's
transcript of the *Meters*) would provide a very clear indication that the
Old English text (or at least part of it) was in verse:

Him wæs lust micel

ðæt he ðiossum leodum   leoð spellode

monnum myrgum   mislic cwidas[22]

The *Proem*, at least, thus identifies itself as verse, and this internal
identification would likely have functioned to alert readers to the presence of verse within Otho A.vi (but see my comments on Oxford,
Bodleian Library, Bodley MS 180 in note 24 below). Further indication of the verse nature of the *Meters* lies in the transitional passages
that precede and follow them, generally using generic terms such as
"*leoð*" and "*fitte*" and descriptive verbs such as "*singan*" and "*gieddian*."
Significantly, the prose and verse portions of this manuscript are very
clearly and carefully separated from each other: each separate section
of the text (whether verse or prose) was intended to begin with a large
(perhaps colored) initial, for which space was left but never filled in.
As a result, it is quite normal for the last line of a section to end well
before the end of the manuscript line is reached, and so portions of

---

[21] O'Keeffe discusses the layout of tenth-century insular copies of the Latin
Boethius in the "introduction" to *Visible Song*, pp. 2-3. O'Keeffe's Plate II
(of Oxford, Bodleian Library, MS Auct. F.I.15, fol. 57v) shows one such
manuscript, in which the Latin verses are lineated (one verse-line per
manuscript line) and rubricated capitals mark the verse-prose boundaries.

[22] Krapp and Dobbie, *ASPR*, vol. 5, p. 153, *Proem*, ll. 3b-5; "For him the
desire was great that he relate in joyful song for men, for this nation, various
sayings."

many of the lines preceding the initials are blank.[23] The Otho A.vi text as a whole, then, stands as a translation of the *Consolation* — in terms of both form and of content — and the very prominent marking of the boundary between the prose portions and the verse portions would have helped readers to negotiate the transitions from prose to verse and back again.[24]

Whereas the poems contained in the translation of Bede's *Historia ecclesiastica* and Boethius's *Consolation* are clearly found in documents of obvious cultural importance, the other clearest examples of verse passages explicitly identified as such in associated prose texts seem far less obviously central to Anglo-Saxon literary culture: these include the verse charms printed under Dobbie's titles *The Nine Herbs Charm*, *Against a Dwarf*, and *For the Water-Elf Disease*.[25] Preserved in London, British Library MSS Harley 585 ("s. xi[1]") and Royal 12 D.xvii ("s. x[med]"),[26] all three of these charms use the verb "*singan*" in their performance instructions and refer to the words to be sung as a song ("*galdor*").

---

[23] Frequently, the blank spaces at the end of a prose or poetic passage also contain heavy punctuation; a clear example occurs at the beginning of *Meter 24* at fol. 87v, line 12 and at the end of the same *Meter*, fol. 88v, line 18. Folio 87v is reproduced as Plate I of O'Keeffe's *Visible Song*. Folio 87, it is worth noting, is probably the best-preserved of the severely damaged leaves that survive from the Otho A.vi manuscript.

[24] Remarkably, the text of the Alfredian Boethius in Oxford, Bodleian Library, Bodley 180 (which has only prose passages corresponding to the *Meters* in Otho A.vi) also uses the same vocabulary of *singan, gieddian, leoð*, and *fitte* to refer to the Old English passages that translate the Latin *Metra*. Readers of Bodley 180 must either understand such terms as referring to the Latin original (if they know it or know of it) or somehow reconcile the generic terms that suggest the presence of poetry with the absence of poetry in the manuscript.

[25] I cite the verse charms in the format of Dobbie's edition because of its convenience and accessibility, though I sometimes disagree with his lineation. For ease of reference, I refer to the *ASPR*'s line numbers, although it is important to note that prose passages and verse passages in those charms that feature both are numbered consecutively.

[26] For the dates of these two books, see Ker, *Catalogue*, pp. 305 and 332.

The *Nine Herbs Charm* consists of sixty-three lines of verse followed by a short paragraph of prose instructions. A point follows the last word of the poetic portion, but no capital or spatial detail is used to indicate the boundary any more clearly. Divisions within the prose paragraph are indicated with capitals, however, and indeed, sections within the poetic passage are far more clearly marked than the poetry-prose boundary, either by a cross within the text, sometimes preceded by a point (before lines 18, 31, 36, and 45),[27] or, in one case, a cross followed by a capital letter, both in the left hand margin (before line 7). While some of the catalogue passages within the poem are pointed fairly heavily (e.g. lines 46-51), it does not appear that the poem as a whole is metrically pointed. The same scribe responsible for the *Nine Herbs Charm* in Harley 585 also recorded the charm *Against a Dwarf.* This charm begins with prose and finishes with verse, but again, the boundary between the two does not seem to be clearly indicated in the manuscript. Nor are the two presented in visually distinctive ways. The point that separates the final word of the poem from the following "*amen*" does little to suggest that this scribe was concerned to mark out the poem as different from the remainder of the text.

The third charm that explicitly identifies a portion of its text as a "*galdor*" to be sung is the charm *For the Water-Elf Disease* in *Bald's Leechbook* (London, British Library, MS Royal 12 D.xvii). The scribe of this charm (who is also responsible for the annals 925-955 in the Parker Chronicle, Cambridge, Corpus Christi College, MS 173; see below) clearly indicates the limits of the verse portion of the charm; the relevant manuscript forms can be seen in the following re-lineated version of the key portions of the charm:

> sing þis gealdor ofer þriwa.
>
> Ic benne awrat   betest beadowræda
> swa benne ne burnon   ne burston
> ne fundian   ne feologan.
> ne hoppettan.   ne wund waxsian.

---

[27] Before line 58 there is also a larger, more ornamental cross in the margin, but well to the left, and definitely of a different character from the other crosses.

> ne dolh diopian.   ac him self heald halewæge.
>
> ne ace þe þon ma   þe eorþan on eare ace.
>
> Sing þis manegum siþum.[28]

Points both precede and follow the verse passage, and capitals are used both to begin the verse and to mark the resumption of prose (where a strikingly large, rounded capital "S" is used, rather than the pointed, insular "s" used elsewhere in the charm).[29] A number of points are present within the verse passage, but they chiefly appear to mark items in the poetic "*ne*-catalogue" and do not represent metrical pointing.[30] As in the texts of Cædmon's *Hymn* in OCCC 279, CUL Kk.3.18, and CCCC 41, the use of capital letters and points at the prose-verse boundaries seems to set off the poetic passage, but metrical pointing is not clearly used as a means of distinguishing the two types of text.

Though they do not explicitly identify their verse portions as poems, a number of the other charms feature prose-poetry juxtapositions, generally with fairly clear internal or contextual indications of the presence of verse. The ritual *For Unfruitful Land*, found on three folios at the end of the *Heliand*-manuscript (London, British Library, Cotton MS Caligula A.vi), contains both sorts of indicator. Unfortunately, the text of this ritual is too long to quote in full, but we can observe that the word "*gealdor*" is used within the first verse passage

---

[28] Royal 12 D.xvii, fol. 125v; "Sing this song over [it] thrice: 'I bound on wounds the best of battle-wreaths, so that the wounds would not burn, nor burst, nor increase, nor discolor, nor throb; nor the wounds grow, nor the injury deepen; but may he hold himself the health-path; nor distress thee any more than earth on an ear aches (?).' Sing this many times." The final verse lines are somewhat obscure, as is much of the language of this charm. Note that the "*x*" of "*waxsian*" is sometimes read as "*-co-*."

[29] A brief alliterating passage sometimes printed as verse near the end of this charm is set off by points, but not by capital letters. Dobbie, *ASPR*, vol. 6, p. cxxxvi, writes in his introduction to this charm, "There are two alliterative formulas, neither of which is metrically regular," but he lineates only the first such passage as verse in his text. See also G. Storms, *Anglo-Saxon Magic* (The Hague: Martinus Nijhoff, 1948), pp. 158ff.

[30] Items in the catalogue of plants in the first prose portion of the charm are likewise each pointed; we might also compare this scribe's general lack of pointing in the two poems copied into CCCC 173. See my comments below on the *Capture of the Five Boroughs*.

(line 32) to identify the presence of verse. Furthermore, a pair of powerful contextual clues mark the transition into the verse passage. Like the other three verse passages of this ritual, the first verse passage is preceded by the instruction to speak the poetic lines aloud: *"cweð þonne þas word"* (line 25).[31] But in addition, the text shifts from instructions in the second person imperative (*"nim," "cweð," "bere,"* and so forth) to prayers in either the first or second person. In the case of the first and last verse passages in the *Unfruitful Land* text, such contextual clues are really the only indicators available to readers to indicate the presence of verse, though points are used at the end of both of these verse passages.[32] The second poetic passage, beginning *"Erce. Erce. Erce. eorþan modor,"* is capitalized, following *"cweð þonne."* and its end coincides with the end of a manuscript line, at which no point is used.[33] After one brief sentence, the third verse passage is introduced with a capital in *"Cweð þonne"*; here no point separates the instruction to speak from the words to be spoken, but this passage does end with a point at the end of line 9 on folio 178r. Prose takes up again on the next line with a capital "N" (which stands partially in the left-hand margin, as do all line-initial capitals in this text). Though the evidence from this charm is difficult to evaluate, it is clear that the *Unfruitful Land* text is far less explicit in visually marking the transition than was a manuscript such as Otho A.vi; one might wonder if the difference in the scale of the texts might have contributed to the differing practices of these manuscripts.[34]

The kinds of contextual cues about the change in genre that operate in the *Unfruitful Land* ritual also function in several of the other charms: *For Loss of Cattle* (Harley 585, CCCC 41); *For Delayed Birth* (Harley 585); *For a Swarm of Bees* (CCCC 41); *Wiþ Blæce* (Harley

[31] "Say then these words."

[32] The first verse passage begins a line; at the end of the previous line, there is some blank space available. It is not clear whether there is room for the first four letters (*"east"*) of the verse text, but it is clearly the largest such space at the end of a line on the page. This space may, then, help mark the boundary point.

[33] "Erce, Erce, Erce, earth's mother," and "say then," respectively.

[34] Compare, however, how the Harley 585 scribe presents the verse-prose boundary in the charm *Against a Sudden Stitch.* See below.

585; not in Krapp and Dobbie, but number 6 in Storms's edition), and, to a lesser degree, in *Against a Sudden Stitch* (Harley 585).[35] In most cases, visual markers of the prose-verse boundaries are used no more effectively or consistently than in the *Unfruitful Land* text, and so we can treat these texts more or less as a group, in which scribes may have seen their primary task as providing texts for recitation rather than as indicating whether the recited texts were conceptualized as poetry or prose.[36] In a striking counter-example, however, the same scribe of Harley 585 responsible for the *Nine Herbs Charm* and *Against a Dwarf* does seem concerned to mark the beginning of the verse portion of *Against a Sudden Stitch* clearly. Here the prose passage that begins the text starts with a capital *wynn* as tall as two lines of writing, and the prose instruction "*wyll in buteran*"[37] is followed by a point and by somewhat more than half a line of blank space. The verse begins at the start of the next line with a capital "H" even larger and more prominent than the capital *wynn* and extending even further into the left-hand margin. Oddly, the final sentence, "*nim þonne þæt seax ado on wætan*"[38] returns to the use of prose and to the second-person imperative, but it is not visually distinguished at all from the end of the poem.[39] Regardless, at the beginning of the poem, the Harley scribe is certainly concerned to mark the transition from prose to verse as a major break; indeed, the boundary is marked here with all the insistence of the boundaries between the *Meters of Boethius* and the prose portions of Cotton Otho A.vi.

---

[35] Dobbie's Charm 11, *A Journey Charm*, is printed entirely as verse, and so is not under consideration here. The lack of contextual cues (chiefly the word "*cweð*" or the like, the shift from imperative instructions to scripted speech, or other similar shifts) suggests that both Dobbie's Charm 12 (*Against a Wen*) and Charm 9 (*For Theft of Cattle*) should be read as entirely verse. Storms prints both this way.

[36] Nor are there any indications that metrical pointing was used in any of the verse charm texts under consideration here.

[37] "boil in butter."

[38] "Take then that sword; put it in [the] liquid."

[39] It is useful to point out that the end of this poem is greatly vexed; see Storms's commentary in *Anglo-Saxon Magic*, pp. 148-50, for a summary of previous attempts to read the final lines.

As in the case of the verse passages explicitly identified in accompanying prose materials, these examples of verse with only internal or contextual clues to their poetic nature only sometimes appear to employ prominent and effective markers of the verse-prose boundary; sometimes these texts use few if any such markers. A single scribe (such as the first principle scribe of Harley 585), as we have seen, might mark the boundary quite clearly in one case (as at the beginning of *Against a Sudden Stitch*) and mark it not at all in another (at the end of *Sudden Stitch*; in *Against a Dwarf*). Though marking this boundary certainly seems to have been perceived as worthwhile (as the investment of time and energy implied by the portions of blank lines and the space reserved for decorated initials in Otho A.vi suggest), it was clearly not mandatory in all cases, and readers often seem to have needed to be able to identify verse (and the boundary between verse and prose) on their own.

In the case of the charms examined so far, however, it is worthwhile to note that the sort of poetry involved is in fact quite far from the sort of "classical" (Sieversian) verse that dominates the modern understanding of Old English verse form. Even at the level of simple alliteration and syllable-counts (to say nothing of more complicated metrical features and patterns), a conservative count would find "faulty" alliteration or meter in at least eight of the *Nine Herbs Charm*'s sixty-three verse lines; three of the nine lines of *Against a Dwarf*; at least four of *For A Sudden Stitch*'s twenty-six poetic lines; and at least four of the six verse lines in *For the Water-Elf Disease*.[40] We see, for example, cases of fourth-stress alliteration (e.g. *Herbs*, line 34; *Water-Elf*, line 13); AABB alliteration (e.g. *Herbs*, line 10; *Water-Elf*, line 12; *Sudden Stitch*, line 16); and no apparent alliteration at all (e.g. *Herbs*, lines 12, 21-22; *Dwarf*, lines 9, 13, and 15). In these charms, verse of this sort

---

[40] An exhaustive survey of the metrical charms would turn up a number of other metrically problematic lines; for just one example, note that all three lines of the first verse passage in *For Delayed Birth* have XXBB alliteration, at least as Dobbie has lineated them. One might, however, compare the very similar passage in *For A Sudden Stitch*, ll. 25-26, which is lineated quite differently. Such inconsistencies in lineating otherwise parallel passages might indicate that interpreting the structure of the verse charms through the lens of "classical" verse is simply inappropriate.

is clearly included in poetic passages explicitly or implicitly identified in their immediate contexts as poetic, and in some of these cases, the verse is visually distinguished from the surrounding prose as effectively as in the examples of Cædmon's *Hymn* from the Old English Bede. And significantly, the Water-Elf Disease charm, which distinguishes prose from verse most effectively, is the very one with the highest percentage of metrically "irregular" lines.[41]

The poems considered in this section, then, which are explicitly or contextually identified as poetic in their original Anglo-Saxon contexts, frequently exhibit the sorts of metrical anomalies that have been disparaged as evidence of a decline in the poetic tradition. While such features as altered alliterative and metrical patterns may indeed represent an alteration of traditional forms, the manuscript evidence of these poems does not suggest that Anglo-Saxons ceased to consider the resulting texts as poetic. To the contrary, the metrically "irregular" charms are as frequently linked with words like "*singan*" and "*galdor*" as are poems of more "classical" form. Further, it is important to note that none of the passages featured metrical pointing as an indicator of generic difference; at the same time, the use of meaningful textual spatialization and capital letters did occasionally function to demarcate the boundary between prose and poetic portions of the texts. The inconsistent use of even these indicators (sometimes in the work of a single scribe, or even a single text) suggests that the prose-poetry boundary did not always need to be clearly marked. The patterns observed in the manuscript record of these poems, however, can help us interpret the record of those poems that are not explicitly or contextually identified as poems in their associated texts.

---

[41] Other charm texts that might be best considered in this section are the *Theft of Cattle* charms (Storms's numbers 11A and 11B), which are recorded in Cambridge, Corpus Christi College, MS 190 (Ker 45; Gneuss 59), the *Textus Roffensis* (Rochester Cathedral Library MS A.3.5; Ker 373), and London, British Library, Cotton Tiberius A.iii (Ker 186; Gneuss 363). Unlike Dobbie's texts of the related charms from Harley 585 and CCCC 41, these charms use the verb "*sing*," which may be intended to apply to both the immediately following Latin text and the Old English passage at the end of the charm (which Dobbie prints as prose). Since these texts are not clear enough in identifying the passage in question as verse, though, I omit them from consideration here.

Thomas A. Bredehoft

Verse in Prose Contexts without Explicit or Contextual Indicators

Without explicit or contextual clues to help readers identify the poems considered in this section, visual features of the presentation of the texts become the only clues capable of indicating the boundary between poetry and prose. And, just as in the first group, there are poems here in which there are no apparent indications of the shift from poetry to prose or *vice versa*. Nevertheless, the sorts of patterns we have seen above can be quite useful in interpreting the manuscript record of the poems in this group, which include a number of poems from the *Anglo-Saxon Chronicle*; *Solomon and Saturn* from Cambridge, Corpus Christi College, MS 422; the brief inscriptional poem on the Brussels Cross; and the so-called *Metrical Epilogue* to CCCC 41.

Since it is the largest and most complex sub-grouping here, it makes sense to begin with the *Chronicle* poems.[42] Although Plummer printed seventeen separate passages from the *Chronicle* as poetry, more

[42] In the following, I use the conventional sigla to refer to the *Chronicle* manuscripts, in which A represents CCCC 173; B stands for London, British Library, Cotton MS Tiberius A.vi; C for Cotton Tiberius B.i; D for Cotton Tiberius B.iv; and E for Oxford, Bodleian Library MS Laud Misc. 636. For recent editions of A, B, and D, see Janet Bately, *MS A, The Anglo-Saxon Chronicle: A Collaborative Edition* 3 (Cambridge: D. S. Brewer, 1986); Simon Taylor, *MS B, The Anglo-Saxon Chronicle: A Collaborative Edition* 4 (Cambridge: D. S. Brewer, 1983); Katherine O'Brien O'Keeffe, *MS C: The Anglo-Saxon Chronicle: A Collaborative Edition* 5 (Cambridge: D. S. Brewer, 2000); and G. P. Cubbin, *MS D, The Anglo-Saxon Chronicle: A Collaborative Edition* 6 (Cambridge: D. S. Brewer, 1996). Charles Plummer, *Two of the Saxon Chronicles Parallel*, 2 vols. (Oxford: Clarendon, 1892-99; rpt. with a note by Dorothy Whitelock, 1952) remains the standard edition of E. Two translations follow Plummer's edition in a page-by-page fashion; they are G. N. Garmonsway, ed. and trans., *The Anglo-Saxon Chronicle* (London: J. M. Dent, 1953) and Michael Swanton, ed. and trans., *The Anglo-Saxon Chronicle* (London: J. M. Dent, 1996). Dorothy Whitelock, with D. C. Douglas and Susie Tucker, eds. and trans., *The Anglo-Saxon Chronicle: A Revised Translation* (New Brunswick, NJ: Rutgers University Press, 1961) attempts to follow all of the manuscripts. Though London, British Library, Cotton MS Domitian A.viii (manuscript F) contains some passages that may preserve some poetic structure, the condensing and rewriting activities of the F-scribe are complex enough to make the formal status of his text especially uncertain, and so I do not consider the F-text here.

recent scholars have not always been able to agree on just how many of these passages really are (in their opinions) poetic.[43] Some passages, such as the 1086 passage on William the Conqueror, have been more or less accepted as poetry, though excluded from the *ASPR* by Dobbie. Other passages, such as the five verse lines in 1067D, are generally excluded entirely from the Old English poetic corpus.[44] For the purposes of this study, I will not exclude any of these passages from my survey, at least not on the grounds of an assessment of their metricality. Certain of the *Chronicle* poems do, however, fall outside of the scope of my survey, because as the sole contents of their respective annals, they are not usefully juxtaposed to prose texts: these are the *Battle of Brunanburh* (937ABCD); the *Coronation of Edgar* (973ABC); and the *Death of Edgar* (975ABC).[45] The annals containing the rest of the passages printed as verse by Plummer (except 942D and possibly 942B; see below) also contain a prose component.

The simplest way to approach the *Chronicle* poems is to take them in the order in which they appear in Plummer's edition. The first of the *Chronicle* poems to share an annal with prose is the *Capture of the Five Boroughs*, in 942ABC. The version of this poem found in manuscript A is especially intriguing: here, the final half-line of the poem appears also to stand as the grammatical subject of the following

---

[43] Six of the passages printed as poems by Plummer were included in the *ASPR*, as noted above. Perhaps because of its origins in separate volumes of the *English Historical Documents* series, Whitelock, Douglas and Tucker's translation agrees with the *ASPR* in identifying poems up through the Conquest, but afterwards it follows Plummer's identification of poetic passages. Robinson and Stanley's *Old English Verse Texts* adds two passages to the *ASPR*'s six: the 975DE poem and the 1086E poem *William the Conqueror*. The most recent translation of the *Chronicle*, Michael Swanton's *The Anglo-Saxon Chronicle* (London: J. M. Dent, 1996) lineates ten passages as poetry, though describing some of those so presented in dismissive ways: the 1075/76 poems, for example, are described in footnotes as "rhythmic epigram[s]" (pp. 219, 212).

[44] Note, however, that this passage is briefly discussed in R. D. Fulk, *History of Old English Meter* (Philadelphia: University of Pennsylvania Press, 1992), p. 258.

[45] To put my criterion for excluding these poems from my survey in another way, I am essentially defining each separate annal as a self-contained "text": consecutive annals are, in my opinion, best conceptualized (at least in the portions of the *Chronicle* that feature poetry) as separate items of text.

prose sentence. The relevant passage stands at the bottom of fol. 27r and the top of fol. 27v in CCCC 173:

> afera eadweardes eadmund cyning onfeng anlaf cyning æt fulluhte. ⁊ þy ylcan geare ymb tela micel fæc he onfeng ræg-enolde cyninge æt bisceopes handa

Swanton translates this as "Edward's son . . . King Edmund. [King Edmund] received King Olaf at baptism, and the same year, after a fairly long while, he received King Rægnald at the bishop's hands."[46] Bately's edition of this manuscript likewise inserts the phrase "*Eadmund cyning*" within brackets.[47] Such editorial interventions aside, it seems clear that this scribe not only fails to mark the boundary between the poem and the following prose visually, but actually seems to allow the syntax of the annal to bridge that boundary, with "*Eadmund cyning*" standing between the two.[48]

Swanton, in the notes to his recent translation of the *Chronicle*, muddies these waters rather than clarifying them. Referring to the prose passage in 942A, he writes:

> These prose lines should probably have been put under 943,

---

[46] Swanton, *Anglo-Saxon Chronicle*, p. 110; ellipsis mine.

[47] Bately, *MS A*, p. 73.

[48] O'Keeffe, *Visible Song*, p. 132, writes: "The end of this poem should be *eadmundcyning*, but the scribe continued on, incorporating the predicate of the next annal into the last line of 27r, the end of his stint. *Onfeng anlafe* appears as an a-verse with vocalic alliteration, and although the following entry is in prose, these two circumstances clearly influenced the scribe to continue writing the 'verse.'" The suggestion that the scribe mistakenly felt that the poem continued at this point is an intriguing one, although a further half-dozen words ought to have been sufficient for any scribe observant enough to identify "*onfeng anlafe*" as a metrically acceptable verse to realize that no more verse was forthcoming. It is, however, possible to hypothesize that A's reading arose from eyeskip or haplography, resulting from an exemplar including a second "*eadmund cyning*"; cf. the form of the material following the 942 poem in BC. Also, note that the stint of scribe 3 of the Parker manuscript actually continues on through annal 955A at the bottom of fol. 27v.

which was left blank in A. The text of A . . . runs the verse
part of this annal straight on to the prose conclusion. B and
C appear to start a new entry beginning "Her King Edmund
. . ." but with no year number.[49]

Clever though such an explanation may be, it does somewhat overstate
its case. In manuscript B, the prose portion does begin with a capital
"H" that is placed in the left-hand margin, but no annal number precedes it (plenty of space is available at the end of the poem, line 11 of
fol. 32v; the annal indicator "*an-. dcccxli*" that precedes the poem is in
an even smaller space at the end of fol. 32v, line 3). The fact that no
annal number appears here, however, is difficult to interpret, because
annal numbers are only included sporadically in this portion of B.[50] In
C, though, a rubricated capital "H" begins the prose passage in question; it is found (after a space the size of fourteen or fifteen letters) on
the same line as the poem's final word. Though an early modern hand
has written the numerals "943" into this space, the annal number for
943 appears in its expected position at the end of the prose sentence on
fol. 142r, line 10.[51]

Difficult as the textual history of the verse and prose portions of
the 942 annal may be to sort out, however, it is fairly clear that manuscripts B and C clearly separate the prose material found in 942A from
the verse that precedes it, while scribe three of the A manuscript runs
the verse into the prose without even a syntactic break. When we recall
that scribe three of the Parker Chronicle likewise copied the charm
For the Water-Elf Disease, where the verse portion of the charm was

---

[49] Swanton, *Anglo-Saxon Chronicle*, p. 110, note 5. The first ellipsis in the
quotation is mine, the second Swanton's.

[50] It is possible that in this portion of B, fruitful annal numbers are intentionally
left blank to allow for their later insertion by a rubricator, while unfruitful
annal numbers are entered by the main scribe. If this is the case, the number
for 941 (which is present) would be "unfruitful," the poem would appear
under 942, and the passage about Anlaf would apparently occur under 943.
The evidence of the B manuscript, then, may not really include a single
annal with both prose and verse here.

[51] Note that most of these details about the B and C records of the 942 annal
are visible in the facsimiles of the passages in Robinson and Stanley, *Old
English Verse Texts*.

bounded by prominent capital letters, it seems reasonable to conclude that (at least for this scribe) the marking of such boundaries was not always mandatory. Likewise, while it seems that the B and C copies of this poem are metrically pointed after the b-lines,[52] the large spaces separating *Capture* from the following prose may be of equal importance for helping readers to move from the poem to the prose (note also the possibly significant use of "marginal space": the B-scribe's use of the left-hand margin for the capital "H").

The poetic passage from annal 959DE, it is generally agreed, is in the style of Wulfstan the homilist.[53] It is a fairly long passage, running to twenty-nine lines in Plummer's edition, and it is preceded in both manuscripts by a brief notice of the death of Eadwig and the accession of Edgar: "*Her eadwig cyning forðferde. ˀ feng eadgar his broþor to rice.*"[54] In both D and E, the poetic passage follows, beginning with a capital "O." The pointing in neither record can be usefully described as metrical (points appear chiefly before the capital letters and before the abbreviation for "*ond*"). Considering that four other capital letters are used in this brief passage, it is difficult to conclude that the initial capi-

---

[52] In this thirteen-line poem, O'Keeffe, *Visible Song*, p. 129, notes that "B and C agree in eleven instances of pointing the b-line."

[53] See Karl Jost, "Wulfstan und die angelsächsische Chronik," *Anglia* 47 (1923), pp. 105-23.

[54] Manuscript D, fol. 52r. "Her Eadwig passed on, and Edgar his brother succeeded to the kingdom."

[55] When we notice that the initial prose portion of the annal is altered from the version preserved in other manuscripts, reading, in B, "*Her forðferde eadwig cing ˀ eadgar his broðor feng to rice*" (see Taylor, *MS B*, p. 54; "Here King Eadwig passed on and his brother Edgar succeeded to the kingdom"), we might hypothesize that the version in DE has been somehow "versified," presumably by Wulfstan as well. It might, after all, be lineated as follows:

> *Her eadwig cyning forðferde. ˀ feng eadgar*
> *his broþor to rice*

The apparent rewriting of Eadwig's death-notice might very well have been intended to make it scan as part of the poem. Of course, if this is the case, there would be no boundary between verse and prose in annal 959. The evidence of the 959 annal, then, is of very uncertain value in this investigation.

tal "O" serves to visually indicate the beginning of a poetic passage.[55]

The brief poetic passage found at the beginning of the 975 annal in D and E, however, is much more clearly poetic in nature (i.e., it is closer to classical verse, and is, in fact, included in Robinson and Stanley's facsimile volume), and presentational features seem to mark this passage as verse in both D and E. In the D manuscript, the poem reads as follows (with modernized spacing and lineation):

> Her eadgar gefor   angla reccend
> westseaxena wine   ⁊ myrcna mundbora.
> Cuð wæs þæt wide   geond feola þeoda
> þæt afaren eadmundes   ofer gatenes beð.
> Cynegas hyne wide   wurðodon \s/wiðe   5
> bugon to þam cyninge   swa him wæs gecynde.
> Næs flota swa rang   ne se here swa strang
> þæt on angelcynne   æs him gefætte
> þa hwile þe se æþela cyning   cynestole gerehte.[56]

Although the poem is not metrically pointed, capitals are used to begin the first, third, fifth, and seventh verse lines; in one case (at the beginning of line five) the capital letter apparently works contrary to the syntax, which suggests continuity between lines four and five. After the point at the end of the poem, there is a blank space at least two letters wide.[57] After this space, we see a capital "H": "*Her eadwerd eadgares sunu feng to rice.*"[58] Since space left like this in the D manuscript often seems to correlate with places where a conflation of multiple source-texts has

---

[56] Manuscript D, fol. 53r. "Here Eadgar passed on, ruler of the Angles, friend of the West Saxons, protector of Mercians. It was widely known among many nations, over the sea [reading '*ganetes*' for '*gatenes*'], that kings widely and greatly honored the son of Eadmund, bowed to the king as was natural to him. There was no fleet so proud, nor army so strong, that in England [they did not] fetch him tribute while the noble king cared for the throne."

[57] Cubbin, *MS D*, p. 46, annal 975 note 2, suggests it is three letters wide. This gap can also be seen in Robinson and Stanley's facsimile of this passage.

[58] "Here Edward, Edgar's son, succeeded to the kingdom."

[59] Similar gaps (and capital letters) separate several passages of the "Mercian Register" from the annals they are joined to in MS D; see Cubbin's notes to annals 905, 906, 910, and 913. The capital "H" in 909D falls at the beginning of a line and so is not preceded by a space, but seems otherwise to fit into this pattern.

occurred in the D-manuscript's textual history,[59] it is tempting to guess that once-separate entries are being brought together here. Even if this is not the case, however, the space, the capital letter, and the repetition of the word "*Her*" indicate an important boundary point within the annal. In 975E, the poem is also followed by a capital letter in the word "*And*" (fol. 38v), which begins a line of writing. Since the previous line of writing is full, no blank space separates poem from prose in the E manuscript, but this version of the poem (in contrast to the D version) does seem to be metrically pointed, with points after every b-line except for 1b (which falls at the end of a manuscript page) and 4b. In addition, the points after 7a and 7b mark the internal rhyme.[60] In both the D and E versions of this poem, then, there seem to be fairly clear presentational features that would help readers identify this passage as verse: metrical pointing in 975E and significant use of spacing and capitals in 975D.

The second Wulfstanian passage in the *Chronicle*, which appears near the end of annal 975D, is (like 959DE) somewhat difficult to assess. Relineated, the passage reads:

> On his dagum   for his iugoðe
> godes wiþærsacan   godes lage bræcon.
> ælfere ealdorman.   ˥ oþre manega.
> ˥ munucregol myrdon.   ˥ mynstra tostæncton.
> ˥ munecas todræfdon.   ˥ godes þeowas fesedon.   5
> þe eadgar kyning het ær   þone halgan biscop
> aþælwod gestalian.   ˥ wydewan bestryptan
> oft. ˥ gelome.   ˥ fela unrihta.
> ˥ yfelra unlaga.   arysan up siððan.

---

[60] Significantly, this rhyming a-line is the only a-line to be pointed in 975E, including 2a, which (since it precedes "˥") would otherwise be a typical position for a point.

[61] Manuscript D, fol. 53v; "In his days, because of his youth, God's enemies broke God's law: ealdorman Ælfere and many others. And they obstructed the monastic rule, and scattered the monasteries, and drove out the monks, and put to flight God's servants, whom King Eadgar had earlier commanded the holy bishop Athelwold to establish. And they despoiled widows, repeatedly and often, and many improprieties and evil unlawfulnesses arose up afterwards. And always after, it grew greatly more evil."

⁊ aa æfter þam hit   yfelode swiðe.⁶¹   10

The passage begins with a large capital "O" at the top of fol. 53v, but since the prose material preceding this goes right up to the end of fol. 53r, the evidence of the capital is of uncertain value. Pointing within the passage might seem to be largely metrical at first glance (seven out of ten b-lines pointed; six out of ten a-lines), but ten of these thirteen points (five of each group) precede the Tironian abbreviation for "*ond.*"⁶² A short sentence about Oslac at the very end of the annal might conceivably be scanned as verse, and once again, the lack of a clear boundary gives us only negative evidence.

The record of the passage Plummer prints as verse in 979DE is not really any clearer. Pointing and capitalization in both the D and E versions seem more concerned to mark this passage's carefully balanced rhetorical style than its metrical structure, which is not always very clear in the first place.⁶³ In the D manuscript the passage is followed by a small blank space and a capital to begin the sentence "*Her feng æþelred to rice,*"⁶⁴ but capitals are common enough in late tenth-century annals in both the D and E texts that this one detail is less than conclusive, at least without the additional evidence of more clearly significant blank space (as in 975D) or more clearly metrical pointing.⁶⁵

In the records of the 1011 poem printed by Plummer (which appears in manuscript C as well as in D and E), even more uncertainties arise. No capitals indicate where this passage begins or ends in any of the manuscripts, and the points in D and E that might mark the

---

⁶² Note also the conventional point before the Tironian "⁊" in the middle of line 8a.

⁶³ Note that Plummer's lineation of this passage is the most tortured of any of the "non-classical" verse passages of the *Chronicle*; if it is indeed poetic, this passage departs more severely from classical standards than the other *Chronicle* passages considered here.

⁶⁴ "Here Æþelred succeeded to the kingdom." Cf. 975D and notes 57 and 59 above.

⁶⁵ The prose passage following the poem in 979E also begins with a capital letter, again used in the word "*And.*" Interestingly, the E scribe thus spells out this frequently-abbreviated word after both the 975E and 979E poems. A fuller examination of other places where the E scribe spells this word in full might be helpful in determining how significant such a circumstance might be.

beginning of the passage suggest different starting points ("*mid him*" is followed by a point in D, suggesting that it belongs with the previous clause; it is preceded by a point in E, suggesting it may belong with the poem). Apparent textual variations, especially in the D and E versions, hint that at some points in this poem's transmission it may have been copied as if it were prose.[66]

The 1036CD poem, interestingly, has also been seen as subject to prose-like copying. Regarding the C manuscript's second scribe and his treatment of this passage, O'Keeffe writes, "There is no indication that he treats these poor verses as anything but prose;"[67] regarding the scribes of 1036D and 1065D, she writes, "for the two rhythmic entries for 1036 and 1065, which C and D share, variation is limited to orthography and substitution (by D) of prose paraphrases for otherwise rhythmical lines."[68] Unfortunately, as O'Keeffe suggests, the entire entry for 1036 is troublesome; her comment, "In Dobbie's edition, the first five 'lines' are printed as prose," seems to raise the possibility that the lines may also be part of the verse.[69] Certainly the C scribe here does not use enough points to indicate truly metrical pointing in any part of the annal, although his spacing of the last half-dozen verse lines suggests he may have recognized their structure, since there appear to be slightly larger spaces between words at verse-boundaries than between other words. The pointing in 1036D is somewhat heavier, including points marking many (but by no means all) of the rhymed pairs in the passage.[70] Ultimately, the boundaries of the verse in the 1036 annal,

---

[66] See the fuller discussion of the scribal response to this short poem in my *Textual Histories: Readings in the Anglo-Saxon Chronicle* (Toronto: University of Toronto Press, 2001).

[67] O'Keeffe, *Visible Song*, p. 135.

[68] O'Keeffe, *Visible* Song, p. 125.

[69] O'Keeffe, *Visible Song*, p. 135.

[70] Although D's text is somewhat different from the C text printed by Dobbie, D has rhymed pairs in lines 7-9, 12, 15-17, 19, 24, and perhaps 25. The notion of rhyme operating in this passage seems to be somewhat more forgiving than most modern notions of rhyme, including at least what we would call "off-rhyme" and possibly including what we would call assonance. Regardless, of these nine pairs, D points both halves of lines 7-9, 15; and the b-lines of lines 16, 19, and 25.

we have to conclude, are not indicated clearly in either manuscript; it is at least remotely possible that the entire annal is in verse, though certainly of a form far from "classical."

The poem in 1057D is, perhaps, even less clearly poetic than that in 1036CD; however, it is certainly not distinguished visually from the surrounding prose any more effectively. It is followed by the phrase "*on þan ilcan gere,*"[71] but since such transitions are common in the prose of the *Chronicle,* this one cannot bear the weight of separating the verse portion of this annal from the prose. The 1065CD poem, on the other hand (copied by scribes working brief stints in both C and D, and hence probably copied within only a few years of one another), is clearly set off from the surrounding prose in both manuscripts. In C, the poem begins at the top of a page; the "H" that begins the poem was apparently left to be added by a rubricator or artist. At the end of the verse passage a third of a line is left blank, and the remaining prose portion of the annal begins with a large "ꞇ" placed in the left-hand margin. In 1065D, the first word of the poem has a large capital "H" placed in the left margin, and the end of the poem (as in 1065C) is followed by a large (we should, perhaps, call it a capital) "ꞇ." The 1065C poem is pointed metrically; the 1065D poem is not. Contextual cues in both manuscripts point to the self-contained nature of the poems: the material preceding the 1065D poem reads "ꞇ *hine man bebyrigde on twelftan dæg on þam illcan minstre:. swa hit her after sægð.*"[72] Although one version of the poem features metrical pointing and the other does not, the degree to which the two versions share features of presentation that serve visually to indicate the limits of the poem is remarkable.

The remaining passages printed by Plummer as poetry can be considered as a group, as all feature rhyme. They appear in annals 1067D; 1075E/1076D (two brief but separate passages in each annal); 1086E, and 1104E. Capitals (preceded by points) appear at the beginning of the passages in 1086E and 1104E, but not in the other cases; in no case are there spatial separators or contextual cues (as there were in 1065CD) to identify or separate the poetry. What we do see in

---

[71] "in the same year"

[72] "And they buried him on Twelfth Day in the same church, as it hereafter says."

these poems, however, is a fairly clear pattern of pointing. Consider, for example, the five lines of the 1067D poem (once again, relineated according to modern conventions):

⁊ cwæð þæt heo hine   ne nanne habban wolde.
gif hire se uplice arfæstnys   geunnan wolde.
þæt heo on mægðhade   mihtigan drihtne.
mid lichoman heortan.   on þisan life sceortan.
on clæne forhæfednysse   cweman mihte.[73]

All five lines here are pointed; all end with rhyme-words (line 1 rhymes with line 2; line 3 with line 5). Line 4 of this poem has rhyme-words in both half-lines and is the only line of the poem pointed on both the a-line and the b-line. Likewise, the rhyme words in 1076D are all pointed (5 in all), as is the b-line of the final, non-rhyming verse; the three b-lines of the brief, related poems in 1075E are all pointed, whereas the only unpointed rhyme word (*"brydeala"*) occurs on a manuscript line-end. The two rhyme words in 1104E are both followed by points (although their significance is difficult to determine, since one occurs before "⁊" and one ends the annal). Of the seventeen unambiguous pairs of rhyme words in the 1086E poem on William the Conqueror, fifteen are pointed after each member of the pair, and the following relineated excerpt is fairly representative:

he forbead þa heortas. swylce eac þa baras.
swa swiðe \he/ lufode þa headeor. swilce he wære heora fæder.
Eac he sætte be þam haran. þæt he mosten freo [.]faran.[74]

In all of these passages, then, points seem to be used to call added attention to the rhyme words; thus they mark the poetic structure as well.

---

[73] Manuscript D, fol. 81r. Above the *"-an"* of *"lichoman"* is written, in the original hand, *"licre,"* as if in substitution, but no mark of deletion is present. Translating without the substitution: "And she said that she would not have him, if the heavenly grace would grant her that she might, with her body's heart, in this short life, please the mighty Lord in maidenhood, with pure abstinence."

[74] Manuscript E, fol. 65r. "He forbade the [hunting of] harts, and so likewise of boars; he greatly loved the stags as if he were their father; likewise he ruled about the hares that they might go free." The erased letter before the last word of the passage quoted appears to have been an "f." At times, the evidence of the 1086E passage is, unfortunately, somewhat difficult to

The results of my survey of the *Chronicle* poems are complex, and a final summary of them might be useful at this point. As we saw when considering poems with implicit or explicit identification of their verse nature, the *Chronicle* poems are sometimes distinguished from surrounding prose very clearly (e.g. 1065CD, 942BC) and sometimes not at all (942A, 1011CDE, 959DE, 1057D). In most cases where we see metrical pointing, it appears in poems also distinguished from prose in other ways (942BC; 1065C; but note 975E), or else appears in the late tradition of pointing rhymes (1067D, 1076D, 1086E, 1104E). And tempting as it might be to conclude that passages such as 959DE, 979DE, 1011CDE, and 1057D are not poetic, since they are not clearly set off from the surrounding prose, the clear example of 942A and the unclear record of 1036CD (which certainly features rhyme and alliteration) should give us pause, as should the earlier examples of similarly undifferentiated poems in this essay.

There remain a number of prose-poetry juxtapositions from outside the *Chronicle*. The two poetic lines on the Brussels Cross appear on silver bands wrapping about the periphery of the cross; they are separated from the accompanying prose inscription only by a bend in the band as it negotiates a corner of the cross. Likewise, the beginning of the prose *Solomon and Saturn* in Cambridge, Corpus Christi College MS 422 is not significantly distinguished from the verse that precedes it at all; the single mark of punctuation at this point on page 6 is, in fact, less heavy than the triple points used three manuscript lines earlier in the poetic portion of the text and eight lines later in the prose. And finally, it is appropriate to end this survey, which focuses so much on the manuscript context of these poems, with a consideration of the so-called *Metrical Epilogue to CCCC 41*. Fred C. Robinson, of course, has convincingly argued (on the strength of the text's "immediate context") that this poem is really the third portion of a tripartite prayer in

---

interpret: it appears that the scribe has pointed the rhyme words relatively regularly, but occasionally the words that follow the points were written close enough to the points to partially obscure them. It is therefore possible that the points in this passage functioned more for the convenience of the scribe (perhaps marking "mini-stints" between examinations of the exemplar) than for the convenience of readers.

the voice of Bede.[75] Considering that each of the three portions of this prayer was intended to begin with a large rubricated or decorated initial and that blank lines are left between the three sections, it is very much worth observing that only the poetic portion of the prayer is written in alternating lines of black ink and red lead: with prominent capitals and space already functioning within this text to mark sections, the scribe manages to mark the prose-verse boundary between the final two sections with this even more striking visual device. The *Metrical Epilogue* stands as a final example, then, of how resourceful a motivated scribe could be in indicating the boundary between poetry and prose.

Conclusions

Two recent comments about the manuscript presentation of Old English poetry, one from a manuscript scholar and one from an editor, might give us pause. The manuscript specialist, Mildred Budny, writes in her recent essay "Old English Poetry in its Material Context" that "The Anglo-Saxons apparently felt no need to distinguish their own vernacular verse from prose in written layout."[76] The editor, G. P. Cubbin, faced with the decision of how to present the poems of the *Chronicle*'s D manuscript, prints them all in long lines across the page, usually footnoting to the effect that "There is nothing in the MS to indicate verse."[77] As I hope this essay has shown, there are, in fact, frequent indicators of the *boundary* between poetry and prose, if not clearly and consistently different modes of presenting the two genres.

What the evidence suggests, I believe, is that poems within prose contexts were, quite often, set apart from the accompanying prose by the same sorts of signals that were frequently used in Anglo-Saxon manuscripts to separate one text from another or to separate major subsections within a text. Examples of the use of capitals, blank space,

---

[75] Fred C. Robinson, "Old English Literature in its Most Immediate Context," *Old English Literature in Context*, ed. John D. Niles (Cambridge: D. S. Brewer, 1980), pp. 11-29.

[76] Budny, "Old English Poetry," p. 40.

[77] See the notes to this effect in Cubbin, *MS D*, annals 937, 942, 959, 975, 1011, 1057, 1065, 1067, and 1076. Cubbin does include line numbers in annal 937D, but only there.

marginal space, or some combination of the three to accomplish this separation of poetry from prose can be seen in *The Meters of Boethius* (Otho A.vi); *Against a Sudden Stitch* (Harley 585, scribe 1); *For the Water-Elf Disease* (Royal 12 D.xvii); Cædmon's *Hymn* (in CCCC 41 and possibly CUL Kk.3.18); and the *Chronicle* poems in annals 942BC, 1065CD, and probably 975D. The existence of such a pattern in these cases is evidence too powerful to be ignored: verse passages within prose contexts were frequently treated by scribes as important sub-sections of their texts and set apart as such by the use of prominent capitals (and the points often used before them) and significant blank or marginal space. The red lead used in the verse passage at the end of CCCC 41 is perhaps best understood as a substitute for these other in-dicators in a case where the capitals and use of space would have clearly been insufficient, since they were already serving another function.

At the same time (and indeed, in the hands of some of the same scribes), verse was often *not* set apart from surrounding prose by these means. Examples include Cædmon's *Hymn* (from Tanner 10, espe-cially); the *Nine Herbs Charm* and *Against a Dwarf* (Harley 585, scribe 1); *For Loss of Cattle* and *For Delayed Birth* (Harley 585, scribe 2); the *Swarm of Bees* charm in CCCC 41; and, again, a number of *Chronicle* poems, but most spectacularly the *Capture of the Five Boroughs* in 942A. Although it might be tempting to blame the lack of differentiation on scribes who failed to appreciate the metrical nature of some of the passages they were copying, the explicit and implicit cues found in the Old English Bede and the Harley charms would demand that we posit a series of scribes who paid little or no attention to the actual content of the texts in their care. Such an argument would function better to explain away the observed evidence than to explain it. At the very least, we must conclude that many poems were not distinguished from the surrounding prose by the use of capitalization and the meaningful use of space, and that the lack of such markers at a particular boundary cannot be used to argue that the associated passage is not poetic.

In addition, the records of these poems suggest some interesting things about the pointing of Old English verse. The clear examples of metrical pointing in the *Chronicle* poems found in 942BC and 1065C involve poems that are *also* set off by capitals and spacing. The clear-est example of metrical pointing that is not also set apart by these

169

other means is the short poem in 975E. Since this poem was excluded from the *ASPR*, it is important to note that the scribe responsible for pointing this passage treated it as verse. Clearly, we ought to hesitate to exclude such texts from the canon of Old English verse when contemporary readers seem to have understood at least some of these texts as poems. Equally important is the use of points to mark poetic rhyme words in 1086E and 1067D (and, to a lesser extent, because of their brevity, in 1076D and 1104E). The pointing of "*rang*" and "*strang*" in 975E is another likely example of this sort of pointing. These points (which serve to call attention to rhyme, a poetic feature that, in a sense, calls attention to itself) argue strongly for a contemporary recognition of the passages as poetic.

Finally, the evidence presented here allows us to draw a handful of specific conclusions about the form of some of the texts considered and about contemporary ideas concerning poetic form and textual identity in Anglo-Saxon England.

> 1. There is no contemporary evidence that would allow us to exclude the late, rhyming poems of the *Chronicle* or other passages of so-called "irregular meter" from the corpus of Old English poetry. These poems as well as those of "classical" form ought to inform modern investigations of both Old English metrics and Anglo-Saxon verse expression. The recognition of the existence of a less narrow and restrictive verse tradition, I believe, might urge us to reconsider the verse form of "irregular" poems such as the *Chronicle* poems or the charms. These poems may well need to be re-edited from a perspective that sees them not as flawed examples of "classical" verse, but rather as examples of a different kind of Old English verse. A better understanding of the possible forms of Old English verse late in the Anglo-Saxon period (including rhyming verse) should help us better to understand how the alliterative poetry of the earlier centuries existed within a developing tradition that may have been neither as metrically conservative nor as closely tied to oral-formulaic processes as has been commonly held.
>
> 2. Since verse texts within prose texts were apparently treated as either continuations of the texts or sub-sections within

them, we should be hesitant to separate such verse from its prose context. A poem like *Solomon and Saturn I*, which is separated from the prose that follows it less insistently than sections within either part are marked, would be best understood (and edited) as a single text containing prose and poetic portions.[78] The same should probably be said of those annals of the *Chronicle* that include both poems and prose. The verse charms, of course, have always been edited with their prose context intact.

3. The pointing that was sometimes used to mark metrical structure in the later Old English period may have been less valuable to readers in initially identifying a passage of verse than the highly visual use of capital letters and meaningful space.[79] At the least, the examples of metrical pointing and rhyme pointing suggest that we still have much to learn about the development of verse pointing during this period.

It is my hope that the descriptions and analyses here will help us better understand the conceptual boundary between poetry and prose in Anglo-Saxon England, fuzzy as that boundary sometimes seems when considering how the two were presented in the manuscripts. I hope also that it might lead to a greater appreciation of the surviving body of

---

[78] Fred C. Robinson, "'Bede's' Envoi to the Old English *History*: An Experiment in Editing," *The Editing of Old English* (Oxford: Basil Blackwell, 1994), pp. 167-79, serves as an edition of the tripartite prayer at the end of CCCC 41, rather than separating the so-called *Metrical Epilogue* from its context.

[79] As I was frequently reminded by Janet Ericksen, one of my colleagues at the NEH seminar in which the first draft of this essay was produced, we may well need to think of Old English manuscripts not as books that were designed to grant easy access to a first-time reader, but rather as books that assumed that readers would consult them many times. Such a perspective may, in fact, be of extraordinary usefulness when considering the pointing and spatialization of Anglo-Saxon manuscripts. A reader who is already familiar with a text that contains both poetry and prose, for example, might be better served by a clear indicator of the boundary between the two (such as a capital letter or noticeable space) than by metrical pointing. If different reading protocols are demanded by poetry and prose, a reader (especially a reader who knows that both verse and prose are present) might wish only for a clear indication of where the transition occurs, rather than requiring that the two sorts of text be accompanied by divergent pointing practices.

Old English poetry that has conventionally been dismissed as "irregular" and hence uninteresting or even non-poetic. At least some poems of the tenth and eleventh centuries were identified as poetic by their scribes and presented as such in the manuscript record, despite the fact that they employed poetic techniques that differed from the forms of "classical" Old English verse (as identified by Sievers). It is certainly likely, after all, that there is still more to say about Old English verse, its forms, and its cultural functions, as well as about familiar but vexed passages where the question of whether they are best read as poetry or prose remains.[80] This investigation, I hope, may serve as a step in the direction of answering such questions.

[80] Consider, for example, the passage in Vercelli homily 2, treated as verse by E. G. Stanley, "*The Judgement of the Damned* (from Cambridge, Corpus Christi College 201 and Other Manuscripts) and the Definition of Old English Verse," *Learning and Literature in Anglo-Saxon England*, ed. Michael Lapidge and Helmut Gneuss (Cambridge: Cambridge University Press, 1985), pp. 363-91, but treated as prose by Donald Scragg, *The Vercelli Homilies*, EETS o.s. 300 (Oxford: Oxford University Press, 1992).

Glastonbury and the Early History
of the Exeter Book

ROBERT M. BUTLER

WHEN LEOFRIC ARRIVED AT CREDITON in April of 1046 to succeed the recently deceased Lyfing as Bishop of Devon and Cornwall,[1] he found there, as he was to tell Pope Leo, a simple village inappropriate for a bishopric, in an area, as he was to tell King Edward, vulnerable to pirate attacks. Four years later, papal and royal authorization in hand, Leofric moved the episcopal see some ten miles south to Exeter, home of the ancient but greatly deteriorated monastery of St. Peter and St. Mary.[2] By the time of Leofric's arrival in 1050, Exeter's holdings had been reduced to two hides of land southwest of Exeter with six or seven cows, one threadbare set of mass-vestments, and five ecclesiastical books, three of them described as "very old" or "very old and worn-out."[3] Leofric seems to have spent the better part of his twenty-two-year tenure at Exeter restoring to it lands it had lost, acquiring a variety of church furnishings, and establishing a respectable library.

---

[1] The diocese had included Worcester as well as Devon and Cornwall but was divided upon Lyfing's death, with Worcester going to Ealdred, abbot of Tavistock and future archbishop of York. See Frank Barlow, "Leofric and His Times," *Leofric of Exeter: Essays in Commemoration of the Foundation of Exeter Cathedral Library in A.D. 1072*, ed. Barlow *et al.* (Exeter: University of Exeter Press, 1972), pp. 1-16, at p. 4, and *passim* for biographical information on Leofric.

[2] Documents concerning the transfer of the see survive on fols. 2r-3v of the Leofric Missal (Oxford, Bodleian Library, MS Bodley 579) and are edited most recently by Patrick W. Conner, *Anglo-Saxon Exeter: A Tenth-Century Cultural History*, Studies in Anglo-Saxon England 4 (Woodbridge, Suffolk: D. S. Brewer, 1993), pp. 215-25. Crediton's susceptibility to *piratarum barbarica* appears on fol. 2v in a narrative prefacing Pope Leo's letter to King Edward agreeing to the transfer (see Conner, pp. 223-24) and is a theme of D & C Exeter 2072, Edward's charter commemorating the event (see Barlow, "Leofric and His Times," pp. 8-9 and citations therein).

[3] In Leofric's donation list; see following discussion and next note.

Robert M. Butler

The sparsity of Exeter holdings in 1050 and Leofric's subsequent additions are detailed in a donation list — an inventory of sorts — written at Exeter undoubtedly under Leofric's auspices within a few years of his death in 1072.[4] This donation list, once part of a Gospel Book at Exeter (now Cambridge, University Library MS Ii.2.11), was removed and sewn into the front of the Exeter Book, probably, as Timothy Graham has shown, by Matthew Parker in the 1560s.[5] It was an apt placement, for the inventory's most famous entry now describes the very volume that it prefaces. About two-thirds into the inventory,

[4] The original draft of the donation list is dated 1069 x 1072 by Max Förster, "The Donations of Leofric to Exeter," *The Exeter Book of Old English Poetry*, ed. R. W. Chambers, Max Förster, and Robin Flower (London: P. Lund, Humphries and Company, 1933), pp. 10-32, at pp. 14-15. Two copies of the list survive in Old English: one is found in the preliminary quire of Oxford, Bodleian Library, MS Auctarium D.2.16 (fols. 1r-2v), a Gospel Book that had once belonged to Leofric; the other, discussed below, occurs in the Exeter Book. Förster's edition of the list (pp. 10-30) is based on the Exeter Book version with variations cited from the Oxford manuscript; he includes also an edition of a surviving copy in Middle English (pp. 30-32). Unless otherwise indicated, I refer throughout to the edition by Conner, *Anglo-Saxon Exeter*, pp. 230-35, also based on the Exeter Book with variations cited. For early printings of the list see Förster, p. 10. For recent editions see Timothy Graham, "A Parkerian Transcript of the List of Bishop Leofric's Procurements for Exeter Cathedral: Matthew Parker, the Exeter Book, and Cambridge University Library MS Ii.2.11," *Transactions of the Cambridge Bibliographical Society* 10 (1996 for 1995), p. 424, n. 12. Michael Lapidge provides a particularly convenient edition of the books in the donation list in his "Surviving Booklists from Anglo-Saxon England," *Learning and Literature in Anglo-Saxon England: Studies Presented to Peter Clemoes on the Occasion of His Sixty-fifth Birthday*, ed. Michael Lapidge and Helmut Gneuss (Cambridge: Cambridge University Press, 1985), pp. 33-89, at pp. 65-69. Exeter's external land holdings, noted above, were at Ide and apparently constituted a single estate. The phrasing of the list (see Conner, *Anglo-Saxon Exeter*, p. 230 §6) makes it probable that the cattle (six cows in the Exeter Book, seven in the Oxford MS) were at Ide rather than Exeter. Books and vestments in Exeter when Leofric arrived are discussed further below.

[5] See Graham, "Parkerian Transcript," particularly pp. 448-51; on the discovery of the connection between the Cambridge MS and the Exeter Book and transfer of the leaves of the donation list, see Bruce Dickins, "The Beheaded Manumission in the Exeter Book," *The Early Cultures of North-West Europe (H. M. Chadwick Memorial Studies)*, ed. Cyril Fox and B. Dickins (Cambridge: Cambridge University Press, 1950), pp. 361-67.

within its list of sixty-six books, appears an entry for · *I* · *mycel englisc boc be gehwilcum þingum on leoðwisan geworht* ("one large English book about various things wrought in poetry"). No one has doubted that the entry describes the Exeter Book itself, which in numbers and variety of poems is the largest of the four surviving codices of Old English poetry, or that the Exeter Book was therefore in Exeter not later than 1072, the *terminus ante quem* for the donation list. It resides there today as Exeter, Cathedral Library, MS 3501.

The Exeter Book was written roughly a century before its appearance in Leofric's inventory, however, and it is this pre-inventory history, and in particular the manuscript's place of origin, that has become a matter of disagreement. In the introduction to the 1933 facsimile edition of the Exeter Book, Robin Flower assigned the production of the codex to a monastery in "the West Country" but one "away from the main centres" of book production.[6] Flower would commit himself no further, but left a thread untucked in noting the similarity between the square *a* of the Exeter Book and that of a Crediton charter of 974.[7] Krapp and Dobbie, in the *ASPR* edition three years later, suggested without elaboration that the Exeter Book "may" have originated in Crediton,[8] and in 1974 Michael Swanton, pointing only to the square *a* of the Crediton charter, said that it was "probably" written there.[9] The square *a*, however, is ubiquitous in the South of the tenth and early eleventh centuries and affords no independent grounds for dating or placing a manuscript.[10] In fact, no thorough investigation to pinpoint the monastery that produced the Exeter Book had been

---

[6] Robin Flower, "The Script of the Exeter Book," *The Exeter Book of Old English Poetry*, pp. 83-90, at pp. 90 and 84.

[7] Flower, "The Script," pp. 84, 89. The charter is Public Records Office MS 30/26/11.

[8] George P. Krapp and E. V. K. Dobbie, Introduction, *The Exeter Book*, ASPR 3 (New York: Columbia University Press, 1966), p. xiv.

[9] Michael J. Swanton, Introduction, *Pages from the Exeter Book*, ed. Michael J. Swanton, Exeter University Occasional Papers (Exeter: Exeter University Press, 1974), p. ii.

[10] See, for example, David Dumville, "English Square Minuscule Script: The Background and Earliest Phases," *Anglo-Saxon England* 16 (1987), pp. 147-79, at p. 153.

published until Patrick W. Conner's 1993 *Anglo-Saxon Exeter*.[11] Conner does not confront the case for a Crediton origin; there is no case to confront. He instead marshals extensive details to argue that the Exeter Book was written at Exeter itself.[12] It is an injustice to reduce the many lines of Conner's argument to one, but perhaps it is fair to say that his case relies most heavily on his analysis of five other impressive manuscripts that, he says, show close historical and paleographical connections to the Exeter Book and that therefore likewise originated in an Exeter scriptorium.[13] In 1996 Richard Gameson published a detailed rejoinder to each of Conner's lines of argument, concentrating also on the five other manuscripts and countering Conner's evidence that any of them, or the Exeter Book, originated in Exeter.[14] Figure 1 indicates a few central details of the debate and, in accordance with Conner's approach, displays the manuscripts in two groups of three. Because the link between the two groups remains uncertain, I restrict my discussion to the manuscripts of Group I. All recent studies of the

---

[11] See n. 2, above.

[12] The most recent edition of the Exeter Book does not attempt an independent study of the origins of the codex but references Conner in noting briefly that "The combined evidence . . . suggests that the manuscript was written at either Crediton or Exeter"; see *The Exeter Anthology of Old English Poetry: An Edition of Exeter Dean and Chapter MS 3501*, ed. Bernard J. Muir (Exeter: University of Exeter Press, 1994), Vol. 1: *Texts*, p. 3.

[13] See especially Conner, *Anglo-Saxon Exeter*, pp. 33-47. The theory of an Exeter origin is but one component of Conner's study, which also includes editions and translations of a number of documents related to pre- and post-Conquest Exeter, a three-booklet theory of the composition of the Exeter Book, and thorough analyses of the paleography and codicology of the codex.

[14] Richard Gameson, "The Origin of the Exeter Book of Old English Poetry," *Anglo-Saxon England* 25 (1996), pp. 135-85. Conner has initiated a response to some of Gameson's objections in his "Exeter's Relics, Exeter's Books," *Essays on Anglo-Saxon and Related Themes in Memory of Lynne Grundy*, ed. Jane Roberts and Janet Nelson, King's College London Medieval Studies (London: King's College London, Centre for Late Antique & Medieval Studies, 2000), pp. 117-56, arguing that Exeter had a scriptorium and other resources necessary to support the production of a manuscript such as the Exeter Book. He also refers therein (p. 152 n. 85) to his forthcoming "The Minster Scriptorium at Exeter."

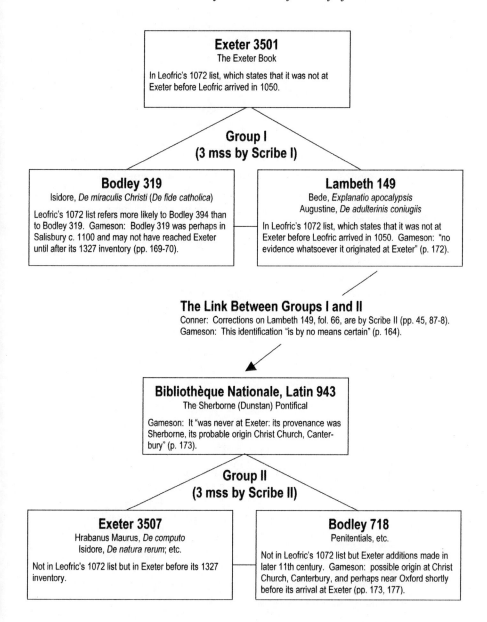

Figure 1: The Exeter Book and Related Manuscripts

Exeter Book have agreed that the three codices of this group — the Exeter Book; Oxford, Bodleian Library, MS Bodley 319; and London, Lambeth Palace, MS 149 — were written in the same scriptorium; most agree that they were probably by the same scribe.[15] Only Conner attributes any of them to Exeter.

One of Gameson's objections, concerning interpretive approaches to Leofric's donation list and one seemingly miscellaneous comment in the list, deserves some additional discussion. The compiler of the list itemizes Leofric's acquisitions for the monastery in three categories — lands, church treasures and ecclesiastical furnishings, and books — pausing after the first two, and midway through the third, to add a brief comment distinguishing Leofric's many gifts to the monastery from those few similar items that were there when he arrived. For the first two categories, such summarizing comments serve as the list's structural markers. In the third category, the Exeter Book is among the many manuscripts distinguished in this way from Exeter's pre-Leofric books.[16] Conner's theory requires that the Exeter Book, having been produced at Exeter a century or so earlier, remain there until Leofric's arrival in 1050. Thus Conner must argue that at least some

---

[15] Flower, who was unaware of Bodley 319, would say only that the Exeter Book and Lambeth 149 "were written, if not in the same scriptorium, in the same narrowly defined script area, and in the same period" ("The Script," p. 85). Based on her study of the rulings of these two manuscripts, Dorothy K. Coveney concluded that "Dr. Flower's cautious statement . . . could safely be amended to 'in the same scriptorium'"; see her "The Ruling of the Exeter Book," *Scriptorium* 12 (1958), pp. 51-55, at p. 55. N. R. Ker first noticed the correspondences in script of Bodley 319, noting that it has "all the features which Dr. Flower lists . . . as common to the Exeter Book and MS Lambeth 149"; see his review of *The Exeter Book of Old English Poetry*, *Medium Ævum* 2 (1933), pp. 224-31, at p. 230 and note. In 1981 I checked Coveney's findings against Bodley 319 (fol. 19r, the first page where rulings are visible) and found a similar page layout and an almost identical procedure for pricking and ruling. Swanton suggests that all three are "in the same hand" (*Pages*, p. ii), and Gameson ("The Origin") and Conner (*Anglo-Saxon Exeter*) accept that all are probably by the same scribe. For the present argument, it is necessary to accept only that the Exeter Book and Lambeth 149 are roughly coeval and were written in the same scriptorium.

[16] On the structure and rhetoric of the list, see Conner, *Anglo-Saxon Exeter*, pp. 226-27. Conner overlooks the disruption of the rhetorical pattern in the list's third category discussed below.

items listed as Leofric's donations, including the Exeter Book, may in actuality have been in Exeter before the bishop arrived; the donation list, that is, cannot always be taken at face value. Both Gameson and Frederick Biggs respond that the list is instead what it declares itself to be in its introduction and conclusion, a record of property Leofric brought into the Exeter monastery during his tenure there.[17] It is no doubt true, as Conner suggests, that memories would have faded between Leofric's arrival at Exeter and the compilation of the list some twenty years later and that inaccuracies may have resulted: Conner notes, for example, that, to conduct a mass before Leofric arrived, the monastery at Exeter would have needed more ecclesiastical accouterments than the list allows it.[18] But while concessions might be allowed for items inadvertently omitted from the list (particularly for those lost during intervening years), no evidence suggests that any property actually included in the list was recorded either deceptively or erroneously. And in the case of the Exeter Book, as we shall see, it would appear that the compiler took deliberate care in recording it as one of Leofric's acquisitions for the monastery.

Having completed the inventory of lands and church furnishings, the compiler turns to the monastery's books. The sequencing of books in the list (service books, followed by two books in English, followed by patristic and other texts in Latin) suggests that he was reading the library's shelves as he wrote. (He had recorded "two great ornamented gospel-books" in the earlier listing of church treasures,[19]

---

[17] Gameson and Biggs question Conner's translation of *gedon* in the list's introduction and *dide* in its conclusion as "brought about" (see Conner, *Anglo-Saxon Exeter*, p. 231 §1 and p. 234 §12), i.e., that Leofric "brought about these things at Exeter" rather than "placed these items in" or "bestowed them upon" the monastery (Gameson, "The Origin," p. 137; cf. Conner, *Anglo-Saxon Exeter*, p. 126). Biggs points out that the final *dide* suggests that with the donation list Leofric was making a payment of sorts in return for God's favor; in this regard, see discussion below. I wish to thank Professor Biggs for forwarding a copy of his paper "The Exeter *Exeter Book*?: Some Linguistic Evidence" (The Annual Meeting of the Medieval Academy of America, Toronto, 17-19 April 1997), which provides a thorough semantic analysis of *gedon* as it is used in Leofric's list and elsewhere.

[18] See Conner, *Anglo-Saxon Exeter*, p. 227.

[19] Conner, *Anglo-Saxon Exeter*, p. 231 §7.

an indication that these two valuable volumes were probably kept separate from the other books.) He records the library's first twenty-eight service books, then *Boetius boc on englisc*, and then the Exeter Book as the *mycel englisc boc be gehwilcum þingum on leoðwisan geworht*. Here he pauses, however, some thirty books shy of finishing, to insert the following comment:

> ꝺ he [Leofric] ne funde on þam minstre þa he to feng boca
> na ma buton .i. capitularię, ꝺ .i. forealdod nihtsang, ꝺ .i.
> pistelboc, ꝺ .ii. forealdode rædingbec swiðe wake, ꝺ .i. wac
> mæssereaf.

> And when he [Leofric] took charge of the minster, he
> did not find any more books except one capitulary, and
> one very old nocturnal antiphoner, and one epistolary,
> and two very old and worn-out Office-lectionaries and
> one worn set of mass-vestments.[20]

The summarizing comment belongs not here, of course, but rather, in keeping with the compiler's rhetorical scheme, at the end of the list of books to mark the close of the inventory's third structural unit. At the present juncture, however, the compiler was confronting on the shelves a sequence containing several greatly aged books — probably all five of those listed in the comment but certainly at least the three described as *forealdod(e)*, as well as the preceding *mycel englisc boc*, which was itself by then about a hundred years old. The compiler had somehow to indicate which of these old books had been donated by Leofric and which had been in the monastery before the bishop arrived. Apparently, the compiler used the summarizing comment earlier than intended to serve just this purpose, taking care to position it — knowingly, we must assume — immediately after the Exeter Book to distinguish it from the next five books as one of Leofric's acquisitions for Exeter.[21]

---

[20] Conner's translation, *Anglo-Saxon Exeter*, p. 233 §7.

[21] This analysis assumes that the five books listed in the comment as antedating Leofric were physically present on the shelves at the time of the inventory. Quite possibly, however, these otherwise unidentifiable manuscripts had been lost by the time of the inventory (or disassembled for other purposes) and were being cited from memory. Such a situation, at least, seems likely in the case of the worn mass-vestments cited in the comment curiously along with

It is possible, of course (and I think probable), that no separate compiler was involved and that Leofric himself drafted the donation list. He had longevity at Exeter and would have known better than anyone else, having acquired most of it himself, how and when property came into the monastery and what had been there when he arrived. We might thus attach all the more weight to the comment's appearance after the entry for the Exeter Book. But whether Leofric wrote the draft or approved the final version, the misplaced comment would have been precisely where he wanted it, for the distinction it makes between a gift and preexisting property would have been of some importance to him. In the penultimate section of the donation list — in a sentence Leofric would surely have drafted himself — the monks of Exeter are asked, in return for all Leofric has done for the monastery, to pray for his soul after his death.[22] The acquisition of the Exeter Book had been one of his accomplishments for Exeter and, his soul at stake, nothing to fib about. And thus the comment, while it does not make it impossible that the Exeter Book was written at Exeter,[23] is particularly problematical to the view that it was in Exeter before Leofric arrived.

And so it would appear fairly certain that Leofric brought the codex to Exeter from elsewhere sometime between 1050 and 1072. But where had he found it? London, Lambeth Palace, Lambeth MS 149, another of Leofric's books and one of the manuscripts originating in

the old books. Surely the vestments were not shelved among the books; but neither, evidently, had they been in their proper place with the other vestments listed in the earlier inventory of such items (i.e., in Conner's §7, *Anglo-Saxon Exeter*, p. 231). They may in fact have been long since discarded, and the sight, or recollection, of the pre-existing manuscripts (all service books) may have triggered memories of services performed in the early days with worn-out books and threadbare vestments, hence the mention of the vestments at this point in the inventory. In either eventuality, however — physical presence or memorial reconstruction — the case remains for books and vestments alike that the comment makes a clear demarcation between items Leofric donated — the Exeter Book in particular — and those he did not.

[22] Conner, *Anglo-Saxon Exeter*, p. 235 §12.

[23] It is conceivable that the codex had been written at Exeter but left there sometime before 1050 to be later recovered by Leofric, who had in a similar manner brought Exeter's former land holdings back to the monastery (see Conner, *Anglo-Saxon Exeter*, p. 230 §§2-3). I cannot find that Conner proposes this possibility, however, and there is little evidence to recommend it.

the same scriptorium as the Exeter Book, suggests a strong possibility for the monastery where Leofric acquired that manuscript, and perhaps along with it the Exeter Book. It thus allows for an alternative reconstruction of the pre-Leofric provenance of both Lambeth 149 and the Exeter Book, as well as of their place of origin.

Lambeth 149 originally contained two texts, Bede's *Explanatio apocalypsis* and Augustine's *De adulterinis coniugiis*.[24] Because Leofric's donation list refers to an *Expositio Bede super apocalipsin* and because Leofric's name appears in Lambeth 149, it is commonly agreed that these are one and the same book.[25] At the top of fol. 138r of this manuscript appears the explicit of the *De adulterinis coniugiis* and, below it, the following colophon:

> Hunc quoque uoluminem Aetheluvardus[26] dux gratia dei ad monasterium sce marie genetricis saluatoris nri condonauit; Quod est in loco qui dicitur [the name of the town has been obliterated]. Hoc autem donum factum est anno ab incarnacione redemptionis nre mxviii. Indi.i. Et factum est ergo post obitum regis eadmundi quod . . . .

> Ealdorman Æthelweard, by the grace of God, gave this volume also to the monastery of St. Mary, mother of our Savior, which is in the place called [the name of the town has been obliterated] in the year of our Savior 1018, the first indiction. And it came to pass therefore after the death of King Edmund that . . . .[27]

---

[24] A second volume, from Lanthony and of the late twelfth or early thirteenth century, was later bound in following the *De adulterinis coniugiis*; see M. R. James, *A Descriptive Catalogue of Manuscripts in the Library of Lambeth Palace: The Medieval Manuscripts* (Cambridge: Cambridge University Press, 1932), pp. 237-39.

[25] The reference occurs in the group of Latin books listed near the end of Leofric's inventory (Conner, *Anglo-Saxon Exeter*, p. 234 §11); that no reference to Augustine's *De adulterinis coniugiis* appears suggests that whoever was taking the inventory did not look beyond the first few leaves of the book.

[26] The *v* in *Aetheluvardus* is added above the line.

[27] I thank Timothy Graham for this translation of the idiomatic *Et factum est . . . quod.*

The last sentence simply stops incomplete. It is followed by a rough *Pater noster* in another, probably later hand, and then, in yet another hand, by Leofric's name (*Leofricus* + *Pater*) in green ink. The name of the town that would identify the monastery of St. Mary was apparently scratched out some time ago. In an effort to recover the reading, someone (presumably much later) applied a reagent, and the name of the town is now so blotted that no trace of a letter can be discovered under ultraviolet light. Both Flower and Joyce Hill discount Frances Rose-Troup's claim that *Exeter*, in one of its early forms, originally filled the space.[28] To their objections I would add that, as indicated above, Leofric's donation list makes it unlikely that the Exeter Book or, on similar grounds, Lambeth 149 had been in Exeter before Leofric's arrival in 1050. Moreover, had the Lambeth MS been donated to Exeter in 1018, there would be no reason for the Exeter monastery to scratch out the name of the town that would verify its ownership of the manuscript. The conclusion seems unavoidable: in 1018 Lambeth 149 was donated not to Exeter but to a monastery of St. Mary elsewhere; sometime between 1050 and 1072 Leofric acquired the manuscript from there and brought it to Exeter. Then, while adding his bishop's name to the leaf, Leofric's scribe would have had some motivation to erase the name of the town of the former owner to give the appearance that Ealdorman Æthelweard had given the manuscript to St. Peter's and St. Mary's at Exeter.[29]

---

[28] Flower, "The Script," p. 87; Joyce Hill, "The Exeter Book and Lambeth Palace Library MS 149: A Reconsideration," *American Notes & Queries* 24 (1986), pp. 112-16 and "The Exeter Book and Lambeth Palace Library MS 149: The Monasterium of Sancta Maria," *American Notes & Queries*, n.s. 1 (1988), pp. 5-8; Frances Rose-Troup, "The Ancient Monastery of St. Mary and St. Peter at Exeter [650-1050]," *Report and Transactions of the Devonshire Association for the Advancement of Science, Literature and Art* 52 (1931), pp. 179-220, at pp. 206-07.

[29] Gameson ("The Origin," p. 170 n. 164) notes that an erasure has also been made in the upper margin of fol. 1r that may have removed additional evidence of earlier ownership. Rose-Troup ("Ancient Monastery," p. 206), Flower ("The Script," p. 87, n. 2), and Hill ("A Reconsideration," p. 114) suggest that the donation inscription postdates the donation itself; Hill refers to the hand of the inscription as "later eleventh century." Thus the donation inscription may have been entered on the folio not too long before Leofric acquired the manuscript and the name of the town erased at Exeter

Hill, who limits her inquiry to Exeter and Crediton, favors Crediton as the recipient of the 1018 donation because Crediton's monastery was dedicated to St. Mary alone and because several of the Latin forms of *Crediton* would fit into the blotted area on the donation inscription, which requires eleven to fourteen of the scribe's letters.[30] Conner favors Tavistock, noting that it, too, was within Æthelweard's domain, was dedicated to St. Mary, and would likewise fill the space nicely.[31] But Conner then says, somewhat surprisingly, that "if the hiatus could be filled, then we should know where the manuscript was probably not written, but that is all."[32] In fact, however, diplomacy may have constrained Æthelweard to restore the manuscript to the monastery that had written it.[33] Moreover, since the *quoque* of the donation inscription makes it clear that at least one other volume was being presented at the same time, it is possible that the Exeter Book and perhaps even Bodley 319, both produced roughly a half-century before the 1018 donation in the same monastery as Lambeth 149, were being returned along with it. Identifying the monastery of St. Mary is thus a matter of some consequence in that it would suggest a strong candidate not only for a pre-Exeter provenance for at least one of these manuscripts, but also for the scriptorium that produced all three.

Flower tells the story of the Æthelweard who donated the manuscript.[34] Grandson-in-law of Æthelweard the Chronicler, our Æthelweard was a member of the most powerful family in southwestern England and ealdorman of the southwestern counties from 1016

shortly thereafter. Gameson, on the other hand, argues that the inscription is contemporary with the donation ("The Origin," p. 17). In either case, it seems unlikely that, between the time of the manuscript's donation and its arrival at Exeter, it would have traveled to another monastery where erasures might have been made.

[30] Hill, "A Reconsideration," p. 115.

[31] Conner, *Anglo-Saxon Exeter*, pp. 35–36; he gives *Attauistoca* as being of the right length (p. 35, n. 14).

[32] Conner, *Anglo-Saxon Exeter*, p. 36.

[33] In personal correspondence of 25 November 2003, Conner explained that his comment above was prompted by the consideration that the manuscript would not have been *given* to the monastery that produced it.

[34] Flower, "The Script," pp. 87–89.

until he was exiled by Cnut in 1020. I count seven monasteries within his domain dedicated to St. Mary alone or to Mary and attendant
saints.[35] These include, in addition to the churches of Exeter, Crediton, Tavistock, and Buckfast, all in Devon, institutions at Sherborne
and Shaftesbury in Dorset and at Glastonbury in Somerset.[36] While
any one might be the monastery in question, the most likely might
be determined through a generally neglected clue on the same folio as
the colophon: the name *æþelwine* (without distinguishing title) in the
upper left margin. In its placement and in its hand, the name seems
to have no connection with the donation inscription and may be no
more than an idle scribble. It nonetheless provides a name of someone
associated somehow and at some point with Lambeth 149.

Better than fifty Æthelwines are recorded for the Old English
period;[37] when the list is narrowed on geographical and chronological grounds, however, three stand out as strong possibilities. First is
Æthelwine Bishop of Wells, who, as Flower first noted, attested a 1018
Crediton charter with Æthelweard.[38] Flower would take the possibilities of this identification no further, however, probably because Wells
was dedicated to St. Andrew and thus could not be the monastery of
donation. But if the marginal *æþelwine* is indeed the man who once
(and apparently twice) served as Bishop of Wells, his name may have
come to the leaf at any time — before or after his episcopacy at Wells
and before or after the 1018 donation. It need not be assumed — indeed it would seem impossible — that Lambeth 149 was presented to
Wells. Wells in any event was not particularly important to the diocese.

---

[35] Æthelweard's district seems to have comprised Devon, Dorset, and Somerset;
see Flower, "The Script," p. 91.

[36] On the location of diocese and churches, see Frank Barlow, *The English
Church 1000-1016: A Constitutional History* (London: Longman, 1963), p.
161. On the names of monasteries and churches, see David Knowles, C. N. L.
Brooke, and Vera C. M. London, eds., *The Heads of Religious Houses: England
and Wales 940-1216* (Cambridge: Cambridge University Press, 1972).

[37] See William Searle, *Onomasticon Anglo-Saxonicum: A List of Anglo-Saxon
Proper Names from the Time of Beda to That of King John* (Cambridge: The
University Press, 1897), s.v. *Æthelwine*.

[38] Flower, "The Script," p. 87, citing Napier and Stevenson, *Crawford
Charters*, p. 9.

Although the nominal bishopric of Somerset, it remained in the tenth century primarily a parish church facing increasing encumbrances on its property; by 1042 it had become "one of the poorer bishoprics."[39] In the meantime it survived quietly in the shadow of the independent monastery at Glastonbury, within walking distance about five miles south.[40]

Glastonbury, the ecclesiastical, political, and cultural center of power in the diocese as well as in Æthelweard's southwestern counties, had been leader under Dunstan of the early reform movement, a training ground for bishops and archbishops, the richest church in England by the time of Doomsday Book, and home of an ancient monastery dedicated to St. Mary. At least eight of Wells's first eleven bishops, up through the time of the donation of the Lambeth MS, had been Glastonbury monks beforehand.[41] Although Æthelwine had come to Wells from Evesham, having served two years there as abbot, he, too, may have been trained earlier at Glastonbury, sometime before his first attestation as abbot of Evesham in 1012.[42] We know only that Lambeth

---

[39] Barlow, *The English Church*, p. 224.

[40] On Wells, see Barlow, p. 224, and J. Armitage Robinson, *The Saxon Bishops of Wells: A Historical Study in the Tenth Century*, British Academy Supplemental Papers 4 (London: Oxford University Press, 1918), pp. 52-55. Glastonbury's independence from diocesan control is indicated in four royal privileges — by Ine (S 250), Edmund the Elder (S 499), Edgar (S 783), and Cnut (S 966) — transcribed by William of Malmesbury into his *De Antiquitate Glastonie Ecclesie* (ed. J. Scott, *The Early History of Glastonbury: An Edition, Translation and Study of William of Malmesbury's* De Antiquitate Glastonie Ecclesie [Woodbridge, Suffolk: D. S. Brewer, 1981], pp. 98-103, 116-19, 122-25, and 132-33, respectively). That some of these may be forgeries merely reinforces Glastonbury's insistence on its independence. Edgar's privilege, for example, states that "neither the Bishop of Wells nor his servants shall have any power at all over this monastery or its parochial churches" (Scott, p. 125). Cnut's privilege of 1032, apparently genuine, does not mention Wells by name but otherwise grants much the same rights as Edgar's, referring not only to the earlier three privileges above, but also to Glastonbury privileges granted by Centwine, Cuthred, Alfred, and Edward (Scott, p. 133). See further, Lesley Abrams, *Anglo-Saxon Glastonbury: Church and Endowment* (Woodbridge, Suffolk: Boydell, 1996), pp. 127-30.

[41] See Robinson, *Saxon Bishops of Wells*, pp. 45-52.

[42] For the dates of Æthelwine's abbacy and episcopacy, see Robinson, p. 50.

149 was written in the latter half of the tenth century — Gameson suggests a date in the 960s or 970s[43] —and came into Æthelweard's hands at some point before his 1018 donation. Had it been in Glastonbury six or more years before the donation, when Æthelwine may have been in training there, he might have written his name on the donation leaf before he went to Evesham and the manuscript went to Æthelweard — that is, before the 1018 donation. It is equally possible that his name appeared on the leaf after the donation — that is, sometime between 1022, when his episcopacy at Wells ended, and his death c. 1027.[44] William of Malmesbury's *Gestis pontificum* indicates that Æthelwine was ejected as Bishop in 1015-1016 and restored, and then ejected again, in 1022.[45] If this is the case, nearby Glastonbury would have served as a ready refuge for Æthelwine, particularly had he spent his earlier years there. Æthelwine may in fact have died at Glastonbury. A thirteenth-century Glastonbury obit-list refers, somewhat confusingly, to an "Æthelwine ealdorman and monk" (*Eilwinus dux et monachus*), obit 26 November.[46] Matthew Blows, the most recent editor of the list, believes that either the name Æthelwine or the title ealdorman is in error.[47] If the title is an error for bishop, then the most likely candidate for the Glastonbury burial is Æthelwine, former Bishop of Wells. And thus Æthelwine may have spent his last five years, from his second

---

[43] Gameson, "The Origin," p. 166.

[44] Æthelwine's death is tentatively assigned to 1027 by William G. Searle, *Anglo-Saxon Bishops, Kings and Nobles: The Succession of the Bishops and the Pedigrees of the Kings and Nobles* (Cambridge: Cambridge University Press, 1899), p. 93.

[45] Robinson (*Saxon Bishops of Wells*) makes no mention of Æthelwine's ejections but had apparently not seen William of Malmesbury's discussion of Bishop Æthelwine. The reference to the *Gestis Pontificum* and to dates of ejection are as cited in Searle, *Anglo-Saxon Bishops*, p. 93.

[46] The list, containing twenty-seven names, occurs on fol. 5v of London, British Library, Add. MS 17450.

[47] M. Blows, "A Glastonbury Obit-List," *The Archaeology and History of Glastonbury Abbey: Essays in Honour of the Ninetieth Birthday of C. A. Ralegh Radford*, ed. Lesley Abrams and James P. Carley (Woodbridge, Suffolk: Boydell, 1981), pp. 257-69, especially p. 267, item 18. Blows dates the list to c. 1239 (p. 257 n. 3) but suggests it is a copy of an earlier exemplar (p. 258).

ejection until his death, as a monk at Glastonbury.[48] If Lambeth 149 had been donated in 1018 to the monastery of St. Mary at Glastonbury, Æthelwine could have had ample opportunity to come into contact with it and inscribe his name therein sometime between 1022 and 1027, if not earlier.

A second possibility for the name on the donation page is Æthelwine "Dei Amicus," ealdorman of East Anglia 962-992, who might seem geographically unlikely to have had contact with a manuscript associated with the Southwest. His father, however, the powerful Æthelstan "Half King," was from a Wessex family with extensive estates principally in Somerset and Dorset.[49] Æthelstan was a close personal friend of Dunstan from early in Dunstan's abbacy at Glastonbury and later a political ally. (According to Dunstan's earliest biographer, the two men shared a vision, while riding together in 946, of King Edmund's death and coming political troubles.[50]) Glastonbury's earliest endowments under Dunstan, including all of Æthelstan's Somerset estates, came from Æthelstan himself or from his brothers.[51] Moreover, Æthelstan, who was virtual regent under Edmund the Elder and Eadred, appears to have had royal charters for Danelaw estates drawn up by a Glastonbury scribe under Dunstan's supervision.[52] In 957 Æth-

---

[48] Glastonbury was always eager to claim its monks who had gone on to assume abbacies, bishoprics, and the archbishopric. The standard early sources of Glastonbury history make no such claim for Æthelwine Bishop of Wells. It may be, however, that had Æthelwine been a troublesome bishop, as his two ejections might suggest, Glastonbury may have been reluctant to acknowledge him as one of its own.

[49] Cyril J. R. Hart, "Æthelstan 'Half King' and His Family," *Anglo-Saxon England 2* (1973), pp. 115-44, at p. 118.

[50] *Sancti Dunstani Vita, Auctore B.*, in William Stubbs, ed., *Memorials of Saint Dunstan: Archbishop of Canterbury* (London, 1874), pp. 44-46. The story is also told in the anonymous *Life of Oswald*; see Douglas Dales, *Dunstan: Saint and Statesman* (Cambridge: Lutterworth Press, 1988), p. 26.

[51] Hart, "Æthelstan 'Half King,'" pp. 119, 120, 124 and n.2 (but cf. Blows, "A Glastonbury Obit-List," p. 268 item 22).

[52] Cyril J. R. Hart, *The Early Charters of Northern England and the North Midlands* (Leicester: Leicester University Press, 1975), pp. 20-21; see also his "Æthelstan 'Half King,'" p. 124 n. 2.

elstan retired as a monk to Glastonbury,[53] bringing additional extensive benefactions,[54] and was buried there after his death. His son Æthelwine would almost certainly have attended the funeral. Æthelwine had been reared together with the young ætheling Edgar in the Half King's household, and as Cyril Hart says, "One cannot doubt that in their childhood both Edgar and Æthelwine came under the influence of Abbot Dunstan of Glastonbury."[55] Æthelwine was brought into the royal court shortly after Edgar's accession,[56] at about the same time Dunstan was appointed Archbishop of Canterbury (960), and succeeded to his father's earldom of East Anglia in 962. As Hart points out, however, Æthelwine continued to maintain close contacts with the monastery of Glastonbury in the Southwest.[57] He endowed Glastonbury with relics[58] and with "100 pounds worth of land and many other goods,"[59] and it was in Glastonbury, while attending another funeral c. 968, that he agreed to found a major monastery at Ramsey.[60] While it is normally assumed, based on *The Chronicle of Ramsey Abbey* and a Ramsey obit-list, that Æthelwine was interred at Ramsey,[61] William of Malmesbury's

---

[53] His retirement is usually given as 956, but see Abrams, *Anglo-Saxon Glastonbury*, p. 122 n. 7, where she thanks Simon Keynes for the revised date.

[54] Hart, "Æthelstan 'Half King,'" pp. 125-26.

[55] Hart, "Æthelstan 'Half King,'" p. 124.

[56] Hart, "Æthelstan 'Half King,'" p. 129.

[57] Hart, "Æthelstan 'Half King,'" p. 136.

[58] See John of Glastonbury's *Cronica sive Antiquitates Glastoniensis*, ed. James P. Carley, trans. D. Townsend, in *The Chronicle of Glastonbury Abbey* (Woodbridge, Suffolk: Boydell, 1985), pp. 20-23. The relics and their possible association with St. Guthlac are discussed further below.

[59] *De Antiquitate*, ed. Scott, p. 85 (the passage may be a later interpolation; see Scott, pp. 195-96). John of Glastonbury (ed. Carley, p. 31) gives the bequest as "a hundred allotments" of land.

[60] Hart, "Æthelstan 'Half King,'" pp. 136-37.

[61] *The Chronicle of Ramsey Abbey* is cited by Hart ("Æthelstan 'Half King,'" p. 135) in the edition by W. Macray, Rolls Series (1858), p. 101. The Ramsey obit-list is cited by Blows ("A Glastonbury Obit-List," p. 267) as it appears in John Leland's *De Rebus Britannicis Collectanea*, ed. T. Hearne, 2nd ed. (London, 1774), Vol. II, pp. 587-88.

De Antiquitate cites Æthelwine's name immediately after his father's as buried in Glastonbury.[62] A Glastonbury burial would account for the otherwise mysterious (or erroneous) reference in the Glastonbury obit-list to an "Æthelwine ealdorman and monk" and would suggest as well that, like his father, Æthelwine had at some point received the tonsure at Glastonbury.[63] Since Æthelwine died in 992, the name *æþel-wine*, if it refers to him, would likely have appeared on the leaf a good while before the 1018 donation, perhaps during one of Æthelwine's stays at Glastonbury. It is likewise possible, given the connection between Æthelstan Half King and the Glastonbury scriptorium, and Æthelwine's own association with Glastonbury, that Lambeth 149 was produced there and passed soon thereafter to father then son, or (as the date of the manuscript's production might suggest rather) directly to son.[64] A further link is provided in Hart's evidence of a family relationship between Ealdorman Æthelwine and the line of Ealdorman Æthelweard the donor.[65] Thus one might envision a chain of events in which Lambeth 149, originating in the Glastonbury scriptorium, came into the keeping of Æthelwine, who passed it on to his kinsman and contemporary Æthelweard the Chronicler, a patron of vernacular

---

[62] *De Antiquitate*, ed. Scott, p. 85. The reference to Æthelstan's and Æthelwine's Glastonbury interments is repeated in slightly different form in John of Glastonbury's *Cronica*, ed. Carley, p. 31.

[63] While Æthelwine may well have desired to be buried beside his father at Glastonbury, the evidence seems clearer for a burial at his own foundation at Ramsey. The dates for the burials do not agree (16 November at Glastonbury, 24 April at Ramsey), and I suspect with Blows ("A Glastonbury Obit-List," p. 267) that an error was made in the Glastonbury list or, more likely, its exemplar. It may be that Ealdorman Æthelwine was conflated therein with the Æthelwine monk at Glastonbury discussed below or with Ealdorman Æthelwine's father, who was indeed both ealdorman and monk. A similar error (or similar exemplar) may account for the references in *De Antiquitate* to Æthelwine's Glastonbury interment. That such errors were made, however (if indeed they were errors) nonetheless suggests that Glastonbury considered itself as having had a close association with Ealdorman Æthelwine.

[64] Æthelwine himself may have had charters drawn up, and celebrated, in the Glastonbury monastery; see n. 74, below.

[65] Hart, "Æthelstan 'Half King,'" p. 138; see also Hart's genealogical chart, p. 117.

190

literature and, like Æthelwine, an active participant in the monastic reform movement.[66] From there, as Flower had conjectured, the book would have passed through the family to the Chronicler's grandson-in-law, Æthelweard the donor.[67] If in the 1018 donation Æthelweard were then returning the Lambeth manuscript to Glastonbury, it would account for the presence on the donation leaf of *Aetheluvardus dux, monasterium sce marie,* and *æþelwine.*

A third possibility for the name on the donation page suggests a more direct connection between Lambeth 149 and Glastonbury. During the abbacy of Dunstan, his brother Wulfric served as manager of the monastery's many estates and amassed for himself property totaling at least 174 hides.[68] Wulfric died while Dunstan was still abbot and, according to the *De Antiquitate,* bequeathed several of his own estates directly to Glastonbury. Three other large estates owned by Wulfric — at Grittleton, Nettleton, and Horton — came to Glastonbury later through "his successor Æthelwine . . . when he donned the monastic habit" (*successor eius Aelwinus . . . assumpto habitu regulari*).[69] A later reference in the *De Antiquitate* makes it clear that it was at

---

[66] It is noteworthy that in 977 Dunstan, then Archbishop of Canterbury, witnessed a charter together with Ealdorman Æthelwine granting land in Cornwall to Æthelweard the Chronicler; see *English Historical Documents c. 500-1042,* ed. Dorothy Whitelock (New York: Eyre and Spottiswoode, 1955), pp. 522-23. On Æthelweard the Chronicler and his family, see Flower, "The Script," pp. 87-90, and *The Chronicle of Æthelweard,* ed. A. Campbell (London, 1962), pp. xii-vi.

[67] Flower, "The Script," p. 90. As discussed earlier, Flower does not propose a specific scriptorium of origin; he suggests only that the Lambeth MS (and the Exeter Book) may have been written for Æthelweard the Chronicler and passed through the family to his grandson-in-law, who donated it "possibly, but not certainly," to Crediton. It is possible also that at some point in the sequence Lambeth 149 passed through Canterbury; see n. 129, below.

[68] See N. Brooks, "The Career of St. Dunstan," *St Dunstan: His Life, Times and Cult,* ed. N. Ramsey, M. Sparks, and T. Tatton-Brown (Woodbridge, Suffolk: D. S. Brewer, 1992), pp. 1-23, at pp. 8-10, and Hart, *Early Charters of Northern England,* pp. 371-72.

[69] *De Antiquitate,* ed. Scott, pp. 114-15; see also pp. 118-19, 130-31, 144-45. On the delayed bequest (which apparently was made first to Wulfric's wife and brought into Glastonbury by Wulfric's *successor* after her death), see Abrams, *Anglo-Saxon Glastonbury,* pp. 132-34, 141, and 179-81.

Glastonbury that this Æthelwine became a monk.[70] In addition to the form *Ælwinus*, the monk's name occurs in the *De Antiquitate* also as *Ælwine*[71] and elsewhere as *Ælwinus*,[72] *Elswyne*,[73] and perhaps *Ælfwino*,[74] and thus his name is variously translated as *Æthelwine* and *Ælfwine*.[75] It is notable, however, that the name *ælwe* appears in the upper left corner of fol. 122v of Lambeth 149,[76] sixteen leaves before the *æþelwine* of the upper left of the donation page. It seems a distinct possibility that the marginal *ælwe* and *æþelwine* of Lambeth 149 refer to the same individual, and to the same Glastonbury monk whose name occurs in such similar forms elsewhere. William's reference to Æthelwine as *successor* to Wulfric may mean that he succeeded to Wulfric's position as estates manager at Glastonbury, that he was Wulfric's heir,

---

[70] See *De Antiquitate*, ed. Scott, p. 119.

[71] Scott, pp. 130, 144.

[72] In John of Glastonbury's *Cronica*, ed. Carley, p. 126; also genitive *Alwini*, p. 42.

[73] In the contents list of the otherwise lost *Liber Terrarem*, where he is also identified as Wulfric's *successor*; see Abrams, *Anglo-Saxon Glastonbury*, p. 132.

[74] In a 975 royal charter (S 802) recording a different land transfer made at the request of *uenerabili propinquo et monacho Ælfwino*, "the king's venerable kinsman and monk Ælfwine," and enacted at Glastonbury before a gathering of all its monks; see Simon Keynes, "The 'Dunstan B' Charters," *Anglo-Saxon England* 23 (1994), pp. 165-93, at pp. 179 and 192-93, who suggests that this monk might be identifiable with Wulfric's *successor* and thus with Dunstan's nephew (and thereby related in turn to the king). Ealdorman Æthelwine "Dei Amicus," however, also occurs as *Ælfwine* (and as *Ælfwynus* and *Ailwynus*; see Searle, *Onomasticon*, p. 27) and was likewise related to the royal household (see Hart, "Æthelstan 'Half King,'" p. 118), and so he may be the *Ælfwino* of the charter. That the transaction involves land in Shropshire, an area probably under Ealdorman Æthelwine's control, and that the charter is of the 'Dunstan B' type, with which Æthelwine's father is associated, might be taken as strengthening this possibility. But, as discussed earlier, if Ealdorman Æthelwine became a Glastonbury monk at some point, 975 would seem too early for him to have done so.

[75] As *Æthelwine* by Scott (ed., *De Antiquitate*) and Townsend (*Cronica*, ed. Carley); as *Ælfwine* by Abrams (*Anglo-Saxon Glastonbury*), Keynes ("'Dunstan B' Charters"), and Hart (*Early Charters of Northern England*).

[76] The name is mentioned only by James (*Lambeth Catalogue*, p. 238).

or that he was Wulfric's son (and thus Dunstan's nephew) — perhaps all three. Wulfric died probably in 951,[77] predeceasing Dunstan by some thirty years, and so apparently died an early death. If Æthelwine was his son, he may have been quite young when his father died and thus may have lived through the 1018 donation.[78] Had the donation been made to Glastonbury, Æthelwine could have placed his name in the manuscript shortly thereafter, an event made the more likely if Æthelwine succeeded also to his father's position as reeve and was in charge of more of Glastonbury's property than its estates. On the other hand, had Lambeth 149 been in Glastonbury before reaching its donor Æthelweard, Æthelwine's name may have been on the leaf already when the donation was made. By Ockham's razor, this Æthelwine — monk at Glastonbury and perhaps nephew to Dunstan and property manager of the monastery — is the most likely of the three Æthelwines to have his name in the Lambeth manuscript. At any event, a Glastonbury customary makes it certain that the feast of one Æthelwine — who might be any of the three —was being kept at Glastonbury by 1248 and probably long before.[79] And so it might be concluded that the marginal *æþelwine* of Lambeth 149 points toward Glastonbury as the home of the manuscript sometime before the donation, or its recipient in 1018, or both.

We can now return briefly to the manuscript's donor, Ealdorman Æthelweard, and to the remaining details of the donation colophon. No trace of Æthelweard seems to have survived from the period following his exile in 1020. But the same obit-list that records the Glastonbury burial of an Æthelwine also records the burial there of an

---

[77] Brooks, "Career of St Dunstan," p. 10.

[78] Æthelwine's youthfulness might explain why his father's estates at Grittleton, Nettleton, and Horton descended first to Æthelwine's mother and only later to Æthelwine, who then apparently transferred them to Glastonbury when he took the habit.

[79] The customary survives in Cambridge, Trinity College, MS R.5.33, datable to 1247/48, about eight years later than the Glastonbury obit-list. Æthelwine occurs among several pre- and post-Conquest monks and lay *benefactrices* listed for minor feast days. The customary is discussed by Blows ("A Glastonbury Obit-List," especially pp. 257-58 and notes 7 and 8) and Scott (*The Early History*, pp. 36-37).

Eilwardus abbas Glast., identifiable with the Æthelweard who served as abbot of Glastonbury c. 1024-1053.[80] Is it possible that Ealdorman Æthelweard returned from exile to the Southwest and took refuge in its foremost monastery at Glastonbury, received the tonsure, assumed the abbacy in 1024, and was buried there in 1053? Like Æthelwine, Abbot Æthelweard was honored at Glastonbury with a minor feast day in celebration of his death, probably because, as Blows suggests, he had been a benefactor of the monastery.[81] If Abbot Æthelweard is the same as the pre-exile Ealdorman Æthelweard, then we might suppose that one of his benefactions to Glastonbury had been Lambeth 149 and any other manuscripts he donated along with it.

The donation inscription concludes with the curious statement "And it came to pass therefore after the death of King Edmund that" and then stops mid-sentence. King Edmund is probably Edmund Ironside, who was buried at Glastonbury before its high altar[82] two years before the donation of the manuscripts, and thus this otherwise unaccountable reference may have been motivated by local pride in the king's recent interment there. If King Edmund is rather Edmund the Elder (obit 946), he too had been buried at Glastonbury, perhaps by Dunstan himself. One final detail concerning the donation inscription: the Latin names for Glastonbury I have found thus far run from 8 to 15 letters in length,[83] the most common, *Glastoniensis*, being 13; Old English forms range from 11 to 14 letters,[84] precisely the number Hill suggests are required for the blotted name of the town on the donation colophon.

---

[80] Blows, "A Glastonbury Obit-List," p. 267 item 16.

[81] Blows, p. 259. The *De Antiquitate* (ed. Scott, p. 135), however, speaks ill of Abbot Æthelweard, accusing him of confiscating for his private purposes the monastery's external estates. Æthelweard's apparent disloyalties to the monastery might be explicable if he came to Glastonbury late and with the experience of an ealdorman accustomed to dealings of the very sort that may have led to his exile.

[82] See *De Antiquitate*, ed. Scott, pp. 85, 133.

[83] *Glasteie, Glastonie, Glastonia, Glastingai, Glastonium, Glastoniensi, Glastingensi, Glestingensi, Glastoniensis, Glastoniensem, Glastoniensibus.*

[84] *Glastinbiry, Glastingebir', Glastingeberi, Glastingbury, Glastingaburi, Glastingebiry, Glastingabery, Glastingaberie, Glæstingeberig, Glæstyngabyrig.*

194

There are, then, some indications — an Æthelwine, an Ealdor-man Æthelweard, a King Edmund, and a monastery of St. Mary in a Southwestern town of the right length — that MS Lambeth 149 was donated to Glastonbury in 1018. Possibly the Exeter Book and Bodley 319, the third of the manuscripts originating in the same scriptorium, were donated along with it. As discussed above, however, it is also possible that Lambeth 149 had a pre-donation Glastonbury provenance. If it had in fact been written at Glastonbury and Æthelweard was later restoring it to its monastery of origin, then it is likewise possible that the Exeter Book and Bodley 319 simply remained at Glastonbury while Lambeth 149 was in Æthelweard's keeping. The three would thus be reunited at the Glastonbury library in 1018 when the Lambeth manuscript was returned. In either eventuality, the Exeter Book would have been in Glastonbury by 1018. And if Lambeth 149 had been written there, paleographical similarities would offer some assurance that the Exeter Book had been also. Gameson, in fact, notes in passing the possibility that Glastonbury produced the Exeter Book[85] but says also that, if it did, we are unlikely ever to know because of the paucity of clearly identifiable Glastonbury manuscripts.[86] Thus he discusses at greater length Christ Church, Canterbury, as the source of a number of related manuscripts and suggests that that center also may have produced the Exeter Book.[87] Evidence beyond that of Lambeth 149, however, suggests rather the Glastonbury origin.

Conner dates the Exeter Book to 950 x 970, others slightly later.[88] During the first six years of Conner's range, Dunstan was abbot

[85] Gameson, "The Origin," p. 179.

[86] Gameson, "The Origin," p. 181.

[87] Gameson, "The Origin," *passim* and p. 179. Gameson argues particularly that Conner's Group II manuscripts (see Figure 1, above) originated at Canterbury. According to Jane Rosenthal, David Dumville (in a letter to her of 16 August 1988) attributed the Exeter Book, Lambeth 149, and Bodley 319 to Canterbury; see her "The Pontifical of St Dunstan," *St Dunstan*, ed. Ramsey, Sparks, and Tatton-Brown, pp. 143-63, at 147-48.

[88] Conner, *Anglo-Saxon Exeter*, pp. 77, 80; Gameson dates it to the 960s or 970s ("The Origin," p. 160); Muir assigns it to c. 965-975 (*The Exeter Anthology*, Vol. I, p. 1); Flower places it "between 970 and 990, and rather early than late in that period" ("The Script," p. 89).

of Glastonbury; following the coronation of Eadwig he spent a year in exile, returning under Edgar in 957 for tours as Bishop of Worcester and then London and succeeding to the archbishopric at Canterbury in 960. It would appear, however, that he continued to control Glastonbury for a considerable time after his elevation,[89] and certainly his influence was felt there throughout the period that the Exeter Book was likely written.

The B. Life of Dunstan offers a glimpse of Glastonbury during this period.[90] Because of the number of Irish pilgrims on its staff, Glastonbury was sometimes known as "Little Ireland."[91] Irish monks provided Dunstan his earliest training in Glastonbury's pre-reform monastery, and in its library he read the works of Irish *peregrini*[92] attracted to the tomb of St. Patrick, legendary founder of Glastonbury, and to the relics and supposed graves of other Irish saints.[93] At Glaston-

[89] Brooks ("Career of St Dunstan," pp. 21-22) points out that no certain successor to Dunstan's abbacy at Glastonbury emerges until 974 and that charter evidence supports Dunstan's continued control.

[90] The B. Life (*Sancti Dunstani Vita, Auctore B.*) is the earliest of five medieval lives of Dunstan (all edited by Stubbs in *Memorials*), written c. 995 by a former member of Dunstan's retinue at Glastonbury; see Michael Lapidge, "B. and the *Vita S. Dunstani*," *St Dunstan*, ed. Ramsey, Sparks, and Tatton-Brown, pp. 247-59. Excerpts of B.'s decidedly difficult Latin are available in translation in Whitelock, *English Historical Documents*, pp. 826-31; summaries and interpretation can be found in Stubbs's Introduction (also collected and ed. by Arthur Hassall, *Historical Introduction to the Rolls Series* [New York: AMS Press, 1902]); J. Armitage Robinson, *The Times of Saint Dunstan* (Oxford: Clarendon, 1923); Eleanor S. Duckett, *Saint Dunstan of Canterbury: A Study of Monastic Reform in the Tenth Century* (London: Collins, 1955); Dales, *Dunstan: Saint and Statesman*; and Brooks, "Career of St Dunstan." A new edition with translation and commentary by Michael Lapidge and M. Winterbottom, *The Early Lives of Dunstan*, is forthcoming in the Oxford Medieval Texts series.

[91] Robinson, *Times of Saint Dunstan*, p. 101. The epithet, originally applied to the nearby dependency of Beckery, where Irish presence was particularly strong, seems to have spread to include Glastonbury as a whole.

[92] See Stubbs, *Memorials*, pp. 10-11; the relevant passage is translated by Whitelock in her *English Historical Documents*, pp. 826-27.

[93] On the Glastonbury cult of St. Patrick, see especially Lesley Abrams, "St Patrick and Glastonbury Abbey: *nihil ex nihilo fit?*" in David N. Dumville's *Saint Patrick, A.D. 493-1993* (Woodbridge, Suffolk: D. S. Brewer, 1993),

bury Dunstan cultivated the manuscript arts of writing (*scribendi*) and drawing (*pingendi*), became accomplished on the harp,[94] and developed "a fondness for the old Saxon songs."[95] (As a young man, Dunstan was dismissed from court and thrown in a muddy pond following rumors that rather than "learning from wholesome books and learned men" he had "learned the idlest poems of ancestral paganism and cultivated the worthless ditties of performers' incantations."[96]) Thus Irish influence, manuscript production, and vernacular poetry were part of the cultural mix at Glastonbury during Dunstan's youth.[97] When he later became abbot (c. 940), his reforms were comparatively mild[98] and, unlike most later reforming abbots, Dunstan seems not to have expelled clerics and

pp. 233-42. Particularly associated with Glastonbury are also the Irish saints Brigit and Indract; on the latter see Michael Lapidge, "The Cult of St. Indract at Glastonbury," *Ireland in Early Mediaeval Europe*, ed. Dorothy Whitelock, Rosamund McKitterick, and David Dumville (Cambridge: Cambridge University Press, 1982), pp. 179-212.

[94] See Stubbs, *Memorials*, p. 20.

[95] Robinson, *Times of Saint Dunstan*, p. 84; on Dunstan's knowledge of Old English poetry see also Duckett, *Saint Dunstan of Canterbury*, p. 38; James P. Carley, *Glastonbury Abbey: The Holy House at the Head of the Moors Adventurous* (Woodbridge, Suffolk: D. S. Brewer, 1998), p. 136; and Dales, *Dunstan: Saint and Statesman*, p. 19.

[96] My thanks to Timothy Graham for this translation of a difficult, and fascinating, passage in the B. Life (for the original, see Stubbs, *Memorials*, p. 11). Dunstan was also a student of Latin poetry and himself composed Latin verses; see Michael Lapidge, "The Hermeneutic Style in Tenth-Century Anglo-Latin Literature," *Anglo-Saxon England* 4 (1975), pp. 67-111, at pp. 95-97 and 108-11, and his "St Dunstan's Latin Poetry," *Anglia* 98 (1980), pp. 101-06.

[97] On the Glastonbury mixture of diverse cultural elements, see further C. H. Slover, "Glastonbury Abbey and the Fusing of English Literary Culture," *Speculum* 10 (1935), pp. 147-60.

[98] Stubbs's account of the softness of Dunstan's reforms (*Memorials*, pp. lxxxv-vi) remains standard and has been supported and supplemented in numerous more recent studies. See, e.g., T. Symons, "*Regularis Concordia*: History and Derivation," *Tenth-Century Studies: Essays in Commemoration of the Millennium of the Council of Winchester and Regularis Concordia*, ed. David Parsons (London: Phillimore, 1975), pp. 37-59 and 214-17, at p. 40; John Godfrey, *The Church in Anglo-Saxon England* (Cambridge: Cambridge University Press, 1962), p. 303; and Brooks, "Career of St Dunstan," p. 13.

other lay priests in favor of exclusively Benedictine regulars.[99] By the mid-tenth century, then, there was at Glastonbury a milieu that might well have allowed for collecting the sorts of secular poetry in the vernacular that predominate in the second half of the Exeter Book.

A conspicuous example is offered by the riddles that fill recto and verso of some twenty folios in this second half. It is difficult to imagine any other monastery, reformed under stricter dictates of spirituality and chastity, that would devote its resources to gathering almost a hundred such riddles, predominately secular, into an expensive manuscript, much less permit transcribing and reciting the several obscene ones. Dunstan, however, appears to have been amenable to such bawdry. His famous "Classbook" (Oxford, Bodleian Library, MS Auctarium F.4.32), which he had almost certainly owned and used at Glastonbury, contains Book I of Ovid's *Ars amatoria*, the only surviving copy of the work from Anglo-Saxon England; its final 26 lines were copied into the Classbook by Hand D, the scribe usually identified with Dunstan himself. While Book I of the *Ars amatoria* is generally inoffensive, it is likely, as Mildred Budny notes, that Dunstan had in his exemplar one or more of the more salacious subsequent Books.[100] Dunstan and Glastonbury seem also to have had a predilection for collecting anthologies of riddles. Oxford, Bodleian Library, MS Rawlinson C.697, containing glosses and variant readings in Hand D, is fairly certain to have been owned and studied closely by Dunstan;[101] it contains, along with two other works in Latin, Aldhelm's *Ænigmata*. Two

---

[99] See Brooks, p. 13; Lapidge has suggested that the author of the B. Life was one such layman and that the school at Glastonbury was readily accessible to non-ecclesiastics ("B. and the *Vita S. Dunstani*," p. 259).

[100] On the *Ars amatoria* and its continuation, see Mildred Budny, "'St Dunstan's Classbook' and Its Frontispiece: Dunstan's Portrait and Autograph," *St Dunstan*, ed. Ramsey, Sparks, and Tatton-Brown, pp. 103-42, at pp. 115 and 122. On the attribution of Hand D to Dunstan, see Budny, "Classbook," p. 136 and *passim*, and citations therein; see also T. A. M. Bishop, "An Early Example of Insular-Caroline," *Transactions of the Cambridge Bibliographical Society* 4 (1968), pp. 396-400.

[101] See Budny, "Classbook," p. 138, and Bishop, p. 399 and plate XXIXc. If, as seems probably, the hand is Dunstan's, it remains uncertain whether Dunstan had written in the manuscript (of continental origin) when he was at Glastonbury or Canterbury.

enigmas by Aldhelm — *Lorica* and *Creatura* — provided the source for Riddles 35 and 40 in the Exeter Book.[102] The 1247/48 catalogue of the Glastonbury library lists two other riddle collections, at least one of which probably survived from the pre-Conquest period. The first, containing *ænigmata multorum*, is now lost, and no evidence survives to suggest when it was written or which riddles it contained. The second, described as "old" (*vetust*), is cited in the catalogue as containing *ænigmata S. Aldelm*[103] but, as James Carley has shown, is probably identifiable with the *Aenigmata Simposii, Aldhelmi, Eusebi, Tautini* that John Leland saw at Glastonbury in the 1530s and that is identifiable in turn with London, British Library, Royal 12.C.23, dated to s. x/xi.[104] Three enigmas by Symphosius (*Simposii*) — *Tinea, Harundo,* and *Flumen et piscis* — provided the source for Riddles 47, 60, and 85 in the Exeter Book.

The first half of the Exeter Book comprises eight long poems, all on clearly Christian themes. The codex opens, appropriately enough, with *The Advent Lyrics (Christ I)*, which devotes two of its "O" antiphons to the Virgin Mary; Mary appears exclusively or prominently in four (numbers 2, 4, 7, and 9) of the twelve lyrics. Thus at Glastonbury's monastery of St. Mary, *The Advent Lyrics* might have been seen as a doubly appropriate opening to the volume. The last

---

[102] For identifications of source enigmas by Aldhelm and (below) by Symphosius, see Krapp and Dobbie's Notes in *The Exeter Book*, pp. 340 ff.

[103] For a reprint of Thomas Hearne's 1726 edition of the library catalogue, see T. W. Williams, *Somerset Mediæval Libraries* (Bristol, 1897), pp. 55-78; the manuscripts cited above are in Williams at pp. 70 and 72, respectively. The *ænigmata multorum*, which were apparently bound in with the Life of Guthlac mentioned below (and with other texts), are also cited in Bertram Colgrave, *Felix's Life of Saint Guthlac: Introduction, Text, Translation and Notes* (Cambridge: Cambridge University Press, 1956), p. 44.

[104] See James P. Carley, "John Leland and the Contents of English Pre-Dissolution Libraries: Glastonbury Abbey," *Scriptorium* 40 (1986), pp. 107-20, at pp. 116-17; and his "Two Pre-Conquest Manuscripts from Glastonbury Abbey," *Anglo-Saxon England* 16 (1987), pp. 197-212, at pp. 201-04. Carley's date accords with that in Helmut Gneuss, *Handlist of Anglo-Saxon Manuscripts: A List of Manuscripts and Manuscript Fragments Written or Owned in England up to 1100* (Tempe: Arizona Center for Medieval and Renaissance Studies, 2001), no. 478.

of the long poems in this half is Cynewulf's *Juliana*. A Glastonbury calendar roughly contemporary with the Exeter Book[105] indicates that the feast day of St. Juliana was celebrated there each February 16,[106] and an early eleventh-century copy of an anonymous *Passio S. Iulianae* (London, British Library, Harley MS 3020) has recently been assigned a Glastonbury provenance.[107]

Of particular note within this half are the two long poems on St. Guthlac (*Guthlac A* and *B*). Guthlac of Crowland was an East Anglian, not a Southwestern saint, and so it is surprising that he was one of only three English saints to be venerated in the highest order at

[105] The calendar, datable to c. 970 x 979, is in the Leofric Missal (discussed below) and printed in Francis Wormald, *English Kalendars before A.D. 1100*, Henry Bradshaw Soc. 72 (London: Harrison and Sons, 1934), pp. 44-55.

[106] Cecilia A. Hotchner, who first proposed in generalized form a Glastonbury origin for the Exeter Book, suggests that manuscripts of *Juliana* and *Christ II*, the second of Cynewulf's poems in the codex, might have come to Glastonbury from Lindisfarne at the same time that the relics of Aidan, Irish founder of Lindisfarne, and other northern saints were brought there; see her *Wessex and Old English Poetry, with Special Consideration of* The Ruin (New York, 1939), pp. 69-76, especially pp. 70-71. The suggestion might be more credible if one could accept her assumption that Cynewulf the poet was Cynewulf Bishop of Lindisfarne. On the transfer of Northumbrian relics to Glastonbury, see D. W. Rollason, *Saints and Relics in Anglo-Saxon England* (Oxford: Blackwell, 1989), p. 152. Two Glastonbury traditions survive in explanation of the translation of the northern saints: that their relics came to Glastonbury in 939-946 as spoils from King Edmund's northern military campaigns (the explanation accepted by Rollason) and that they were brought there for safekeeping during the Danish invasions; see Francis Wormald, "The Liturgical Calendar of Glastonbury Abbey," *Festschrift Bernhard Bischoff zu seinem 65. Geburtstag dargebracht von Freunden Kollegen and Schülern*, ed. Johanne Autenrieth and Franz Brunhölzl (Stuttgart: A Hiersemann, 1971), p. 343.

[107] See James P. Carley, "More Pre-Conquest Manuscripts from Glastonbury Abbey," *Anglo-Saxon England* 23 (1994), pp. 265-81, at pp. 277-79. The *Passio S. Iulianae* provided the Latin source for Cynewulf's *Juliana*. While Juliana is normally celebrated on February 16, the version of the *passio* in Harley 3020 gives her commemoration as February 13. The Harley version thus belongs to a family of recensions different from that probably used by Cynewulf, on which see Lapidge, "Cynewulf and the *Passio S. Iulianae*," *Unlocking the Wordhord: Anglo-Saxon Studies in Memory of Edward B. Irving, Jr*, ed. Mark C. Amodio and Katherine O'Brien O'Keeffe (Toronto: University of Toronto Press, 2003), pp. 147-55.

Glastonbury.[108] As Carley explains, however, St. Guthlac was apparently confused at Glastonbury with one of its own early abbots, also named Guthlac (c. 824-851),[109] and thus St. Guthlac, like St. Patrick, came to be culted there.[110] Bertram Colgrave believes that some of the remains of St. Guthlac may have arrived at Glastonbury sometime before 970 x 979.[111] Thus it would seem a good possibility that these arrived among the relics mentioned above given to Glastonbury by the East Anglian ealdormen Æthelstan Half King and his son Æthelwine. Before his retirement to Glastonbury in 957, Æthelstan lived probably on the edge of the fens not far from Guthlac's hermitage in Crowland, and Æthelwine, considered Crowland Abbey's "patron and protector," provided the land for the refoundation of that institution 974 x 984.[112] The ealdormen, then, with their immediate connections to Crowland on the one hand and close ties to Dunstan and Glastonbury on the other, may have been endowing a Guthlac cult developing at Glastonbury at about the time the Exeter Book was written. The veneration of Guthlac was to spread throughout the South but appears to have been cultivated particularly at Glastonbury. An additional shrine to Guthlac was donated to Glastonbury in 1045,[113] and eventually Glastonbury would claim to hold *magna pars Sancti Gutlaci anachorite*.[114] One of

---

[108] He is ranked along with Cuthbert and Augustine in the Glastonbury calendar in the Leofric Missal; see Wormald, *English Kalendars*, pp. 46, 47, 48.

[109] William of Malmesbury mentions briefly an Abbot Guthlac (*Cuthlac abbas*) who in 824 sold a parcel of land at *Brunham* (apparently owned privately) and from the proceeds of 500 *solidi* gave 300 to the monks at Glastonbury; Guthlac seems to have been succeeded as abbot by Ealmund in 851 (see *De Antiquitate*, ed. Scott, pp. 110-13).

[110] Carley, *Glastonbury Abbey*, pp. 8-9; and Carley, ed., *Cronica*, p. 275 n. 31.

[111] Colgrave, *Felix's Life of Saint Guthlac*, p. 9.

[112] Hart, "Æthelstan 'Half King,'" pp. 122, 137.

[113] See Scott, ed., *De Antiquitate*, pp. 139-40. The shrine was given to Glastonbury, along with shrines of George and Oswald, by Brihtwold, a Glastonbury monk and Bishop of Ramsbury, apparently upon Brihtwold's burial at Glastonbury in 1045.

[114] John of Glastonbury's *Cronica* (ed. Carley, p. 18) attributes a large gift of Guthlac's remains to Henry of Blois, Bishop of Winchester.

Glastonbury's island dependencies, possibly Marchey, more probably Nyland, held a chapel dedicated to St. Guthlac.[115] Three lives of St. Guthlac, one of them containing also the *ænigmata multorum* noted above, are listed in the 1247/48 inventory of the Glastonbury library;[116] John Leland recorded that he saw a Life of Guthlac that he thought was by Bede in the Glastonbury library.[117] In actuality this latter was probably a copy of Felix's Latin *Vita Sancti Guthlac* (c. 714),[118] the source for *Guthlac B* of the Exeter Book.

The immediately preceding *Guthlac A* has no known direct source in the traditional sense; a recent article by Patrick Conner, however, finds in it the strong influence of the *Regula Sancti Benedictii* and Smaragdus's *Expositio Regulam Sancti Benedicti* and thus dates its composition to the time of the tenth-century reforms and specifically to a period contemporary with the compilation of the Exeter Book.[119] (Conner sees the poem as offering a model for the individual soul struggling to live the monastic life under a new order.) While Benedict's *Regula* might have been found in virtually any reformed monastery, Smaragdus's *Expositio* appears to have been somewhat rarer. I have been able to identify only two extant pre-Conquest copies: one — Paris, Bibliothèque Nationale, lat. 4210 — is unattributed and may be too late to have influenced the Exeter Book poem;[120] the other —

---

[115] Philip A. Rahtz and S. M. Hirst, *Beckery Chapel, Glastonbury, 1967-8* (Glastonbury, 1974), pp. 11-12.

[116] See Williams, *Somerset Mediæval Libraries*, p. 70; the three Glastonbury lives, as they appear in the 1247/48 catalogue, are listed also in Colgrave, *Felix's Life of Saint Guthlac*, p. 44, and Carley, "Two Pre-Conquest Manuscripts," p. 201.

[117] J. Leland, *Collectanea*, Vol. 3, p. 154; cited by Carley, ed., *Cronica*, p. 275 n. 31.

[118] Carley, "John Leland," p. 114, item 12; see also Carley, "Two Pre-Conquest Manuscripts," p. 201 n. 17.

[119] Patrick W. Conner, "Source Studies, The Old English *Guthlac A* and the English Benedictine Reformation," *Revue bénédictine* 103 (1993), pp. 380-413; he suggests a date of composition in the late 960s (p. 409). See also Conner's *Anglo-Saxon Exeter*, pp. 162-63.

[120] Helmut Gneuss dates the manuscript s. x/xi (*Handlist*, no. 883) and accepts T. A. M. Bishop's assignment of Fécamp as a provenance; Bishop, however, had dated the manuscript to the tenth century (see his *English Caroline Minuscule* [Oxford: Clarendon, 1971], p. 2).

Cambridge, Cambridge University Library, Ee.2.4 — contains Hand D and was probably used by Dunstan at Glastonbury (and may have been transcribed there) not long after 943.[121] In a complementary study of *Guthlac A*, Christopher A. Jones, while stopping short of embracing fully a tenth-century composition, emphasizes the relevance of the poem's themes to recently reformed monasteries of the period and suggests that it may have been written to appeal especially to the monks of a particular (unspecified) monastery attempting to appropriate Guthlac as its own.[122] Jones points out that among the poem's epithets for its hero are *foregenga*, which can in a monastic setting mean "forerunner," and *hyrde*, which can mean "pastor" or "abbot."[123] At Glastonbury the terms would undoubtedly have reinforced the monastery's association of its own Abbot Guthlac of about a century earlier with the St. Guthlac chronicled in the poem. While Felix's *Vita* repeatedly identifies Crowland as the locus of its action, *Guthlac A* leaves the setting unspecified, allowing an audience to make its own associations.[124] The poem's topography would have been particularly suggestive for Glastonbury monks. In the Exeter Book, Guthlac erects an isolated home on one of the green hills (*grene beorgas*) in the fenlands (*mearclond, westen*). Glastonbury's Tor, rising several hundred feet above the monastery, looked down over a series of green hills to the surrounding Somerset fenlands below. I do not suggest that either of the Guthlac poems had been written at or for Glastonbury, but only that both of them — *Guthlac A* in particular — would have evoked in Glastonbury monks keen feelings of identification and a sense that the poems concerned one of their own forebears. And thus a compilation of the

---

[121] Also fols. 1, 1*, and 2 of Oxford, Bodleian Library, MS lat. theol. c. On the manuscript see Gneuss, *Handlist*, no. 3; Bishop, *English Caroline Minuscule*, p. 2, and Bishop, "Insular- Caroline," pp. 396-400; and Budny, "Classbook," p. 137.

[122] Christopher A. Jones, "Envisioning the *Cenobium* in the Old English *Guthlac A*," *Mediaeval Studies* 57 (1995), pp. 259-91, especially pp. 269 and 271.

[123] Jones, p. 279.

[124] As Jones suggests (pp. 260-61), *Guthlac A* omits any mention of Repton, where, as Felix's *Vita* recounts, Guthlac received the tonsure and served for two years before departing for Crowland.

Exeter Book at Glastonbury might explain why the Guthlac poems, appearing immediately after the opening poems to Christ, receive pride of place in the codex.

A fire swept Glastonbury in 1184, destroying many of its pre-Conquest manuscripts; perhaps as many as a thousand more volumes were lost in the Dissolution.[125] Some managed to survive both devastations, however, whether through the rescuing efforts of monks,[126] through Glastonbury's earlier donations to other monasteries,[127] or through Dunstan's having brought them to Worcester,[128] London, or Canterbury.[129] And while we thus have scant paleographical data to aid

---

[125] On the Glastonbury library and the tragedies that befell it, see Carley, *Glastonbury Abbey*, pp. 132-44, and the citations therein.

[126] This was evidently the case with Dunstan's "Classbook," which appears to have remained at Glastonbury until at least the Dissolution; see Budny, "Classbook," p. 124.

[127] This may have occurred with Cambridge, Corpus Christi College, MS 183, written 934 x 939 and containing a copy of Bede's *Vita S. Cuthberti* and other texts related to Cuthbert; it was probably commissioned by King Æthelstan and presented by him to the community of St. Cuthbert at Chester-le-Street. Simon Keynes sees a Glastonbury origin for the manuscript as a "reasonable possibility"; David Dumville terms a Glastonbury origin "most likely." See Keynes, "King Æthelstan's Books," *Learning and Literature in Anglo-Saxon England*, ed. Lapidge and Gneuss, pp. 143-201, at p. 184; and Dumville, "English Square Minuscule: The Background and Earliest Phases," p. 174. (But see also Dumville's retreat from this attribution in his "English Square Minuscule Script: The Mid-Century Phases," *Anglo-Saxon England* 23 [1994], pp. 133-64, at p. 136 n. 18.) It is possible that Bodley 319, which may have been used at Salisbury c. 1100 (see Gameson, "The Origin," pp. 169-70), also owes its survival to a Glastonbury donation.

[128] Oxford, Bodleian Library, Hatton 30 contains the inscription *Dunstan abbas hunc libellum scribere iussitis* and is almost certain to have been written in Glastonbury during Dunstan's abbacy; it was in Worcester probably shortly thereafter, and as Dumville says, "It is a reasonable probability that it came with or to Dunstan when (after his continental exile) he was bishop of Worcester in 957 x 959, although other and later routes cannot of course be ruled out" ("English Caroline Script: The Mid-Century Phases," p. 149).

[129] The 'Utrecht Psalter' (London, British Library, Harley MS 603), from Reims, came to England probably during the tenth century and was in Canterbury during the eleventh. It has been suggested that it may have served as a model for the illustrations of Christ in Dunstan's "Classbook" and that it therefore "may have passed through Glastonbury on its way

in identifying other Glastonbury manuscripts, there seems a strong possibility that, as John Higgitt has argued, several texts of uncertain origin or assigned elsewhere on questionable grounds had been produced at Glastonbury.[130] The limited paleographical evidence supports the suggestion that the Exeter Book, Lambeth 149, and Bodley 319 are among these.

In his meticulous analysis of the script of these three manuscripts, Conner compares individual letter formations to those of thirty other tenth-century manuscripts and inscriptions, including two manuscripts of probably Glastonbury origin: Cambridge, Corpus Christi College 183 and Oxford, Bodleian Library, Hatton 30.[131] These two, while constituting a small percentage of the base of comparison, show a remarkably high incidence of correspondence with formations in the Exeter Book. Congruence is especially apparent in many of the more distinctive morphologies of the Exeter Book: the Form II square *a* in combination with the older *oc* form (in CCCC 183); the tall *i* (in Hatton 30); the *o* with tendencies toward pointing at the bottom and a hook at the left shoulder (an especially close form in Hatton 30); the *p* with a curling bow or projecting serif (a close match in Hatton 30); the *t* with cross-stroke extended to the left in initial position and, in final position, a concluding curl and dot (both forms in CCCC 183); and the *u* with wedged tops and concluding serif at the line (earliest

---

to Canterbury"; see J. Higgitt, "Glastonbury, Dunstan, Monasticism and Manuscripts," *Art History* 2 (1979), pp. 279 and 282. If Gameson is correct in suggesting that corrections to Lambeth 149 were made at Canterbury ("The Origin," p. 179), it may be that that manuscript likewise traveled from Glastonbury to Canterbury before coming into Ealdorman Æthelweard's hands sometime before 1018.

[130] Higgitt, pp. 275-90.

[131] On these two manuscripts, see notes 127 and 128, above. For Conner's comparison of forms, see *Anglo-Saxon Exeter*, pp. 60-76, where he refers to CCCC 183 as "Æthelstan 934 x 939" and to Hatton 30 as "Glastonbury Augustine 940 x 957." (Through an apparent misprint on pp. 56-57, two differing referents for "Æthelstan 934 x 939" are given; I have tried to take the misprint into account in the following discussion.) Conner's comparisons to Glastonbury manuscripts are based on the few plates available in print; a larger sampling of the manuscripts in full might, of course, have yielded greater correspondences in paleographical features.

forms in Hatton 30). Such correspondences should not be overstated: a glance at the published plates ensures that in general aspect and ductus the scripts of these two manuscripts are different from that of the Exeter Book.[132] And those rare features of the Exeter Book — the hairline ticks that begin the top strokes of *g* and *t*, and the horizontal stroke bowing over and completing the bowl of the *d* then ending in a dot — are nowhere to be found in manuscripts attributed to Glastonbury.

Nonetheless, the similarities between Glastonbury texts and the Exeter Book apparently lie behind Conner's most specific proposal for the origin of the Exeter Book. As Conner notes, the Exeter monastery was reformed by Abbot Sidemann, who arrived in Exeter from his former monastery of Glastonbury, together with a team of other monks from Glastonbury, in 968. Conner thus suggests that the Exeter Book was written at Exeter by one of these Glastonbury monks, if not by Sidemann himself.[133] As discussed above, however, there are difficulties in locating the Exeter Book at Exeter before 1050, and the theory of a Glastonbury-trained scribe working at Exeter encounters a further problem. Conner's *terminus ante quem* of 970 for the Exeter Book would leave two years following Sidemann's arrival for Exeter to compile and transcribe the volume, and it seems unlikely that the monastery, in the early throes of refoundation, would devote its scriptorium and the talents of a gifted scribe to producing a large volume of vernacular secular poetry (including obscene riddles) in lieu of the essential texts of the reform movement. It is far easier to suppose that

---

[132] For CCCC 183, see Keynes, "King Æthelstan's Books," plate X, and, especially, Mildred Budny, *Insular, Anglo-Saxon, and Early Anglo-Norman Manuscript Art at Corpus Christi College, Cambridge: An Illustrated Catalogue* (Kalamazoo, MI: Medieval Institute Publications, 1997), Vol. II: *Plates*, plates 110-52. For Hatton 30, see Budny, "Classbook," plate 8f, and Andrew G. Watson, *Catalogue of Dated and Datable Manuscripts c. 435-1600 in Oxford Libraries* (Oxford: Clarendon, 1984), Vol. II, plate 14. Humphrey Wanley's *Book of Specimens* (Longleat House, MS 345), containing a brief but strikingly accurate imitation of the script of Hatton 30, was recently discovered by Simon Keynes and reproduced as part of his paper, "Humphrey Wanley's 'Book of Specimens,'" The 33rd International Congress on Medieval Studies, Kalamazoo, 8 May 1998.

[133] Conner, *Anglo-Saxon Exeter*, p. 85.

Glastonbury, which had already a well established library of ecclesiastical and patristic works, had the leisure and resources to produce a poetry book and that Glastonbury itself was responsible for the similarity in letter forms in the Exeter Book, CCCC 183, and Hatton 30.[134]

Among the manuscripts that Gameson compares to the Exeter Book is Cambridge, Corpus Christi College, MS 57, containing a *Regula sancti Benedicti*, Usuard's *Martyrologium*, and Smaragdus's *Diadema monachorum*. Written c. 1000, by which time "the life seems to have gone out of the script,"[135] the volume nonetheless shows a close paleographical resemblance to the Exeter Book, in letter formations as well as in general aspect, display scripts, and decoration.[136] As two entries on fol. 94v make certain, CCCC 57 was at Abingdon by the 1040s; however, while Canterbury and (especially) Abingdon are strong candidates, its place of origin remains unknown, and the fact that its single scribe used throughout a traditional square minuscule rather than the English Caroline minuscule then standard for Latin texts at Abingdon might be taken to argue against production there.[137] The manuscript

---

[134] Conner (*Anglo-Saxon Exeter*, pp. 85-86) raises two main objections to a Glastonbury origin. He argues first that a Glastonbury scribe would have shown more influence of the emerging Caroline minuscule, which appears rarely (if at all) in the Exeter Book. The same objection might be made, of course, to Conner's own theory that a Glastonbury-trained scribe wrote the codex in Exeter. Moreover, Dumville has argued that the birthplace of the English form of Caroline minuscule was not Glastonbury, as T. A. M. Bishop had believed, but Canterbury ("English Square Minuscule Script: The Mid-Century Phases," pp. 151-52; Dumville also refers there to his *English Caroline Script*, ch. 3). And thus there is no necessity that a Glastonbury scribe exhibit Caroline features, particularly if his style was intentionally archaic. Conner's second objection is that Glastonbury shows no evidence of producing texts in the vernacular. I would note again, however, the paucity of surviving Glastonbury manuscripts and would refer to C. Hohler's suggestion (discussed below) that an Old English copy of Bede's *Ecclesiastical History* was written at Glastonbury. Moreover, I would suggest that Glastonbury's evident interest in Latin secular literature outweighs its lack of surviving manuscripts in English.

[135] Gameson, "The Origin," p. 176.

[136] Gameson, "The Origin," pp. 175-76.

[137] For a thorough description of the manuscript, with analyses of contents, codicology and script, origins, and medieval uses, see Timothy Graham, "Cambridge, Corpus Christi College 57 and Its Anglo-Saxon Users," *Anglo-Saxon Manuscripts and Their Heritage*, ed. Philip Pulsiano and Elaine M. Treharne (Aldershot and Brookfield, VT: Ashgate, 1998), pp. 21-69 and plates 1-10. I thank Professor Graham for allowing me to use a pre-publication copy of this article for the present study.

copy of the *Martyrologium* contains Usuard's own entry for St. Patrick at 17 March. As Dumville points out, however, among the several interpolations in the *Martyrologium* is another entry for Patrick, this one under 24 August, which Dumville translates as follows:

> In Ireland the holy abbot Patricius and Gildardus the confessor. Patrick is said to have been the first teacher of the Irish; but, because he could not discipline them, he departed on pilgrimage. He came to Glastonbury Abbey and, growing famous for his miraculous powers, ended his life there. Even to the present his corporeal relics are seen to attest that.[138]

Although the addition gives quite clearly the Glastonbury view of Patrick, Dumville declines to assign it a locale or date pending further study. Likewise, on so little evidence, CCCC 57 in its entirety certainly cannot be assigned either a Glastonbury provenance or origin, but it might be suggested that Glastonbury be added to the list of possible houses when such questions are considered. At the least, it seems clear that the manuscript shows Glastonbury influence in the interpolated entry for Patrick, and so it is possible that Glastonbury may likewise have influenced its script. Abingdon was reformed by Æthelwold, who had trained as a monk under Dunstan in Glastonbury and who probably brought with him to Abingdon a Glastonbury style of handwriting or Glastonbury texts for imitation, the influence of which might still have been felt at Abingdon late in the tenth century when CCCC 57 was probably written. And so there seems some possibility that an insular square minuscule with a clear affinity to that of the Exeter Book was being written at Glastonbury earlier in the century.

If, as suggested by the historical and literary evidence and supported by the limited paleographical data available, the Exeter Book and Lambeth 149 were written at Glastonbury, and were there together in 1018 when Æthelweard donated the latter, how then did they get to Exeter before 1072 in time for Leofric's inventory? For nineteen of Leofric's twenty-two years as Bishop of Exeter, Æthelnoth was Abbot of Glastonbury (1053-1077). According to William of Malmesbury, Æthelnoth sold off enough church treasure to precipitate the eleventh-century decline of the monastery at Glastonbury.[139] An estate at

---

[138] David Dumville, "St. Patrick in an Anglo-Saxon Martyrology," in his *Saint Patrick*, pp. 243-44, at p. 244.

[139] *De Antiquitate*, ed. Scott, pp. 134-35.

Culmstock that Leofric acquired (or reacquired) for Exeter had earlier belonged to Glastonbury, and it appears likely that Leofric purchased it from either Æthelnoth's predecessor or Æthelnoth himself.[140] And, as itemized below, many of the treasures that William lists as sold by Æthelnoth show striking correspondences to items the Exeter inventory lists as acquired by Leofric.

Table 1: Glastonbury Sales and Exeter Purchases

Sold by Æthelnoth at Glastonbury[141]	*Purchased by Leofric for Exeter*[142]
2 gospel-books	2 great ornamented gospel-books[143]
1 altar worth 20 marks	1 ornamented altar
1 wonderfully large censer of gold and silver	1 silver incense boat with 1 silver incense spoon
1 processional cross	2 great ornamented crosses
25 other crosses	2 episcopal crosses
	2 little silver pendant crosses

[140] Leofric's inventory cites Culmstock as the first of Exeter's lost estates restored by Leofric (see Conner, *Anglo-Saxon Exeter*, p. 231 §3); it was in Leofric's possession by 1066. Glastonbury appears to have owned substantial lands in Culmstock well into the tenth century, though the matter is uncertain; see Abrams, *Anglo-Saxon Glastonbury*, pp. 101-03, for a full discussion. (The view that the property came to Exeter during Æthelstan's reign [Förster, "The Donations," p. 18, n. 21] is based on a charter forged in the time of Leofric.) If Leofric acquired the property early in his tenure, he may have done so from Æthelnoth's predecessor, Æthelweard (1024-1053), who William says "confiscated lands outside the church" while Æthelnoth "removed ornaments from within it" (*De Antiquitate*, ed. Scott, p. 135).

[141] *De Antiquitate* (ed. and trans. Scott), p. 139.

[142] Trans. Conner, *Anglo-Saxon Exeter*, pp. 231-33 §7; details on vestments by Förster, "The Donations," p. 22 n. 51.

[143] One of these is almost certainly the 'Bodleian Gospels' (Oxford, Bodleian Library, MS Auctarium D.2.16); see Förster, "The Donations," p. 21 n. 46.

Sold by Æthelnoth at Glastonbury	Purchased by Leofric for Exeter
1 chalice of 20 marks of silver and 4 of gold	5 silver chalices
1 chalice of less weight but greater value	
other ornaments of gold and silver	2 ornamented cruets
	4 ornamented horns
	1 silver pipe [etc.]
1 precious alb of silk 19 copes with palls . . . with gold & gems 1 stole 1 chasuble 1 maniple	5 full sets of mass-vestments [5 albs, 5 amices, 5 girdles, 5 stoles, 5 chasubles 5 maniples]
2 candlesticks[144]	2 great ornamental candlesticks

We may never know if any of these items were identical, but clearly, Glastonbury was selling when Exeter was buying. It has been suggested that the account of plundering from Glastonbury may include only those items maintained in its treasury,[145] and so an unknown

[144] The wording of the *De Antiquitate* makes it uncertain that Glastonbury sold these candlesticks. They are listed after the items above and along with other property that appears to have been in Glastonbury's possession when William was writing. The same situation obtains with Glastonbury's shrines to saints Guthlac, George, and Oswald; although Leofric's inventory cites "three ornamented reliquaries," William's quotation of the verses on the Glastonbury shrines would seem to indicate that he had seen them and that they should not therefore be identified with those Leofric purchased.

[145] Higgitt, "Glastonbury," p. 276. Higgitt is apparently referring to the passage in *De Antiquitate* that provides the listing above. This passage, it should be added, is concerned only with the benefactions of Brihtwold, Glastonbury monk and bishop of Ramsbury, and the loss of many of them through Æthelnoth. It is likely that, if Æthelnoth's plundering led to the decline of Glastonbury, he sold off far more monastic property than the items listed by William.

number of other items, in particular volumes beyond the two gospel books listed above, may have been lost through Æthelnoth. There seems some likelihood that at least two of Leofric's books came from Glastonbury. The first, the famous Leofric Missal (Oxford, Bodleian Library, MS Bodley 579), is generally assigned a Glastonbury provenance in the mid to late tenth century; it appears in the following century in Leofric's inventory. Precisely how and when the Leofric Missal came to Exeter is uncertain, but it would seem quite possible that Leofric acquired it, too, from Æthelnoth.[146]

The second volume, now Cambridge, Corpus Christi College, MS 41, was omitted from the Exeter donation list, but since it bears

---

[146] Of continental origin, the Leofric Missal became an amalgam of materials written or stitched in in England at various times and places. It has thus a gnarled history that poses problems for dating and tracing. It is generally agreed that the volume was in Glastonbury by c. 979, when three gatherings containing a Glastonbury calendar and associated tables were added. Its whereabouts thereafter are unknown until its appearance in the Exeter inventory of c. 1072, which specifies it as one of Leofric's acquisitions. In her unpublished dissertation, E. M. Drage argues that the Leofric Missal was in Exeter before the time of Leofric (see her "Bishop Leofric and the Exeter Cathedral Chapter, 1050-1072: A Reassessment of the Manuscript Evidence" [University of Oxford, 1978], pp. 71-141; my citations are those of Conner, *Anglo-Saxon Exeter*, p. 18 n. 49). Conner follows with the theory that the missal's Glastonbury materials were either copied or bound in not at Glastonbury but at Exeter, sometime after 968, when Exeter was refounded by Glastonbury monks (*Anglo-Saxon Exeter*, p. 18). (For Conner's more recent work on the early provenance of the Leofric Missal, see his "Exeter's Relics, Exeter's Books," *passim*.) Förster had thought that Leofric brought the volume directly from the continent to Exeter ("The Donations," p. 25 n. 77), and Dumville would place it at Canterbury and then Tavistock before its arrival at Exeter (see his *Liturgy and the Ecclesiastical History of Late Anglo-Saxon England: Four Studies*, Studies in Anglo-Saxon History 5 [Woodbridge, Suffolk: D. S. Brewer, 1992], pp. 39-65, and briefer references in his "English Square Minuscule Script: The Mid-Century Phases," pp. 143-44 and 149). I have followed the traditional view of a Glastonbury provenance, on which see R. Deshman, "The Leofric Missal and Tenth-Century Art," *Anglo-Saxon England* 6 (1967), pp. 145-73; Higgitt, "Glastonbury," pp. 277-78 and 281-82; and C. E. Hohler, "Some Service-Books of the Later Saxon Church," *Tenth-Century Studies*, ed. Parsons, pp. 60-83 and 217-27, at pp. 69-70 and 78-80. The missal contains Exeter records and is probably one of the two *fulle mæssebec* in Leofric's inventory (see Conner, *Anglo-Saxon Exeter*, p. 232 '9).

an inscription documenting Leofric's gift of the volume to Exeter, it was undoubtedly in the Exeter monastery by 1072. A working copy in English of Bede's *Ecclesiastical History*, the manuscript has unusually wide margins that allowed a slightly later hand to archive a wide variety of homilies, liturgical materials, poetic charms in Latin and Old English, and ninety-three lines of the Old English poem *Solomon and Saturn*.[147] The main Bede text was written in a Southern scriptorium in the first half of the eleventh century;[148] the marginal texts were probably all added before mid-century and thus before Leofric found and brought the volume to Exeter sometime after 1050.[149] The question thus arises again: where had Leofric found it? One the basis of the

[147] Descriptions of the manuscript can be found in N. R. Ker, *Catalogue of Manuscripts Containing Anglo-Saxon* (Oxford: Clarendon, 1957), pp. 43-45; M. R. James, *A Descriptive Catalogue of the Manuscripts in the Library of Corpus Christi College Cambridge* (Cambridge: Cambridge University Press, 1912), Vol. I, no. 41; Budny, *Catalogue*, Vol. I: *Text*, pp. 501-13 ff.; and in three studies by R. J. S. Grant: *Cambridge, Corpus Christi College 41: The Loricas and the Missal* (Amsterdam: Rodopi, 1978); *Three Homilies from Cambridge, Corpus Christi College 41: The Assumption, St Michael and the Passion* (Ottawa: Tecumseh Press, 1982); and "Description of Cambridge, Corpus Christi College, MS 41," forthcoming in *Anglo-Saxon Manuscripts in Microfiche Facsimile*, ed. A. N. Doane and Philip Pulsiano (Binghamton: State University of New York Press, 1994 ff.). For a study of the first sixteen pages of the volume, see Sarah Larratt Keefer, "Margin as Archive: The Liturgical Marginalia of a Manuscript of the Old English Bede," *Traditio* 51 (1996), pp. 147-77.

[148] Ker, *Catalogue*, pp. 43-45; the place and date are accepted by Budny, *Catalogue*, Vol. I, p. 507, and Grant, "Description."

[149] Grant ("Description") says, "The greatest likelihood is that the additional matter was already in the margins when Leofric obtained the manuscript . . . ." Budny (*Catalogue*, Vol. I, p. 509) is more cautious, noting the possibility that Leofric may have obtained the volume while he was still at Crediton (1046-1050) and suggesting that it therefore "may have acquired some or many of its additions while it belonged to Leofric before coming to Exeter." No evidence is available to support the theory of a Crediton provenance, however, and that CCCC 41 does not appear in Leofric's inventory (1069 x 1072) might indicate that Leofric came by it late, after the inventory had been completed.

sorts of liturgical materials entered and the appearance of four stanzas from St. Sechnall's hymn to St. Patrick, Christopher Hohler attributes the marginalia to a secular priest living "somewhere near the obvious centre of the cultus of St. Patrick in England (namely Glastonbury)."[150] It might be added that in the margin's charm against theft of cattle appears an invocation not only to St. Patrick but also to Brigit, the Irish saint whose relics Glastonbury claimed and who was said to have lived for a period on Glastonbury's island of Beckery.[151] (If, as Hohler suggests, the marginalia were entered by the priest at a small minster or, as several have proposed, the manuscript proper originated in a provincial center,[152] Beckery — about a mile from Glastonbury — would seem a most likely candidate.) In fact, as Raymond Grant has noted, Irish influence is also to be found in *Solomon and Saturn* and in all six homilies of the margin,[153] an influence that might be traceable to the Irish monks at Glastonbury. The second of the marginal homilies, on the assumption of Mary, was probably read aloud at the Feast of the Assumption, an occasion of particular importance at Glastonbury. William of Malmesbury lists the feast adjacent to those for Mary's nativity and the dedication of the church as three of the six special festivals at which Glastonbury monks were allotted generous extra servings of mead and food,[154] and a Glastonbury calendar assigns the Feast of the Assumption its highest liturgical grading.[155] In what may be no more than a remarkable happenstance, the fourth marginal homily of CCCC 41 (on the Ascension) contains a speech of Christ to the damned (beginning *Ego te, O homo*) that runs parallel to that in *Christ III* of the Exeter

---

[150] C. Hohler, Review of *Cambridge, Corpus Christi College 41: The Loricas and the Missal*, by Raymond J. S. Grant, *Medium Ævum* 49 (1980), pp. 275-81, at pp. 275-76.

[151] On the charm, see Grant, "Description"; on Brigit at Glastonbury, see *De Antiquitate* (ed. Scott), pp. 60-61.

[152] See Hohler, Review, p. 276; Budny, *Catalogue*, Vol. I, p. 508; Keefer, "Margin as Archive," p. 147; Grant, *Three Homilies*, p. 1; and Grant, "Description."

[153] Grant, *Three Homilies*, pp. 6 ff., and Grant, "Description."

[154] *De Antiquitate* (ed. Scott), pp. 162-63.

[155] See Wormald, "The Liturgical Calendar of Glastonbury Abbey," p. 335 under August 15.

Book (beginning *Hwæt, ic þec mon,* l. 1379).[156] It may be happenstance also that, among the additions to CCCC 41, the only two Anglo-Saxon names to occur are *Ælfwine* (interlined on p. 155) and *Ælfwerd* (in the outer margin of p. 242).[157] As discussed earlier, *Ælfwine* is a variant of *Æthelwine,* the name that appears in the margin of the donation leaf of Lambeth 149, and can thus be associated with Glastonbury through any of three persons. Of these three, Bishop Æthelwine lived on after his episcopacy at Wells until 1027, and Æthelwine/Ælfwine, monk (and possibly reeve) at Glastonbury, likely lived into the early eleventh century; thus either may have been alive and in Glastonbury when the name came to be written into CCCC 41. For the second name, *Ælfwerd,* Glastonbury had two abbots whose names and dates would fit: Ælfweard (975 x 985-1009)[158] and Ælfweard/Æthelweard (*Eilwardus,* 1024-1053), the latter of whom (also as discussed earlier) is conceivably identifiable with the Ealdorman Æthelweard who donated Lambeth 149 in 1018.

While there is thus some hint of a relationship between CCCC 41 and both the Exeter Book and Lambeth 149, my point is simply that the two names in CCCC 41, together with the appearance of the Glastonbury saints Patrick and Brigit and the indications of Irish influence throughout the marginalia, would seem to corroborate Hohler's view that the manuscript was at or near Glastonbury before about 1050. If indeed the marginalia were entered there, we might have a later example of the way the poems of the Exeter Book (particularly the shorter poems of the second half, with its similarly eclectic mix

---

[156] A similar address occurs also in Vercelli homily 8. The speech derives from a sermon once believed to have been by St. Augustine but now attributed to Caesarius of Arles (see Grant, *Three Homilies,* p. 7), and so the three related passages may simply have been based on the same or similar sources; it is possible, however, that a close study of parallels between the speech as it appears in CCCC 41 homily 4 (which remains unpublished) and in the Exeter Book would reveal further connections between the two manuscripts. *Christ III* is quoted as in Krapp and Dobbie, *The Exeter Book,* p. 49.

[157] Budny, *Catalogue,* Vol. I, p. 507.

[158] See S. Foot, "Glastonbury's Early Abbots," *The Archaeology and History of Glastonbury Abbey,* ed. Abrams and Carley, pp. 163-89, at p. 184 item 19 and p. 189 item 19.

of the religious and secular) may have been archived at Glastonbury before being copied into the final codex. Moreover, if CCCC 41 were in Glastonbury along with the two gospel books, the Leofric Missal, Lambeth 149, and the Exeter Book when Leofric was collecting books, it is easy to imagine that he simply acquired them all at Æthelnoth's rummage sale and brought them to Exeter sometime before 1072.

We thus arrive full cycle, to the *mycel englisc boc* shelved in Exeter's monastic library by the time of Leofric's death. Short of the discovery of some striking new piece of evidence, any case for the earlier history and origin of the Exeter Book is of necessity circumstantial. One might wish for more certainty, for a definitive attribution might be brought to bear on readings of many of the volume's poems and would surely influence our understanding of tenth-century literary culture. I hope to have raised a number of issues relevant to such an attribution. Until greater assurance can be had, however, I would suggest that the cumulative possibilities offered by the 1018 donation inscription, the literary milieu of Glastonbury under Dunstan, the concerns of several Exeter Book poems, the few paleographical analogues at hand, and the apparent transactions between Glastonbury and Exeter point us not toward Crediton, Exeter, or Canterbury — the other houses having a claim to the manuscript's production — but rather to the monastery of St. Mary at Glastonbury during or shortly after the abbacy of Dunstan.

Parker's Purposes for His Manuscripts: Matthew Parker in the Context of his Early Career and Sixteenth-Century Church Reform

NANCY BASLER BJORKLUND

ATTHEW PARKER (1504-1575), noted in history as archbishop of Canterbury during the reign of Elizabeth I, has also attracted scholarly attention for his outstanding collection of medieval manuscripts, now preserved chiefly in the Parker Library at Corpus Christi College, Cambridge. Scholars generally agree that by assembling the priceless volumes during the 1560s and 1570s, he rescued them from neglect and possible ruin following the dispersal of the monastic libraries.[1] Researchers have also pointed out Parker's role in reviving the study of Old English in the sixteenth century and for sponsoring publications using Anglo-Saxon typeface. Both Timothy Graham and R. I. Page, for instance, have recently presented evidence that Parker and his circle depended upon the manuscripts to gain knowledge of Old English and to publish documents in which that language was used.[2]

---

[1] The origin and composition of Parker's library have been widely studied. See, for example, R. I. Page, "Christopher Marlowe and the Library of Matthew Parker," *Notes and Queries* (1997), pp. 510-14; Pamela Black, "Matthew Parker's Search for Cranmer's 'great notable written books,'" *The Library* 29 (1974), pp. 312-22; Bruce Dickins, "The Making of the Parker Library," *Transactions of the Cambridge Bibliographical Society* 4 (1972), pp. 19-34; W. W. Greg, "Books and Bookmen in the Correspondence of Archbishop Parker," *The Library*, 4th ser., 16 (1935), pp. 243-79; M. R. James, *A Descriptive Catalogue of the Manuscripts in the Library of Corpus Christi College* (Cambridge: Cambridge University Press, 1909 and 1912) and "The Sources of Archbishop Parker's Collection of Manuscripts at Corpus Christi College, Cambridge," *Cambridge Antiquarian Society*, Octavo Publication, No. 32 (1899); and S. W. Kershaw, "Archbishop Parker, Collector and Author," *The Library*, 2nd ser., (1900), pp. 379-83.

[2] Timothy Graham, "The Beginnings of Old English Studies: Evidence from the Manuscripts of Matthew Parker," *Back to the Manuscripts*, ed. Shuji Sato (Tokyo: Centre for Medieval English Studies, 1997), pp. 29-50; R. I. Page, *Matthew Parker and His Books* (Kalamazoo, MI: Medieval Institute Publications, 1993), pp. 87-105. See also John Bromwich, The First Book Printed in Anglo-Saxon Types," *Transactions of the Cambridge Bibliographical Society* 3 (1962), pp. 265-291; N. R. Ker, *Catalogue of Manuscripts Containing*

217

Yet in spite of this broad scholarly examination, a number of questions about Parker and his manuscripts remain. R. I. Page, at the conclusion of his study of Parker and his books, calls for further study on the still unresolved problem of establishing Parker's purposes in assembling, annotating, and studying his collection.[3] Scholars have suggested a variety of answers, but have failed to produce a comprehensive picture of Parker's motivations. Furthermore, misunderstandings of Parker's purposes have led to denigration of the man himself: his early intellectual pursuits have been ignored, his scholarship questioned, his personal use of the manuscripts disputed, his interests dismissed as antiquarian, his publications branded as pure propaganda, and his editorial activities thoroughly denounced.[4] Parker himself sometimes contributed to the confusion by failing to sign his own publications or state his opinions boldly. Historians have further compounded the problem by focusing their attention upon Parker's fifteen years as a prelate and neglecting his earlier career of thirty years. The ecclesi-

---

Anglo-Saxon (Oxford: Clarendon Press, 1957; rpt. with Supplement, 1990), pp. lxiii, 41-122; Peter Lucas, "A Testimonye of Verye Ancient Tyme? Some Manuscript Models for the Parkerian Anglo-Saxon Type Design," *Of the Making of Books: Medieval Manuscripts, Their Scribes and Readers*, ed. P. R. Robinson and R. Zim (Aldershot: Ashgate, 1997), pp. 147-88; and C. E. Wright, "The Dispersal of the Monastic Libraries and the Beginnings of Anglo-Saxon Studies. Matthew Parker and His Circle: A Preliminary Study," *Transactions of the Cambridge Bibliographical Society* 3 (1951): pp. 208-237.

[3] Page, *Matthew Parker and His Books*, p. 105.

[4] See criticisms of Parker's editing in F. J. Madden, ed., *Historia Anglorum*, by Matthew Paris (London: HMSO, 1866; rpt. Liechtenstein: Kraus, 1970), vol. 1, pp. xx, xxxi-xxxvii, lvii n. 3; H. R. Luard, ed., *Chronica Majora*, by Matthew Paris (1872-1880; rpt. Wiesbaden: Kraus, 1964-5), vol. 2, pp. xxii-xxviii, and vol. 5, p. xvii; and W. H. Stevenson, ed., *Asser's Life of King Alfred* (1904; rpt. Oxford: Clarendon, 1959), pp. xvii-xx. Studies of Parker's use of manuscripts include Eleanor N. Adams, *Old English Scholarship in England from 1566-1800*, Yale Studies in English 55 (1917; rpt. Hamden, CT: Archon, 1970), pp. 11-41, 157-59; Theodore H. Leinbaugh, "Ælfric's *Sermo de Sacrificio in Die Pascae*: Anglican Polemic in the Sixteenth and Seventeenth Centuries," *Anglo-Saxon Scholarship: The First Three Centuries*, ed. Carl T. Berkhout and Milton McC. Gatch (Boston: Hall, 1982), pp. 51-68; F. J. Levy, *Tudor Historical Thought* (San Marino, CA: Huntington Library, 1967), pp. 114-213; May McKisack, *Medieval History in the Tudor Age* (Oxford: Clarendon, 1971), pp. 26-49.

astical career that preceded his elevation, however, provides a key to understanding the archbishop and his intentions.[5] This paper will provide evidence that Parker's chief purpose in collecting, annotating, and studying his library was to defend the concepts of church reform that he had adopted before he became archbishop. Consideration of his early career in its sixteenth-century reformation context may lead to greater understanding of the man and dispel a series of misconceptions about him.

The first misconception to be discarded is that little may be known about Parker's early intellectual interests or intentions. A related supposition is that he may have lacked serious purposes and have pursued manuscript study simply as a leisure-time activity. Historian F. J. Levy, for instance, writes that it is impossible to say why Parker turned to a historical justification of the church as a way to spend his leisure: "we know too little of his intellectual interests prior to his elevation."[6] Yet a number of sixteenth-century sources reveal Parker's concerns before his consecration as archbishop. Parker's Latin secretary

---

[5] The following details of Parker's life are known: born in Norwich, he was educated at Corpus Christi College, Cambridge, received his Bachelor of Arts degree in 1525, and was made a priest and Fellow of his College in 1527. He became Master of Arts in 1528, Bachelor of Divinity in 1535, and Doctor of Divinity in 1538. Having served as chaplain at the court of Anne Boleyn, he received her appointment as dean of Stoke-by-Clare, a college of secular priests in Suffolk. Henry VIII appointed him Master of Corpus Christi College in 1544, and he was twice elected vice-chancellor of Cambridge University (1545 and 1549). During the reign of Henry VIII he was presented to the rectories of Ashen, Burlingham, and Landbeach, and was installed prebendary in the church of Ely; under Edward VI he became prebendary at Lincoln, then dean of Lincoln. Dispossessed of all his livings during Mary's reign, he then became Elizabeth's first Archbishop of Canterbury in 1559, until his death in 1575. See his "Memoranda" in John Bruce and Thomas Perowne, eds., *Correspondence of Matthew Parker, D.D.* (1853, rpt. New York: Johnson Reprint Corp., 1968), pp. vi-x. Standard biographies include John Strype, *The Life and Acts of Matthew Parker* (1711; rpt. Oxford: Clarendon, 1820 and 1821); W. F. Hook, *Lives of the Archbishops of Canterbury* (London, 1872), vol. 9, pp. 492-507; William H. Kennedy, *Archbishop Parker* (London: Isaac Pitman, 1908); Edith Perry, *Under Four Tudors* (London: Allen & Unwin, 1964); and V. J. K. Brook, *A Life of Archbishop Parker* (Oxford: Clarendon, 1962).

[6] Levy, pp. 115.

John Joscelyn wrote two biographies under the Archbishop's supervision: the "Historiola," published as *The Life off the 70. Archbishopp off Canterbury . . .* , and the "Matthaeus," a concluding chapter in Parker's *De Antiquitate Britannicae Ecclesiae*. Most of Parker's correspondence has been printed, along with his "Memoranda" of important life events. John Foxe's *Acts and Monuments* identifies Parker with a group of early reformers. Volumes of personal papers survive at the Parker Library of Corpus Christi College, Cambridge. Furthermore, Foxe's *Acts and Monuments* identifies Parker with a group of Cambridge church reformers during the 1520s and 1530s.[7]

These sources document Parker's serious intellectual interest in church reform throughout his life. During the three decades preceding his archiepiscopal consecration, the English church underwent a series of wrenching changes, as Henry VIII removed it from Roman Catholic jurisdiction, Edward VI allowed it more Protestant-style reforms, and Mary I returned it to the Roman Catholic fold. Throughout these years Parker sided with the reformers who wished to restore the church to a purity it had presumably possessed before becoming corrupted by medieval traditions. He personally favored several reform measures even before they became legal, notably the marriage of clergy and the use of vernacular scriptures. He opposed teachings and traditions not taught by scriptures or the early church, such as the doctrine of transubstantiation and the superstitions sometimes accompanying the veneration of relics and images. When he became archbishop he continued his long-held support of these reform measures, and his manuscript library became his chief tool.

A further misconception holds that Parker was not himself a scholar and did not personally conduct research using his manuscripts. Eleanor Adams writes, "Parker was noted for his conservatism, his even balance, and his executive ability, rather than for his scholarship," add-

[7] "Historiola," Cambridge, Corpus Christi College, MS 489, no. 4; John Joscelyn, *The life off the 70. Archbishopp off Canterbury presentlye Sittinge. . . .* [Geneva] 1574, and "Matthaeus," in Matthew Parker, *De Antiquitate Britannicae Ecclesiae et privilegiis Ecclesiae Cantuariensis, cum Archiepiscopis ejusdem 70.* (London, 1572), printed in Strype, vol. 3, pp. 269-307; Bruce and Perowne, *Correspondence*; John Foxe, *Acts & Monuments* (London: John Day [1563]), p. 477 (irregular pagination).

ing that "Parker had a great man's genius for making others work."[8] R. I. Page has observed that "Parker was not a research student. Rather a director of research, with . . . research assistants."[9] Although Parker in his later years did employ researchers in his household, he himself remained an industrious student of his own manuscripts, continuing an intellectual pattern begun early in life. At Cambridge he had excelled as a scholar, earning an ability-based scholarship during his first year at Corpus Christi College and finishing the normal four-year liberal arts course in three and a half years. After receiving his Master of Arts degree in 1527, he concentrated his theological studies on the early church fathers and councils, which after four or five years of intensive research he declared himself to have mastered. He was made Bachelor of Divinity in 1535 and Doctor of Divinity in 1538.[10] His scholarly activities continued through the 1550s, when he conceptualized a reformed church based on the teachings of patristic Christianity. Collaborating with the continental scholar and reformer Martin Bucer, he helped to produce the "Florilegium Patristicum," a source book of theological opinions gleaned from patristic studies, intended as a model for sixteenth-century reforms.[11] As archbishop he continued personally to scrutinize historic texts as guides for church practice.

Recent scholarship has helped to correct yet another mistaken concept, that Archbishop Parker rarely annotated his manuscripts for personal use. N. R. Ker, for instance, had asserted: "Writing in Parker's hand occurs in very few manuscripts. He was a busy man who left the making of marginalia to others."[12] C. E. Wright concurred: "The use of . . . red chalk for pagination and rulings make it unlikely that for this sort of tedious work the Archbishop would have time to spare."[13] But

---

[8]   Adams, pp. 14, 40.

[9]   Page, p. 92.

[10] *Correspondence*, p. vii; Joscelyn, *Life*, p. A3r; Strype, vol. 3, p. 275.

[11] CCCC MS 418; Martin Bucer and Matthew Parker, "Florilegium Patristicum," ed. Pierre Fraenkel, *Martini Buceri opera latina* 3 (Leiden: Brill, 1988).

[12] Ker, p. lii.

[13] Wright, p. 228.

the scholarly Parker took time to examine and mark his manuscripts. Recent work at the Parker Library, begun by the Research Group on Manuscript Evidence and continued by Timothy Graham and R. I. Page, has shown that his distinctive, identifiable hand is found in many places, not just in pagination but in marginalia and other markings.[14]

The larger significance of Parker's personal annotations is that most of them relate to church reform. A number of his markings may be found, for example, on passages regarding clerical marriage. Parker, a married clergyman, diligently hunted up evidence that the church had not always enforced clerical celibacy. Cambridge, Corpus Christi College MS 44, a Pontifical of Canterbury and Ely dating from the eleventh and sixteenth centuries, bears Parker's marginal notations, "*In orationibus in admoniti[onibus] in Benedictionibus null[a] mention celibatus*" (p. 235). In CCCC MS 190, a Latin and Old English penitential that includes a section about the sons of priests, Parker's hand-written title conveys harsh criticism of those who condemn priestly marriage (p. 361). In CCCC MS 191, an eleventh-century Latin and Old English copy of the enlarged version of the Rule of Chrodegang of Metz, Parker marked a passage noting that the lower orders of clergy would not be damned for having children and a wife while preaching Christ (p. 164). In CCCC MS 265, an eleventh-century volume of penitentials and other church documents, Parker underlined a passage attesting to the existence of married clergy and drew a hand in the margin pointing to it (p. 169). In CCCC MS 342, a copy of the Rochester Chronicle, Parker's marginal note observes that there were married clerics in the days of John Pecham, Archbishop of Canterbury (fol. 110r). CCCC MS 373 bears Parker's annotation regarding episcopal letters endorsing clerical marriage (fol. 32r). Although some of Parker's annotations indicate his interest in place names and Old English,[15] many more relate to reform issues.

This evidence helps to dispel another mistaken idea: that Parker's interest in his manuscripts was primarily antiquarian, an enjoyment of

---

[14]The Research Group on Manuscript Evidence, 1989-1994, identified and located several styles of Parker's hand among his manuscripts. See Graham, pp. 30, 35-37; and Page, pp. 87-94, 125-17.

[15]Graham, pp. 35-38.

the old volumes above all for their rarity and great age. Eleanor Adams, for instance, writes, "the underlying interest [in Old English records] was antiquarian, even with the Reformers . . . ."[16] As his notations on the marriage of clergy imply, however, Parker was a reformer first and an antiquarian second. Believing that a study of medieval manuscripts would increase the perceived value of church reform in his own age, he used historical texts to contrast alleged errors of the past with contemporary religious enlightenment. The preface to one of his publications, *The Gospel of the fower Evangelists*, states:

> Among other great and manifold fruites which dayly ensue by the studyes of good me*n* . . . there is none . . . more needefull, then the opening to this our age the tymes of old antiquities. The defecte whereof, what inconuenience it hath bredde to the Church of Christ . . . for want of true history, truth hath lacked witnesse, tyme wanted light, new thynges were reputed for olde, and olde for new, errour em- brased for veritie, superstition for religion, true iudgement darkened through preposterous perswasion, for that, men litle vnderstanding, or not well expending what passed be- fore, could little or nothing iudge of thinges present, being forced to beleue, not what truth was in deede, but what pleased them, which had the guiding of them, so that they being blindly led by other, as blinde as ther selues, both fell into the pit . . . and all for ignorance of auncient testimonies & truthes of antiquitie.[17]

Parker intended any antiquarian study to reveal how far the church had wandered away from its earliest teachings. Indeed, church history as a guide for reform may well have furnished the original in- spiration for Parker's manuscript collection. In 1561 he received a letter from Matthias Flacius Illyricus, who represented continental reformers seeking to borrow manuscripts on which to base a new history of the

---

[16] Adams, p. 12.

[17] John Foxe, preface to *The Gospels of the fower Evangelistes translated in the olde Saxons tyme out of Latin into the vulgare toung of the Saxons, newly collected out of auncient monumentes of the sayd Saxons and now published for testimonie of the same* (London, 1571), fol. Aiir (omitted letters supplied in italics).

church justifying its reform. Flacius's suggestion that such rare hand-
written volumes should be brought together into well-known places
sparked Parker's interest in locating and utilizing English manuscripts.
Parker complied with Flacius's request, but first sought advice from
John Bale, himself a manuscript collector and church historian. Bale's
information about extant manuscripts in England further inspired
Parker to locate, preserve, and print them.[18] In 1568 the Queen's Privy
Council granted Parker special oversight in the "conservation of such
ancient records and monuments," previously kept in monasteries but
now in the hands of private persons.[19] With this authority he acquired
and borrowed many of the volumes on which he based his own historical publications. By 1572, having enlisted John Joscelyn's scholarly
and literary skills, he produced a history of the English church, the
De Antiquitate Britannicae Ecclesiae.[20] Preservation and publication of
manuscript material were two of Parker's goals, but both were rooted
in the church reform movement.

As Parker studied the manuscripts, he encountered texts in Old
English, a language that he helped to revive, promote, and enlist in the
cause of church reform. Fascinated by the vocabulary and grammar of
the language, he attempted to teach himself by studying interlined and
bilingual passages, but may have gained no more than a rudimentary
knowledge. He found especially helpful the eleventh-century Latin and
Old English Rule of St. Benedict, now Cambridge, Corpus Christi College, MS 178, Part II, and observed the volume's usefulness in language
study: "In hoc libro facilius discitur Lingua Saxonica" (p. 291) [see
Plate 1]. Parker was not the first sixteenth-century figure to become
interested in those texts, for Robert Talbot, Robert Recorde, and John
Leland had studied some of them before him, occasionally sharing and

---

[18] *Correspondence,* pp. 139-141; Norman L. Jones, "Matthew Parker, John
Bale, and the Magdeburg Centuriators," *Sixteenth Century Journal* 12, no.
3 (1981): pp. 35-49. Bale to Parker, 30 July 1560, in Cambridge, Cambridge
University Library MS. Add. 7489; printed in H. R. Luard, ed., "A
Letter from Bishop Bale to Archbishop Parker," *Cambridge Antiquarian
Communications* 3 (1879): pp. 157-73; Madden, xvii-xix.

[19] *Correspondence,* pp. 327-28.

[20] Joscelyn's hand-written drafts survive in London, British Library, Cotton
MSS Vitellius D.vii and E.xiv.

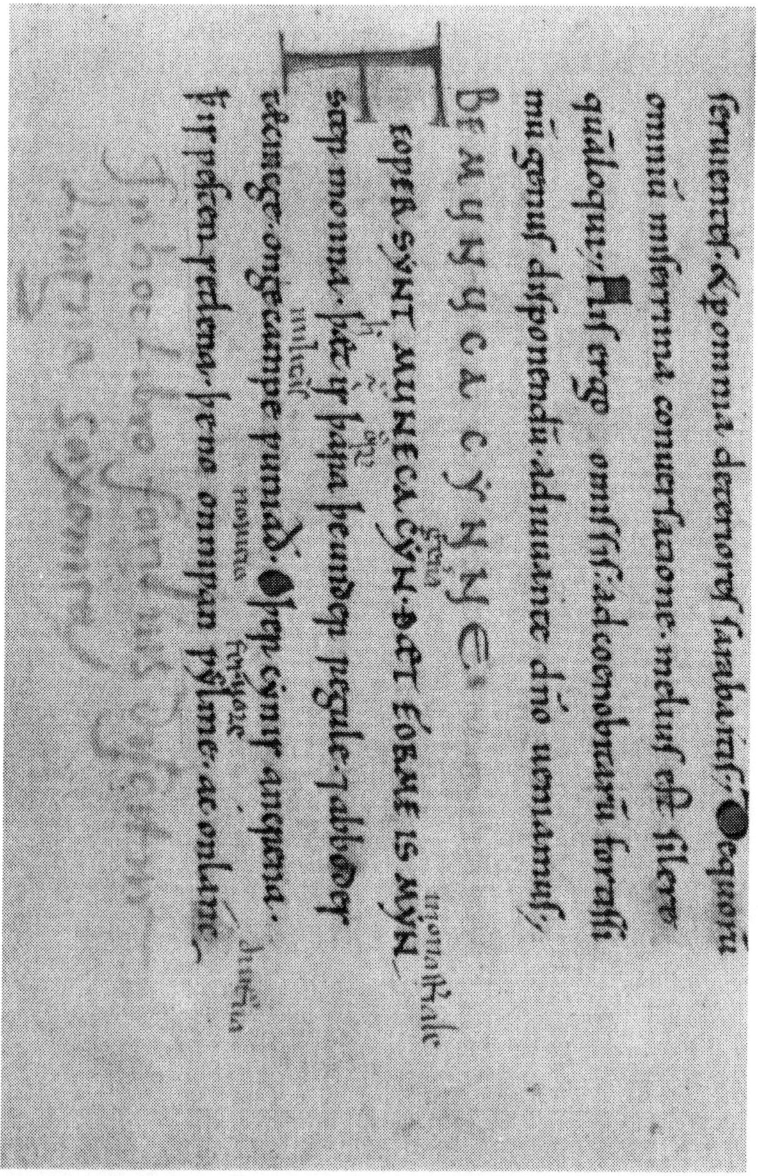

Plate 1. MS CCCC 178, p. 291, the 11th century Latin and Old English rule of St. Benedict, showing Parker's hand-written notation.

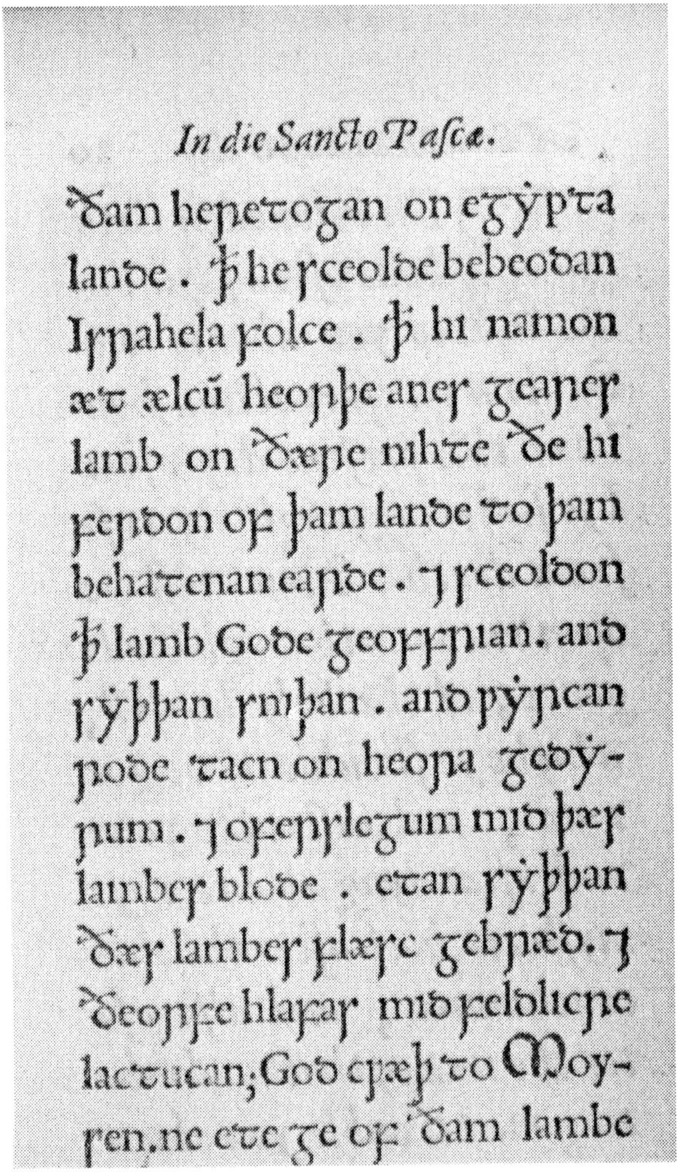

In die Sancto Pasca.

ðam heꞃetoȝan on eȝypta
lande . þ he ꞃceolde bebeodan
Iꞃꞃahela folce . þ hi namon
æt ælcū heoꞃþe aneꞃ ȝeaꞃeꞃ
lamb on ðæꞃe nihte ðe hi
feꞃdon of þam lande to þam
behatenan eaꞃðe . ꞽ ꞃceoldon
þ lamb Gode ȝeoffꞃian. and
ꞃyþþan ꞃniþan . and pyꞃcan
ꞃode tacn on heoꞃa ȝeoð-
num . ꞽ ofeꞃꞃleȝum mið þæꞃ
lambeꞃ blode . etan ꞃyþþan
ðæꞃ lambeꞃ flæꞃc ȝebꞃæd. ꞽ
ðeoꞃꞽe hlafaꞃ mið felðlicꞃe
lactucan; God cꞃæþ to Moy-
ꞃen.ne ete ȝe of ðam lambe

Plate 2. Parker commissioned this Old English typeface for *A testimonie of antiquitie*, CCCC SP. 281, fol. 20v (detail).

annotating the volumes that later fell into Parker's hands. During the 1560s and early 1570s he gathered into his household scholars who could devote themselves to understanding the Old English texts. Joscelyn laid the foundations for further study with annotations, transcripts, and an early Old English dictionary, but without Parker's inspiration and patronage the work would never have proceeded.[21] Joscelyn's biography of Parker gives due credit to the archbishop for directing the team that collected, preserved and deciphered the manuscripts:

> Therefore in seekinge upp the chronicles off the Brittones and Inglishe Saxons/ which lay hidden every wheare contemned and buried in forgetfullnes/ and through ignoraunce of the Languages not wel understanded/ his owen especially/ and his mens diligence wanted not. And to the end/ that these antiquities might last longe/ and be carefully kept/ he caused them/ beinge broughte into one place to be well bounde and truely covered.[22]

Parker's interest in Old English dovetailed conveniently with his interest in church reform, and he commandeered Old English manuscripts to refute such Roman Catholic teachings as transubstantiation and clerical celibacy.[23] By publishing Old English texts he attempted to prove the sixteenth-century reforms were doctrinal restorations rather than innovations.

A misunderstanding of this effort has led to the assertion that Parker pulled evidence from his historical volumes to create propaganda or justification for the ecclesiastical innovations his church had

---

[21] I thank Timothy Graham for his help in locating Corpus Christi College manuscript references. See also Graham, pp. 30-42; and Judith Sanders Gale, "John Joscelyn's Notebook: A Study of the Contents and Sources of British Library Cotton MS. Vitellius D.vii" (M. Phil. thesis, University of Nottingham, 1978).

[22] Joscelyn, *Life*, Cir & v.

[23] See, for example, *A testimonie of antiquitie, shewing the auncient fayth in the Church of England touching the sacrament of the body and bloude of the Lord here publikely preached, and also received in the Saxons tyme, above 600. yeares agoe* ([1566]; rpt. Amsterdam: Theatrum Orbis Terrarum, 1970); and Foxe, *Gospels*.

recently adopted. David Douglas, for example, notes, "the chief impulse which inspired his work was undoubtedly a polemical hope that perhaps he might find in the primitive ecclesiastical polity of the Anglo-Saxons a prototype of the reformed church over which he had been called to preside."[24] C. E. Wright states, "on Parker as Primate rested the responsibility for securing the necessary material to supply the official propaganda for those constitutional and doctrinal principles on which the 'Ecclesia Anglicana' was to be established."[25] N. R. Ker observes that Archbishop Parker and his household sought out Old English manuscripts "as a means of promoting the 'Ecclesia Anglicana.'" May McKisack writes, "the driving force behind all this antiquarian activity was Parker's desire to present the history of the Church of England in a way that would justify the Elizabethan settlement."[26] J. R. Hall speaks of Parker's looking to the past in an attempt to find precedent for Anglican doctrine.[27] Finally, Theodore H. Leinbaugh refers to Parker's first Old English publication as "Anglican polemic" and claims that the text was deliberately mistranslated to "enforce the Anglican view-point."[28] These observations deserve closer examination.

Although it is true that Parker defended the teachings of the Elizabethan church, the assertions quoted above distort the picture by reversing cause and effect. The authors assume that Parker defended certain ecclesiastical doctrines because his church had adopted them. But it is more accurate to state that his church adopted those doctrines because Parker and other reformers had long defended them. Archbishop Parker played a major role in formulating the articles of belief

---

[24] David Douglas, *English Scholars* (London: J. Cape, 1939), p. 61.

[25] Wright, pp. 226-27.

[26] McKisack, p. 39.

[27] J. H. Hall, "Old English Literature," in *Scholarly Editing*, ed. D. C. Greetham (New York: Modern Language Association of America, 1995), pp. 150-51.

[28] Leinbaugh, pp. 51-52. R. I. Page has refuted Leinbaugh's charges of deliberate mistranslation; see *Notes and Queries* (October, 1983), pp. 444-45.

[29] Charles Hardwick, *History of the Articles of Religion* (London, 1886). Parker's personally written text in Parker MS 121, pp. 233-53, shows his hand at work.

that in 1563 became the official creed of the Elizabethan church.[29] Similar to the Forty-two articles adopted under Edward VI, the Elizabethan Thirty-nine articles reflected long-standing reformist positions, among them rejection of transubstantiation, acceptance of clerical marriage, and elimination of non-scriptural teachings. The following examples show not only that Parker supported these tenets with his manuscript-based publications in the 1560s and early 1570s, but he had also endorsed the same doctrines at least thirty years earlier.

Parker's first manuscript publication attacked the Roman Catholic doctrine of transubstantiation. In 1566 he published *A testimonie of antiquitie*, a 600-year-old sermon arguing for the spiritual presence of Christ in the sacrament. Translated from Latin by the abbot Ælfric in the late tenth century, the sermon appears in a number of manuscripts, implying its widespread use and authority in Anglo-Saxon times. Parker had the sermon printed in both contemporary English and Old English, for which he commissioned the first Old English types to be cast at his own expense [see Plate 2].[30] The sixteenth-century preface states simply that the volume was to "reveale unto us what hath ben the state of our church in England from tyme to tyme," but the sermon is later declared to be "agaynst the bodely presence" in the sacramental elements (fol. 3r & v). The text speaks of receiving "ghostlye, Christ bodye" (fol. 27r). If sixteenth-century readers needed help in understanding the point, a marginal note states boldly: "No transubstantiation." The sermon then explains the differences between Christ's natural body, "borne of the flesh of Marie," and the sacrament, "gathered of many cornes: without bloude, and bone" (fol. 35r, 36r).[31] Parker published the sermon to refute the Roman Catholics,

---

[30] *A testimonie of antiquitie.* See also Bromwich, pp. 265-91, and Lucas, pp. 147-88.

[31] Of two miraculous stories in the text that seemed to support transubstantiation, Parker correctly observed that they had been "infarced" or interpolated into the sermon as found in CCCC MS 198 and elsewhere. He discovered the same stories in a completely different homily from CCCC MS 162. See Page, *Books*, pp. 96-97, and Leinbaugh, pp. 54-55.

who claimed a long, unbroken history for their belief in transubstantiation.[32] His publication supported the Elizabethan article maintaining that transubstantiation was "repugnant to the plain words of Scripture" and that "the faithful should not believe in 'the real and bodily presence,' on the ground that Christ's body cannot be present in many places at once."[33]

If Parker was defending an Elizabethan doctrine, he was also restating an opinion he had adopted some thirty years before. As a young preacher during the mid 1530s at Clare, Suffolk, he made the point to his congregation that "Christ once died, and died no more," refuting the Roman Catholic teaching that Christ was sacrificed anew at every mass. This and other reformist opinions so upset conservative parishioners that they sent a list of charges against him to the Lord Chancellor, who quickly sided with Parker and refused to censure him.[34] Parker became known for his opposition to transubstantiation. When, under Edward VI, that doctrine was officially discarded, ecclesiastical authorities insisted that the stone altars in parish churches, on which Christ's body presumably had been offered repeatedly in the mass, were to be replaced with plain wooden tables. The Bishop of Ely, needing a spokesman to preach the necessity of this replacement, called upon Parker to do the job.[35] When he became archbishop Parker continued to oppose transubstantiation, using added support from his manuscripts.

A second doctrine Parker defended in his manuscript-based publications was the right of the clergy to be married. Soon after *A testimonie*, Parker published *A Defence of priestes mariages* to reinforce the thirty-first Article of 1563, which stated that since no divine com-

---

[32] "Wherfore what may we nowe thinke of that great consent, wherof the Romanistes have long made vaunte, to witte, their doctrine to have continued many hundred yeares as it were lincked together with a continuall chaine, wherof hath been no breche at any time. Truely this their so great affirmation hath uttered unto us no truth . . . ." *A testimonie*, fol. 18r.

[33] Article xxviii of 1563. See Hardwick, p. 329; A. G. Dickens, *English Reformation* (New York: Schocken Books, 1964), p. 253.

[34] *Correspondence*, p. 7.

[35] "Register of Bishops Goodrich, Thyrlby and Cox," *Ely Diocesan Remembrancer* (Ely: 1885-1915), p. 451.

mandment is given to clergymen to vow celibacy, they may marry at
their own discretion. The complex history of *A Defence* begins with
a manuscript written during the 1550s by a man who, according to
Parker's preface, died before completing it. That man may have been
John Ponet, to whom the entire work has been attributed and who
had promised such a work in reply to Thomas Martin, a defender of
clerical celibacy.[36] The unfinished treatise apparently fell into the hands
of Parker, who greatly expanded the text while he was in hiding during Mary's reign.[37] His Memoranda entry of 1557 proudly proclaims:
"I have written a defence of the marriage of priests against Thomas
Martin." When he became archbishop, he acquired from John Bale further historical references to married clergy, along with the encourage-
ment to print them.[38] Parker impatiently tucked some of his newfound
evidence into the Preface to *A testimonie*, then published *A Defence*
approximately a year later. Additional manuscript references coming
into his hands soon necessitated a second edition, augmented from 274
pages to 359 and replete with Old English references.[39]

Parker defended the right of the clergy to marry not only because his church taught it, but also because as a reformist, married
priest, he believed in it. Certain early reformers had argued that the
rule of celibacy was unscriptural and unrealistic, and when in the 1530s

---

[36]Strype, vol. 2, pp. 446-48.

[37] *Correspondence*, ix. See also Strype, vol 1, pp. 66-67; and W. H. Frere, *The
Marian Reaction in its Relation to the English Clergy* (London, 1896), pp.
73-75 n. 1.

[38] Bale to Parker, 30 July, 1560: Luard, ed., "A Letter," pp. 169-71; Madden,
pp. xviii-xix.

[39] *A testimonie*, fol. 6r-8v, 14r-15v; *A Defence of priestes mariages, stablysshed by the
imperiall lawes of the realme of Englande, agaynst ... Thomas Martin ...* (London:
Richarde Jugge, n.d.). On Parker's use of manuscripts in the expanded version,
see Page, *Books*, pp. 89-95.

[40] See, for instance, Robert Barnes, "That by God's worde it is lawfull for
Priestes that hath not the gift of chastitie, to marry Wives" (1534), cited
in John K. Yost, "The Reformation Defense of Clerical Marriage in the
Reigns of Henry VIII and Edward VI," *Church History* 50 (June 1981), pp.
152-53; *Letters and Papers, foreign & domestic, of the reign of Henry VIII*, ed.
James Gairdner (1828-1912, rpt. Vaduz: Kraus, 1965), vol. 9: no. 812; vol.
10: no. 82; vol. 12, pt 1: no. 990 and pt. 2: no. 450.

England broke with Rome, a number of priests took wives.[40] By the late 1530s, Parker had pledged himself to marry Margaret Harlston, the daughter of a Norfolk gentleman. Before a ceremony could take place, however, Henry VIII in 1539 signed the Act of Six Articles, making married priests felons and liable to the death penalty. Since marriage seemed out of the question, Matthew and Margaret simply lived together without a ceremony.[41] When Henry VIII died in 1547 and his son Edward VI came to the throne, Parker anticipated quick legalization of clerical marriage. Unfortunately, his wedding ceremony pre-dated the passage of the statutes that would make it lawful, and the Parkers' first son was deemed illegitimate and unable to inherit goods or property. During Mary's Roman Catholic regime, Parker forfeited his career and was deprived of his entire livelihood for refusing to abandon his wife and family. By the time he became Elizabeth's archbishop he was prepared to fight for the right of the clergy to marry, and he did so despite the Queen's disapproval.[42] She could not, however, prevent the church from adopting this tenet, one in which reformists like Parker already believed.

Another reformist concept that Parker defended both in his early career and later with his manuscripts was the elimination of non-scriptural and allegedly erroneous teachings that the church had adopted over the centuries. To reveal the differences between medieval beliefs and those taught by the reformed sixteenth-century church, he printed the works of leading monastic chroniclers, making their texts broadly accessible for the first time. In 1567 he produced an edition of Matthew Paris's *Flores Historiarum*, which recorded events from the beginning of the world to 1307. Subsequent discovery of better manuscripts caused him to print a revised edition of the *Flores* in 1570, followed in 1571 by Paris's *Chronica Majora*, covering the period from William the Conqueror's reign through that of Henry III. Following the 1572 publication of his own chronicle, *De Antiquitate*, Parker produced in 1574 the *Historia Brevis* as well as the *Ypodigma Neustriae* of Thomas Walsingham, covering the period from the reign of Edward I to that

---

[41] *Correspondence*, p. x. Parker's Memoranda indicates three years of cohabitation before marriage, the Matthaeus seven years. See Strype, vol. 3, p. 285.

[42] *Correspondence*, pp. viii-x, 66, 148, 156-57.

of Henry V. In the same year he published *Ælfredi Regis Res Gestae*, an account of Alfred the Great, printed in Latin but with Old English typeface. Including *A testimonie*, *A Defence*, and the Old English edition of the Gospels, Parker produced ten major historical volumes as well as several minor works during a brief but energetic eight-year period.[43]

He expressed several motivations behind this publishing zeal. First, as the preface to the *Historia Brevis* states, he wished to make the texts widely available to readers. Second, he wished to present examples from church history as a guide for the present, as the *Life* explains:

> to knowe the religion off thancient fatheres/ and those especiallye which were/ off the Englishe churche . . . he endevored to sett out in printe/ certaine off those aunciente monumentes/ whearoff he knew very fewe examples to be extante/ and which he thoughte woulde be most profitable for the posterytye/ to instructe them/ in the faythe and religion off the elders.[44]

Third and most significantly, he wished to expose the superstition and ignorance that he believed had corrupted the church and led it away from scriptural teachings. His preface to Walsingham speaks of fables and extravagant tales in Matthew Paris's accounts, expressing doubt that anyone in contemporary England was so stupid and insensible as to believe in them. He relates how in recent times darkness had been pushed away and light spread by the gospels; former ignorance,

---

[43] *Flores historiarum. Elegans . . . rerum, praesertim Britannicarum . . . ad annum Domini 1307 narratio, quam Matthaeus Westmonasteriensis monachus . . . Flores Historiarum scripsit*, ed. M. Parker (London, 1567); *Matthaei Paris historia maior (à Guilielmo Conquaestore; ad ultimum annum Henrici tertii . . .* , ed. Matthew Parker, (London, 1571); Thomas Walsingham, *Historia brevis Thomae Walsingham, ab Edwardo primo, ad Henricum quintum*, (London, 1574); *Ypodigma neustriae vel Normaniae: per Thomam de Walsingham*, (London: John Day, 1574); Asser, Bp. of Sherborne, *Ælfredi Regis res gestae* (London, 1574). On Parker's use of manuscripts for publications, see Page, *Books*, pp. 58-60. Additional historical works from Parker and his circle include John Joscelyn, ed., *De Excidio et conquestum Britanniae*, by Gildas (London, 1568), *Epistolae duae D. Volusiani episcopi Carthaginensis* (London, 1569), and *Catalogus Cancellariorum . . . Cantebrigiensi* (London, 1572).

[44] Joscelyn, *Life*, fol. Cir-Ciiv.

error, false rites, and ceremonies had all vanished like a vapor.[45] The preface to *A testimonie* also observes that Ælfric's church was "full of blindnes and ignoraunce: full of childysh servitude to ceremonies, as it was longe before and after."[46]

Parker believed that the antidote to such ignorance was a return to scriptural authority, a belief that dated back to his Cambridge student days. Admiring early sixteenth-century Christian humanists for their knowledge of ancient languages and texts, he praised John Colet and William Warner, who delivered biblical university lectures, ignored the pronouncements of scholastics, and "returned all things to the rule of sacred scripture."[47] Parker collected and studied the works of Erasmus, who, although remaining loyal to the Roman church, urged scripture-based reforms.[48] The text of Erasmus's definitive Latin and Greek New Testament of 1516 inspired the Cambridge reformer Thomas Bilney, whose circle Parker joined. Bilney taught that "Christ hath not been purely preached now a long time," and that churchmen, "leaving the word of God, have taught their own traditions." He rejected non-scriptural observances such as pilgrimages, pardons, worship of images, and invocation of saints when used as a means of salvation, believing that only a simple faith in Christ was necessary.[49] Although Bilney was burned at the stake in 1532, Parker adopted his teachings and by the mid-1530s was preaching a similar message: that ritualistic ceremonies were in vain unless accompanied by faith in Christ and that the veneration of relics could too easily turn into superstitious worship of them. He spoke of bringing people from "blindness and superstitions . . . to the truth and right worship of God," and he criticized those who accepted "superstition and papistical dregs." He attempted to justify his own teachings both by scripture and by "the most approved authors in Christ's church."[50]

---

[45] Preface to *Historia Brevis*, ¶iiv-¶iiiv.

[46] *A testimonie*, fol. 16v.

[47] *De Antiquitate*, p. 353.

[48] Erasmus's works in the Parker Library include CCCC S.P. 23, 139, 167, 186, 205, 235, 266, 278, 280, and 328.

[49] Foxe, *Acts & Monuments* [1563], pp. 465-79 (irregular pagination).

[50] *Correspondence*, pp. 7-12.

Parker's reliance upon scripture to rid the church of ignorance and superstition fits well with yet another of his goals: to promote the use of vernacular scriptures. As archbishop he enlisted his learned bishops in translating a new, reliable English version of the Bible for both the clergy and the laity to use, the so-called "Bishops' Bible" of 1568, for which Parker himself did much of the work.[51] To garner support for vernacular scriptures, he produced an Old English edition of the gospels, showing that translations into the people's language were nothing new. *The Gospels of the fower Evangelistes translated in the olde Saxons tyme out of Latin into the vulgare toung of the Saxons* reproduced the Old English text with a contemporary English version in smaller print. John Foxe's preface underscores the value of this historical model and invokes the authority of King Alfred:

> . . . if any shall doubt of the auncient vsage therof, whether they had the Scriptures in their language of old time, here he may haue a proofe of so much translated into our old Englishe tounge, the diuers translations wherof, and in diuerse ages, be yet extant to be seene . . . . As for the bokes of holy Scripture they were sorted by Alfrede, as by thys edition may appeare, to be read to the people . . . for the better instruction of the people in their common prayers.[52]

The preface goes on to laud Parker's persistent efforts in publication and to refute the critics' charge that the Elizabethan church introduced innovations:

> Wherein we have to see how much we are beholden to the reuerend, and learned father in God, Matthew Archbishop of Cant. a cheefe and a famous trauailler, in thys Church of England, by whose industrious diligence and learned labours, this booke, with others moe, hath bene collected & searched out of the Saxons Monuments: so likewise have we to vnderstand & conceaue, by the edition hereof, how the

---

[51] *The holie bible* [Bishops' version] (London, 1568). *Correspondence*, pp. 248, 256, 262, 265, 290, and 334-38.

[52] Foxe, preface to *The Gospels*, fol. Aiiir, Aiiiir.

religion presently taught and professed in the Church at thys
present, is no new reformation of thinges lately begonne,
which were not before, but rather a reduction of the Church
to the Pristine state of olde conformitie, which once it had,
and almost lost by discontinuance of a fewe later yeares.[53]

Parker's interest in promoting vernacular scriptures dated back
to the 1530s, when he received his first appointment as dean of Stoke-
by-Clare, a college of secular priests in Suffolk. There he instituted
scripture readings and lectures four days a week, "the fyrst half hower
[in] the vulgare tong for the capacite of those that be unlernyd, & then
the next half hower in the laten tong."[54] Since he seems to have begun
these bilingual readings by 1536, Parker was ahead of his time and
slightly ahead of the law. Complete English translations of the Bible
existed, but the officially sanctioned "Thomas Matthew" Bible would
not be licensed for sale until the following year. Parker's interest in
vernacular scripture continued during Mary's reign. With his career in
limbo and church services once again in Latin, he took advantage of his
"literary leisure" to write a metrical version of the Psalms in English.
Looking ahead to some future day when English would once more be
used in the church, he accompanied his text with collects and musical
notations for use in corporate worship.[55]

One final point remains to be addressed regarding Parker's purposes as he used his manuscripts. He has been accused of inflicting
upon the volumes a series of editorial blunders and crimes, inexcusable
even in the light of his zeal for church reform. Critics indict him for
taking outrageous liberties with his manuscripts and published texts,
mixing material from several sources without explaining how or why,
interpolating and rearranging them at will. He or his editors revised
wording, composition, and order, sometimes inflicting permanent
damage to the manuscripts. For doing so he has incurred the wrath of
later editors and manuscript-keepers, whose indictments have sullied

---

[53] Foxe, preface to *The Gospels*, ¶iir.

[54] CCCC MS 108, p. 158.

[55] *Correspondence*, pp. viii-ix; *The Whole Psalter translated into English Metre,
which contayneth an hundreth and fifty Psalmes* (London, 1577); Inner Temple
MS Misc. 36.

his reputation to this day. For example, Sir Frederic Madden, the nine-teenth-century Keeper of the British Library manuscripts and probably Parker's most severe critic, argued that Parker as an editor

> was sadly deficient in critical ability, and in the knowledge acquired only by the careful collation of manuscripts . . . . His edition [of Matthew Paris], in truth, is a mere piece of patchwork, and exhibits an utter disregard of the ordinary rules to be observed in publishing an historical work.[56]

H. R. Luard, a nineteenth-century editor of Matthew Paris's *Chronica Majora*, remarks,

> It has been unfortunate for the estimate of Matthew Paris . . . that he found so utterly untrustworthy an editor as arch-bishop Parker, or whoever it was whom he employed to edit the work . . . . Parker has not the slightest scruple in altering what he does not understand, or changing words or expres-sions that he does not like.

Luard goes on to list pages of errors introduced by Parker and perpetu-ated in later editions.[57] William H. Stevenson, the early twentieth-cen-tury editor of Asser's *Life of King Alfred*, writes of Parker,

> he took the greatest liberties with the texts, correcting the style and spelling, interpolating from other works, and com-mitting such sins that a modern scholar has been moved to describe his editing as 'wicked' and 'fantastic.'[58]

Timothy Graham points out the damage to the manuscripts which Parker's erasures and other alterations caused:

> The purpose of such erasures was probably to tidy up the appearance of manuscripts that reached Parker in an incom-plete state. The effect of the erasures is lamentable . . . . Parker was . . . responsible for some permanent losses. He occasionally caused leaves to be removed from the begin-ning or end of manuscripts . . . . The alterations that Parker caused to be made to manuscripts while they belonged to

[56] Madden, preface to *Historia Anglorum*, vol I, p. xx. See also pp. xxxi-xxxvii.

[57] Luard, preface to *Chronica Majora*, vol. 2, pp. xxii-xxviii.

[58] Stevenson, p. xvii.

him included altering their structure by removing leaves from one manuscript and inserting them into another, or by combining originally separate manuscripts.[59]

Although it is true that Parker rearranged his manuscripts, altered the texts, and violated modern rules of editing, several points may be made in his defense. First, today's editorial procedures have not always been standard practice. Parker knew nothing of what Madden called the "ordinary rules" of publishing because they did not exist in his day. He followed the practices he knew, those of the medieval scribes and editors before him who at their discretion repeatedly added to, deleted from, and reassembled parts of manuscripts.[60] Parker has been condemned for failing to meet standards not set until centuries later.

Second, scholarly editing styles vary according to the goals of the editor. If an editor intends primarily to preserve the historical accuracy of a text, corrections will be kept to a minimum. If, however, the goal is to ensure comprehension of the text, the editor may use scholarly judgement in introducing alterations to eliminate obvious problems.[61] Madden, Luard, and Stevenson aimed at preserving the accuracy of their texts and therefore corrected very little. Parker, envisioning the texts as vehicles for ecclesiastical reform, needed them to be comprehensible and therefore boldly rectified textual problems. He corrected errors made by medieval scribes in grammar, wording, and composition.[62] He also filled in missing or damaged parts as he saw fit. For example, when the year 1307 was found to be missing from his best *Flores Historiarum* source, he filled it in with additions from other historical manuscripts. He deleted redundancies, rearranged pages, and added missing leaves. Although his amendments sometimes included

---

[59] Graham, pp. 42-44. See also Ker, pp. xl-xlii, lii-liii, and lxii-lxiii.

[60] Madden himself (pp. xxviii, liii) noted in manuscripts of the *Flores Historiarum* medieval omissions and insertions of a local character, "according to the views of the respective scribes," along with errors to be corrected.

[61] See G. Thomas Tanselle, "The Varieties of Scholarly Editing," in *Scholarly Editing*, pp. 9-30.

[62] Luard, vol 2, pp. xxiii-xxvii.

errors of their own, he at least made his version clear and readable. Since he hoped to restore the texts to what he believed the original authors intended, he could say without a qualm that he did not add to nor diminish them with anything of himself.[63] He altered texts as medieval scribes had done before him and as other manuscript collectors would do after him.[64] These practices may seem inexcusable today, but Parker justified his "improvements" because they rendered his texts more understandable and potentially more persuasive.

Parker also altered manuscripts to extend their beauty, value, and life. When he found the Vespasian Psalter with a missing leaf, he resolved to have it repaired and wrote to a fellow collector, Sir William Cecil:

> I had thought to have made up the want of the beginning of the Psalter, for it wanteth the first psalm, and three verses in the second psalm, and methought the leaf going before the xxvith psalm would have been a meet beginning before the whole Psalter, having David sitting with his harp or psaltery . . . which I was in mind to have caused Lylye to have counterfeited in antiquity, &c., but that I called to remembrance that ye have a singular artificer to adorn the same, which your honour shall do well to have the monument finished, or else I will cause it to be done and remitted again to your library . . . . So that [such treasures] may be preserved within the realm, and not sent over by covetous stationers, or spoiled in the poticaries' shops.[65]

Parker considered artful restoration a responsible course of action, without which some manuscripts might have landed on the scrap heap.

For a final word in Parker's defense, it should be noted that he wished to bring important manuscripts to print in spite of the difficulties that plagued the process in its early stages. He lacked the benefit

---

[63] Matthew Parker, preface to *Ælfredi Regis Res Gestae* (London, 1574) fol. Bir.

[64] The great seventeenth-century collector Robert Cotton often separated and reassembled part of his manuscripts at his own discretion. See Ker, p. liv.

[65] Parker to Sir William Cecil (24th January, 1565-1566), *Correspondence*, pp. 253-54.

of a complete corpus of manuscripts and sometimes had to rely on defective sources, making necessary later revised editions. He lacked procedural rules for print shops, and thus printers' ink sometimes damaged manuscript pages. He lacked skilled type-designers and faced major problems producing texts in Old English typeface. Trained as a theological scholar, he lacked sophisticated editorial skills. And yet, undaunted by these difficulties, he still managed to publish historical works that otherwise would long have remained obscure. He intended them to provide church and society with sources of wisdom for generations to come.[66] As imperfect as his results may have been, he deserves credit for his pioneering efforts.

Parker continued his manuscript work until shortly before he died. He published his last manuscript text at the advanced age of about 71, but by then declining health had robbed him of his former vigor, and his eyesight had begun to fail. His red chalk letters, used only after he became archbishop, appear far larger than his earlier-written letters. Having done his part for scholarship and publication, he allowed his younger assistants to assume the burden of work. Even so, less than three months before he died, he continued personal manuscript work, making some transcripts of his own. He wrote to Cecil (Lord Burghley) in mid-February, 1574/5, anticipating the death that came in May, "I toy out my time, partly with copying books . . . . And thus, till Almighty God cometh, I repose myself in patience."[67]

Parker's purposes in collecting, annotating, and studying his manuscript collection centered upon his lifelong interest in church reform. Although modern scholars may fault his handling of the manuscripts, Parker needs to be understood in the context of his own century and the reformation movement that early captured his loyalty. He collected the manuscripts in order to save them for posterity, to promote the study of Old English, and to make English history more accessible. But above all, he wished to promote his reform agenda, especially the marriage of clergy, the use of vernacular scriptures, and the

---

[66] See Catherine Hall, "The One-Way Trail: Some Observations on CCC MS 101 and G&CC MS 427," *Transactions of the Cambridge Bibliographical Society* 11, no. 3 (1998), p. 283.

[67] Parker to Lord Burghley, 18th February, [1574-5], *Correspondence*, p. 474.

rejection of transubstantiation. His objective was a more enlightened church, free of corruption and adhering to scriptural standards. In the words of his admittedly flattering biographer, Parker was determined that,

> by the heavenly doctrine of the worde/ [he] should bringe againe into the lighte the congregation off Christ/ which nowe a greate while hath miserably lyen hidden/ and over-whelmed in grosse darknes/ by the traditions off men.[68]

Matthew Parker's standing and character have suffered much at the hands of those unfamiliar with his context and purposes. A new appreciation of his early career, reforming interests, and sixteenth-century context may help to refine our understanding of the man and refurbish his reputation.

[68] Joscelyn, *Life*, fol. Bixr-v

Index of Manuscripts

General Index

Abelard, Peter, 48

Abingdon, 208-09

Acta Apostolorum Apocrypha, 83

Acts of Andrew, 59, 62

Acts of Matthew, 59

Acts of Peter, 58-60

Adamnan, vision of, 35, 51

Adams, Eleanor, 220, 223

Adso of Montier-en-Der, 75-81, 86

Ælfric, 18, 32-33, 41-48, 51, 57-58, 60-66, 72, 77, 79, 81, 90, 111, 119, 122, 126-28, 130, 135, 229; Catholic Homilies, 41, 61, 83-86, 122, 125, 127-28; *De auguriis*, 125; *De duodecim abusivis*, 125; *De falsis diis*, 125, 130; *De initio creaturae*, 129-31, 137; *De sanguine prohibito*, 134, 136-37; *De septiformi spiritu*, 133, 135-37; *De temporibus anni*, 128; *De tribus ordinibus saeculi*, 125; *De xii abusivis*, 130; *Grammar*, 6, 96-120, 126; *Hexameron*, 124, 128-31, 136; *Interrogationes Sigewulfi*, 125, 127, 129-32, 134, 136-37; *Lives of the Saints*, 125-26, 130; on the Assumption, 41, 42, 57, 61; on copying from an exemplar, 18, 78; on visions, 32-33, 61; *Passio Apostolorum Petri et Pauli*, 83-86; *Preface to Genesis*, 126; *Preface to the Catholic Homilies*, 75-80, 125; silent days, 62; translations of apocrypha, 58, 60

Ælfwerd, 215

Ælfwine, 193, 215

Ælfwino, 193

ælwe, 193

Ælwinus, 193

Æthelnoth, abbot, 209, 210-12, 216

Æthelstan Half King, 189-91, 193, 202

Æthelweard the Chronicler, 185

Æthelweard, abbot, 195

Æthelweard, ealdorman, 183-88, 191-92, 194-96, 206, 209, 210, 215

Æthelwine, "Dei Amicus", 189, 190-91, 193, 202

Æthelwine, Bishop of Wells, 186-89, 215

Æthelwine, monk, 192-94, 215

Æthelwold, 43, 47, 117, 209

Against a Dwarf, 150-51, 154-55, 170

246

Printed in the United States
21322LVS00004B/58-204

9 780937 058831